Understanding and Managing Diversity

SECOND EDITION

Understanding and Managing Diversity

Readings, Cases, and Exercises

Carol P. Harvey
Assumption College

M. June Allard
Worcester State College

Prentice Hall
Upper Saddle River, NJ 07458

Library of Congress Cataloging-in-Publication Data

Harvey, Carol P.
   Understanding and managing diversity: readings, cases, and exercises/Carol P.
   Harvey, M. June Allard.—2nd ed.
       p.   cm.
   Rev. ed. of: Understanding diversity: readings, cases, and exercises / Carol P.
   Harvey, M. June Allard. c1995
   Includes bibliographical references and index.
   ISBN 0–13–029264–8
   1. Minorities—Employment—United States.   2. Multiculturalism—United
States.   3. Personnel management—United States.   I. Allard, M. June   II. Harvey,
Carol P. Understanding diversity.   III. Title.
HF5549.5.M5 H37 2002
658.3′0089—dc21   2001036163

Acquisitions Editor: Melissa Steffens
Editor-in-Chief: Jeff Shelstad
Executive Editor (Editorial): David Shafer
Assistant Editor: Jessica Sabloff
Media Project Manager: Michele Faranda
Marketing Manager: Shannon Moore
Managing Editor (Production): John Roberts
Production Editor: Renata Butera
Permissions Coordinator: Suzanne Grappi
Associate Director, Manufacturing: Vincent Scelta
Production Manager: Arnold Vila
Manufacturing Buyer: Diane Peirano
Design Manager: Pat Smythe
Art Director: Jayne Conte
Cover Design: Bruce Kenselaar
Cover Illustration/Photo: Reza Estakhrian/Stone
Manager, Print Production: Christina Mahon
Composition: BookMasters, Inc.
Full-Service Project Management: BookMasters, Inc.
Printer/Binder: Courier-Westford

10   9   8   7   6   5   4   3
ISBN 0-13-029264-8

Dedicated to our good friend and colleague,
the late Dr. Jean F. Smelewicz

Dedicated to my good friend and colleague

Contents

SECTION III: PERSPECTIVES ON SOME DIMENSIONS OF DIVERSITY

SECTION IV: PERSPECTIVES ON DIVERSITY: CASES

Introduction

Since the first edition was published 6 years ago, the workforce has become increasingly diverse; the focus of diversity initiatives has changed from compliance with the law to understanding individual differences to using diversity to gain a competitive edge in the marketplace; and international business has become the norm rather than the exception. Because of these changes, the ability to understand and appreciate individual differences and to work productively, particularly on teams, with people who may be different from us is now recognized as a necessary management skill. As a result, we have rewritten this text to reflect the needs for both individual understanding of differences and organizational systemic change.

Many in the majority groups think that diversity is "evolutionary," that is, progress has been made and will continue to happen. To them, diversity will become a nonissue. Although this position does have a historical basis, it fails to recognize the complexity of the diverse workforce. So far, diversity programs seem to have gone through three phases: first, the legalistic/quota approach; second, an attempt to generalize the differences attributed to specific demographic groups; and third, the current attempts by organizations to "manage differences."

- The social movements of the 1960s and 1970s did lead to important diversity legislation, such as The Civil Rights Act of 1964. However, many managers and organizations interpreted these laws as simply requiring them to hire demographically diverse employees, particularly women and racial minorities, to fill "quotas." Few changes were made in organizational policies, procedures, and cultures. Diversity initiatives were quantitative rather than qualitative.
- In the second phase, understanding differences, emphasis was put on awareness of the cultures, values, and sensitivity to the characteristics of individual groups. Although these are important to understand, such as the importance of family and language to many Hispanics, not all members of these groups exhibit the same behaviors or hold the identical values. Generalization failed to account for individual differences within the groups and led to additional stereotypes. However, this approach did make a contribution because it opened up the possibilities that diverse communication styles and values had merit. The understanding differences approach primarily relied on ad hoc training programs for individuals that did little to inspire organizations to develop and implement ways to relate the utilization of the talents of the more diverse workforce to the attainment of organizational goals.
- The third and current phase, often called *managing differences,* is based on the premise that organizations can learn to "manage" people's differences in ways that will make workers more productive and more compatible team members. Although the most difficult to implement, the value of this approach is that it has identified the need for organizations, not just individuals, to change their ways of thinking about diversity and to take appropriate action. For example, a workforce composed of large numbers of parents of young children may require some rethinking of the structure of the workday, the composition of benefit

packages, and heavy requirements for business-related travel in order to advance. Organizations need to do more than talk about diversity as a value and offer training programs that have no accountability for implementation. They must "walk the talk" by integrating systemic changes into their ways of doing business.

Rather than consider this as evolutionary process, we would consider it as revolutionary. Change will not just "happen" in the passive sense. To become an integral part of an organization's strategic planning process will require complex changes in both the ways that individuals think about people different from themselves and also in the ways that organizations work. A heterogeneous workforce is incompatible with homogeneous management policies and procedures.

The authors of this book share a common perspective based on their teaching experience. First, students learn about diversity through the more active methods of teaching and learning. Lecture is probably the least effective pedagogy for this subject. Increasing student awareness and understanding of others' perspectives must be the foundation of diversity education. Consequently, this edition includes many cases, experiential exercises, and assignments that lend themselves to high levels of student involvement and lively discussions. Second, we respect and appreciate the diversity of the knowledge that our contributors have to offer. Many of them have devoted their lives to specialized areas of study. Our experience in teaching about diversity for almost 10 years is that challenging long-held beliefs through exposure to different perspectives can lead to change in thinking and behavior. For this reason, we have sought out contributors to write about their specialized areas. Third, this text reflects the need to move students into the analysis of the ways that organizations have attempted to implement diversity initiatives to make students aware of how difficult and complex it is to develop and to implement successful organizational changes in response to fluid business environments.

OBJECTIVES OF THIS BOOK

To Provide Effective Up-to-Date Classroom Material for Courses that Involve Issues of Workplace Diversity.

In terms of research, we have listened to faculty who used our first edition and those who did not. We have surveyed students to determine their needs and preferences. We have studied syllabi from diversity, organizational behavior, human resource, and social science courses that focus on diversity. As a result, we have chosen and written material to meet the needs of these audiences. The articles, exercises, and cases in this book are written for classroom use. We have attempted to make them challenging but interesting. Our focus is on raising student understanding of the complexity of diversity by encouraging them to examine their personal perspectives as well as to analyze and evaluate organizational diversity initiatives. Matrices found in the *Instructor's Manual* provide suggestions for using specific text material as a supplement to organizational behavior, management, and human resource courses.

To Allow Instructors Maximum Flexibility in the Way that They Use this Material.

We understand that classes vary in length, size, and the degree of student homogeneity or heterogeneity. We have attempted to accommodate these variations by including material appropriate for different situations. We offer exercises that can be done in as little as 10 minutes of a 50-minute class as well as more complex exercises that require long blocks of time for processing and discussion. The *Instructor's Manual* provides guidance and suggestions for material that meets the need variations in class length, size, and composition.

To Present Students with Multiple Perspectives and Expanding Viewpoints on Workforce Diversity Issues.

Diversity is a complex, developing, multifaceted topic. Many of its roots lie within the social sciences. Some of our authors are from the fields of psychology, sociology, law, history, and anthropology as well as management and organizational behavior. We think that this broad perspective adds richness and depth to the text material.

To Provide a Comprehensive Instructor's Package Consisting of an Extensive *Instructor's Manual* and PowerPoint Slides.

Diversity is a difficult subject to teach. We have tried to provide the instructor with a comprehensive supplement that meets the needs of both the novice and the experienced teacher. In addition to outlines, practical and detailed guidelines for cases and exercises, we have included optional assignments, additional resources, capstone, and Internet assignments, and topic matrices. The latter will be particularly helpful to instructors who want to use this book as a supplement to organizational behavior and human resource classes. PowerPoint slides are available to adopters.

CHANGES FROM THE FIRST EDITION

- A shift in perspective from understanding individual differences to the need for systemic changes in the ways that organizations think about and meet the needs of their diverse employees. We believe that those who will develop and implement these changes need to begin with an examination of their personal beliefs and biases. However, to be effective, diversity initiatives must progress from the individual to the organizational level.
- A broadened focus and definition of diversity. The first edition was focused on primary aspects of diversity such as race, ethnicity, age, sexual orientation, and physical and mental abilities. The second edition expands coverage to include such secondary aspects of diversity as social class, religion, and military experience. In addition, there is material that explores diversity in terms of communication styles, nonprofit organizations, and international business.

- We have added innovative material on religion, values, gender and communication, social class, Native Americans, Generation X, employment law in Canada, innovative work models for older workers, and personality disorders under the ADA law.
- Some popular material from the first edition has been expanded and updated such as The Cracker Barrel Case, Briarwood, Distinguishing Difference and Conflict, and the Workforce IQs (American and Canadian versions). In addition, new cases on recent controversial diversity issues such as Tailhook, Smith Barney, Barry Winchell, and so on, are included.

ORGANIZATION OF THE BOOK

To provide a logical order, the text is divided into five sections: Perspectives on Diversity; Perspectives on Organizations and Diversity; Perspectives on Some Dimensions of Diversity; Perspectives on Diversity: Cases; and Perspectives on Experiencing Diversity: Exercises. To reflect the organizational perspective of this text, the structure goes from the macro to the micro environment.

Section I opens with Allard's extensive analysis of the models that attempt to explain the complex topic of diversity from many theoretical perspectives. We intend this article to be both an introduction and a frequently consulted reference for both the student and the instructor. Both Miner's and Sowell's works are intended to provide a global perspective to the topic of diversity.

Section II addresses the implications and the complexity of managing diversity at the organizational level. Although the focus here is on systemic change (Cox and Blake, Dass and B. Parker, Sherer and Harvey), other authors (C. Parker and Ofori-Dankwa and Julian) point out pitfalls that organizations need to avoid.

Section III provides in-depth coverage of some individual aspects of diversity: gender (Tannen and Thompson), race and sexual orientation (McIntosh), sexual orientation (Hunt), social class (Aguirre), and religion (Rao).

Section IV presents students with complex cases for analysis and discussion. It is easy to say what organizations and individuals "should" do but more difficult to deal with the realities of what they do. All of the cases in this section are based on true events. Some like "Nightmare on Wall Street" (Ligos) and "Tailhook" (Dawson and Chunis) are easily identified. Others have the names and places changed for privacy reasons. Many contain complex intersections of diversity issues such as culture, organizational politics, gender (Athanassiou and McNett) and sexual harassment, nonprofit management, and ADA law (Oliver and Bartholomew).

Section V offers a wide variety of experiential materials. Instructors have four different ways to incorporate an exercise on values into their classes (Ashamalla, Aurelio, Schmidt-Wilk, and Allard's "I AM . . ."). Short exercises (Hunt's, Allard's "Musical Chairs" and "Treasure Hunts") are icebreakers that quickly get students' attention. Longer exercises (Kunsler, Parker, and Klein) provide the opportunity for students to deepen their understanding of difference. Other material is more suitable for out-of-class assignments using the Internet (Sherer) and groups (Harvey's "Diversity Audit" and Allard's "Create an Exercise").

Acknowledgments

This book represents a real diverse team effort. First, we wish to thank all of the contributing authors for sharing their knowledge, expertise, and talents. Their diverse perspectives are the heart and soul of this book.

We are grateful to our reviewers for their support and constructive suggestions. We have reread your suggestions many times and tried to incorporate your ideas into this second edition. Our thanks to Dr. Ellen Ernst Kossek, Michigan State University; Dr. Marybeth Kardatzke, Montgomery College; Professor Andy C. Saucedo, Dona Ana Branch Community College; and Dr. Kathleen J. Powers, Willamette University.

Thank you to students and work-studies, who have tirelessly pretested our cases and exercises, offered ideas, answered our questionnaires, and helped us in so many ways. We appreciate the suggestions of our colleagues who teach in this field who gave us ideas for Internet, film, and print resources.

It has been a privilege to work with the staff at Prentice Hall. We are particularly indebted to Melissa Steffens, our editor, who believed in this project.

Each of us wishes to thank our academic institutions that provided support, encouragement, and facilities. Particular thanks go to Diane Bleau of the Business Studies Department at Assumption College, whose clerical and technological skills were so important to the completion of this book. Our librarians, Pamela McKay of Worcester State College and Carol Maksian and Larry Spongberg of Assumption College, were invaluable resources.

Extra special thanks go to Francis S. Harvey, Jr., Kevin, and David Harvey for their patience and continued support throughout this project.

Carol P. Harvey, Ed.D.
Associate Professor
Assumption College
500 Salisbury St.
Worcester MA 01609-1296

508 767-7459
charvey@assumption.edu.

M. June Allard, Ph.D.
Chair of the Psychology Department
Worcester State College
486 Chandler Street
Worcester, MA 01602

508 929-8789
jallard@worcester.edu

Carol P. Harvey is an associate professor and has been chair of Business Studies at Assumption College. She has an Ed.D. from the University of Massachusetts at Amherst, an MBA and a certificate of advanced graduate studies from Northeastern University, and an MA in psychology from Assumption College. She was formerly employed as a manager for the Xerox Corporation. Her research interests include implementing organizational diversity initiatives and improving critical-thinking skills in the college classroom.

M. June Allard (Ph.D., Michigan State University), is professor and chair of psychology at Worcester State College. She is a social and experimental psychologist with research, teaching, and consulting interests in international and cross-cultural psychology and in program assessment and evaluation. Prior to teaching, she worked as a senior scientist in the R & D industry. A lifelong world traveler, she teaches research and evaluation courses internationally.

Understanding and Managing Diversity

SECTION ONE
Perspectives on Diversity

Theoretical Underpinnings of Diversity

M. June Allard
Worcester State College

"Our most serious problems are social problems for which there are no technical solutions, only human solutions."
— REP. GEORGE E. BROWN, JR.[1]
*Chairman of the House Committee
on Science, Space, and Technology*

"It is very helpful to suggest that diversity is not so much an end in itself as it is a condition of our society and a condition of the world in which we live."
— FRANK WONG[2]
*Vice President for Academic Affairs
University of Redlands*

DIVERSITY AND CULTURE

Diversity

By the early 1990s, the melting pot and assimilation ideas of earlier decades had given way to the realities that not all people were "meltable" and that the numbers of "unmeltables" were increasing. In the wake of legislation designed to open doors and right wrongs, the concerns were those of compliance with the law, the entitlement to employment, and the moral issues of fairness.

As employment gates opened further, concern shifted to recognizing and understanding individual differences. Diversity modelers focused first on developing sensitivity to "differentness" and more recently on managing diversity.

Where once we talked of acculturation and then of acceptance and of accommodation, we now speak of appreciation and integration. No longer do we think in terms of assimilation; instead, we think of "managing" diversity.

Just what is this diversity we want to manage? There is no easy answer because there is no real consensus. For some, diversity refers to racial, ethnic, and gender differences, and for others it includes a much broader range of differences among people, such as religion, social class, and age.

In this book, we consciously define diversity very broadly to include the multitude of social, cultural, physical, and environmental differences among people that

3

impact the way they think and behave. Diversity for us includes race, ethnicity, gender, physical abilities, sexual orientation, age, religion, social class, and many other dimensions.

We are in accord with Loden & Rosener, who see it as "this vast array of physical and cultural differences that constitute the spectrum of human diversity,"[3] and with R. Roosevelt Thomas: " . . . I mean the whole nature of the modern workforce—in terms of age, educational differences, background, nationality, and a multitude of other factors."[4]

Culture

Whatever the definition, whatever the model of diversity, it is clear that understanding, or valuing, or managing it requires some insight into its cultural underpinnings. With this in mind, we begin this book with a brief discussion on culture. We hope, thereby, to provide a broad background against which to examine the diversity issues faced today in organizations of all kinds.

Culture defines how we look at life in general, and it guides how we respond to characteristics such as race, ethnicity, physical attributes, age, social class, and education. It shapes our responses to these qualities both within us and in other people.

At the broad social level, culture tells us who we are, that is, what groups we belong to, how we should behave and " . . . gives us attitudes about 'them,' the people who are different from us. It tells us what should be important as well as how to act in various situations."[5]

Culture envelopes us so completely that often we do not realize that there are different ways of dealing with the world, that others may have a different outlook on life, a different logic, a different way of responding to people and situations.

Culture permeates all aspects of organizations. Organizations themselves have cultures; organizational managers behave in terms of both organizational and personal cultural backgrounds, as do workers who bring diverse cultural backgrounds to their organizations. In corporate and nonprofit organizations, the culture of the consumer is of key importance to marketing considerations. In multinational organizations, successful operation depends upon compatibility with host-country cultures.

Organizational cultures are reflected in the way they manage people, that is, in who they hire, how they evaluate them, and who they promote. For example, some organizations do not value nationalities unaccustomed to looking managers in the eye, or older workers, or women who are not assertive, or cultural deviations in dress styles running counter to organizational dress codes. Too, some corporations reflect the cultures of their industries. Women, for example, find far less acceptance in the manufacturing sector than in the services sector, whereas older workers are less welcome in dot-coms than in manufacturing; gays and lesbians are more accepted in fashion, advertising, and the arts than in many other industries.

For organizations now coping with a plurality of identity-conscious groups, the management of diversity not only involves moral considerations; it also requires consideration of the influence of cultural complexity, cultural change, and cultural judgments (stereotypes).

Cultural Complexity

The complexity of our cultural backgrounds vastly increases the difficulty of managing a diverse workforce. Not only are there differences in values *among* cultures, but there are vast differences *within* cultures, as well. Culture is not the same for every member of any single group. We all belong to many groups that influence our behavior and beliefs. Certainly not all blacks behave the same way nor do they have identical values; neither do all women, all Latinos, all members of the upper middle class, nor all members of any other group.

We are born with gender, race, and ethnicity memberships, and we acquire even more identities as we go through life. We become easterners, accountants, and Democrats. The values and beliefs of our group memberships are not always consistent with each other, and the relative importance of each of our groups to us is not the same for everyone. Family is a far more important membership for some than it is for others, as is religious affiliation or professional affiliation. The importance to us of particular memberships affects not only our own behavior, but it affects how we interpret the behavior of others, as well.

Cultural Change

Perhaps because of the completeness of its influence in our lives, we tend to think of culture as an object or a thing, but culture is neither concrete nor stable. Rather, it is a state or condition that changes and evolves. One has only to think of how often our country's international friends and enemies change or of the things that have changed between our parent's generation and our own or even within our own lifetime to realize this.[6,7,8]

The fact that cultures change in what they value and in the behaviors they prescribe compounds the difficulty in understanding other cultural groups. On the other hand, this makes it clear that insensitivity, bias, and intolerance can be unlearned; they can be replaced with understanding and acceptance. This is a welcome note for all kinds of organizations struggling to deal with diversity issues.

Cultural Judgments (Stereotypes)

Among the most important aspects of our cultural backgrounds are the dimensions of judgment provided for assessing others. For those groups with whom we have little contact, our culture provides us with a predetermined set of attitudes and a prescription for interacting. It provides us with stereotypes, those labels by which we typecast all members of a group as though they were clones from an inflexible mold. Stereotypes organize the unknown world for us, but at the same time they constrain us with tunnel vision. They encourage us to perceive all members of one group as welfare cheats, of another group as lazy, of another as musical, and another as mechanical. Individual differences and character are lost in stereotyping.

In an organization, even the best-intentioned manager who relies on stereotypes in dealing with others runs the risk of making incorrect assessments of people and their behavior, of creating misunderstanding and conflict, and of blocking opportunities for others. "Giving too much attention to the cultural group runs the risk of stereotyping the individual as a member of that cultural group and forgetting individual uniqueness."[9] Cultural judgments based on stereotypes are useful, but they are not an adequate basis for dealing with diversity or with the accompanying legal and social judgments of fairness and inclusion.

WEAVING DIVERSITY INTO ORGANIZATIONAL FABRIC

Organizational Frameworks

Changing social, legal, and business circumstances exert heavy pressures on organizations to develop "initiatives" to deal with the growing complexity of diversity concerns. These initiatives generally take two forms:

- policies (including policies of action and inaction)
- formal training programs

Policies   From a theoretical perspective, models of diversity policy can be thought of as evolving from singular and simplistic to more complex and comprehensive. However, farsighted early modelers, such as R. Roosevelt Thomas, saw well beyond single dimensions and simple solutions. Today, actual practices range all the way from minimal compliance (or even noncompliance) with the law at one extreme to active promotion of diversity and well-articulated international practices at the other. Whether due to dislike or disinterest, the bottom line is that theory is way ahead of practice; few organizations have comprehensive diversity policies, and most initiatives still seem to be limited to relatively simple hiring quotas or sexual harassment training efforts.[10]

Policy Evolution   Traditional approaches to diversity are either based on an assimilation "discrimination-and-fairness" theme . . . ("they" should adjust to our ways and be like us) or on a differentiation "access-and-legitimacy" theme that matches the demographic characteristics of people to those of the marketplace.[11]

These approaches go beyond the traditional Equal Employment Opportunity/ Affirmative Action concern with employing adequate numbers of minorities, as they often provide some mentoring and career development. In these approaches, however, the "staff . . . gets diversified, but the work does not."[12]

A third theme of "learning-and-effectiveness" connecting diversity to the "actual *doing* of work" emerged in the mid 1990s. This approach is premised on integration: "We are all on the same team *with* our differences—not *despite* them." This trend, popularly known as *multiculturalism,* appreciates diversity while respecting the uniqueness of the individual.[13,14]

Diversity policies grow out of social and business pressures: The diversity-under-duress policies are powered by a pressing problem; equal opportunity policies are a legal necessity; augmented affirmative action policies come from legal and political forces; valuing differences policies emerge from social pressures for inclusiveness; and managing diversity policies are economically-based strategies tying progress to organizational goals, cultures, structures, policies, and reward systems.[15]

In essence, policy modeling began at one extreme (assimilation into the workforce), swung to the opposite extreme (differentiation based on diversity), and came back to a more central position of integration incorporating elements of both extremes.

Assimilation		**Differentiation**		**Integration**
Treat Everyone the Same	$\longrightarrow$	Capitalize on Differences	$\longrightarrow$	Appreciate Difference and Respect Uniqueness

Policy Evolution

Diversity integration is the frontier in policy modeling today. Integration policies include practices such as flex time, mentoring, network building, overseas assignments, work and family life initiatives, job assignments with supportive superiors, and assignments to task forces to promote peer relationships.[16] Broader strategies include tailoring procedures to group and individual needs, recruitment, career development, upward mobility, two-way manager-employee feedback, accountability, systems approaches such as redesigning work, global computer networks, consensus building, structural change accommodations, and recruiting.[17]

Diversity "engineering" may be the most "advanced" thinking, but it is not for everyone. Not all theorists have embraced the idea, nor have all workers or organizational leaders. Some find the focus on diversity per se too limiting; others object to the idea of managing it. Modelers and CEOs of international corporations voice concern that the current focus on valuing and managing differences concentrates on differences and ignores commonalities[18]; white males see the emphasis on differences as divisive.[19]

The whole idea of managing diversity is questioned by Gormley.[20] She points out that to manage diversity is to defeat the real purpose; "managing" implies control, and control runs counter to "the incorporation of equals." Still other CEOs object to highlighting the "managing of diversity." "Businesses do not become great because they manage diversity well; well-managed businesses naturally take advantage of the diversity of their workforce."[21]

We now find organizations at all stages in diversity management efforts. They make different levels of commitment, and they start at different points. Because thinking has gone way beyond legal compliance concerns, it is tempting to assume that organizational efforts have, too. Unfortunately, this is not the case. Although organizational efforts are found all along the continuum, most are concentrated in the beginning stages.

Some organizations still resist operating at even the minimal legal level—compliance with the law. One has only to listen to the news to hear that Company X or even Government Agency Y "today made an out-of-court settlement with workers who claimed unfair treatment in hiring and promotion." For example, the U.S. Office of Education and Coca-Cola recently settled long-standing discrimination suits; Microsoft faces a $5 billion racial-bias lawsuit; the Adam's Mark hotel chain has been sued at least seven times in the last decade for discrimination; and Eagle Global Logistics, a large freight delivery firm, faces a racial-bias lawsuit.

At the other extreme, some organizations have moved vigorously to incorporate multicultural initiatives into their operations. This is evidenced by groups that draw up lists of the "best companies to work for" in terms of accommodating differences. Even further along the continuum, business magazines such as *Working Woman* carry reports of proactive, aggressive diversity recruiting efforts and of U.S. corporations succeeding internationally because of their sensitivity to the cultural values of their host countries.

Diversity Training

Diversity policy is one important component of organizational initiatives; diversity training is the other. Training programs are at the most visible core of an organization's diversity efforts, and many corporations see training as the "be all and end all" of dealing with diversity, no matter how limited the training effort. Training programs are not alike, however; as concepts of diversity differ greatly in purpose and scope; so do the training programs derived from them.[22,23]

Self-Awareness   With the exception of programs focused on complying with employment laws, however, some form of "other awareness," that is, sensitivity to "others," is a common denominator in training. Other awareness begins with self-awareness. A basic premise of most sensitivity training is that "to understand others, you must first understand yourself." We all carry cultural software that programs our perspectives and judgments. We wear our cultural cloaks so closely wrapped about us that we don't realize how they affect what we sense and do.

Sensitivity training, then, sets out to help individuals recognize their own cultural identities and their biases. This is more complicated than it might appear for self-identity means different things to different people. Different cultures produce different self-concepts and these in turn lead to different behaviors.

For example, in many Western cultures where there is an *independent construal of self,* the individual is defined in terms of his/her personal characteristics such as abilities, personality, and intelligence. Individualism, self-expression, and personal achievement are valued. In non-Western, collectivistic cultures, however, individuals focus more on their relationships, their connectedness to others. In these cultures where there is an *interdependent construal of self,* harmony is valued more than individual achievement. " . . . individuals . . . strive to meet or even create duties, obligations, and social responsibilities."[24,25,26]

Loden's dimensions of diversity model provides an example of the first approach (independent construal of self). In Loden's model, individuals are defined and distinguished from each other both in terms of primary dimensions such as age, race, and gender (core characteristics that do not change) and in terms of secondary characteristics such as education, religion, and income that can change.[27] Figure 1-1 presents Loden's diversity wheel.

In contrast, the Szapocznik and Kurtines model is an interdependent construal of self approach that rests upon the individual's group memberships. In this model, each person wears several layers of cultural clothing. Closest is the cultural cloak of the family. Additional layers are added by the diverse cultures in the environment

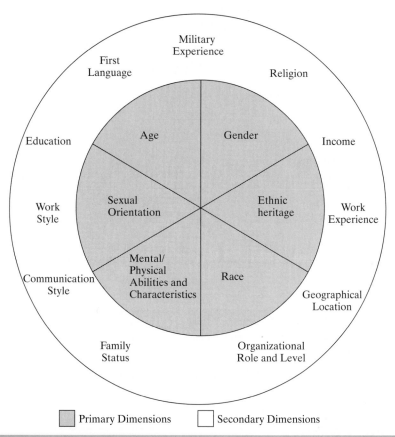

Primary Dimensions   Secondary Dimensions

FIGURE 1-1 Dimensions of Diversity

Source: From Loden, Marilyn, *Implementing Diversity*, 1996, Business One Irwin, p. 16.

in which the family is enveloped. This model recognizes that the individual faces the pulls of diverse generations as well as the pulls of a diverse environment outside of the family.[28]

Locke developed a similar, but even more comprehensive *interdependent* model (see Figure 1–2). Locke's model encompasses global and large cultural factors as well as community, family, and individual influences on the individual. Awareness of self and awareness of cultural diversity are both included in this model.[29]

"Other" Awareness   After self-awareness, training generally moves toward developing sensitivity to the cultures of others. The key to "other awareness" is recognition that others view the world differently. The training aim here is to develop an empathic understanding of others, an understanding of why various cultures have adopted the different traditions that support their ways of living. " . . . The culturally sensitive individual must be cognizant of world events and how members of various cultures translate those events into personal meaning."[30]

Learning Stages   Developing sensitivity to others is a learning process that is thought to occur in stages.[31,32,33] Modifying stages originally described by Hoopes,

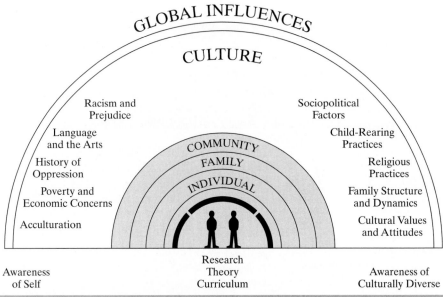

FIGURE 1-2 Multicultural Understanding

Source: From Locke, Don C., *Inceasing Multicultural Understanding: A Comprehensive Model*, 2/e, 1998, p. 2.

Bennett, for example, models learning stages in terms of the individual's awareness and acceptance of difference.[34]

Stage	Perspective
Denial	Differences are unseen, unrecognized: "As long as they all speak English, there's no problem."
Defense	Differences are seen, but judged negatively: "They just aren't aggressive enough to . . ."
Minimization	Differences are seen, but considered minor, unimportant: "Technology is bringing cultural uniformity to the developed world."
Acceptance	Differences are seen and accepted: "I always bone up on a new country before I go there."
Adaptation	Differences are "understood"; viewer can put himself/herself in shoes of others: "To solve this dispute, I have to change my approach."
Integration	Viewer's self-identity is not tied tightly to any one culture: "Everywhere is home, if you know enough about how things work here."

Derived from Bennett & Bennett

Changing the Organization

   . . . any process designed to "value," "manage," or "increase" diversity is fundamentally a change effort.

WITHERSPOON AND WOHLERT[35]

Powerful social forces are combining with diversity concerns to change social circumstances and mandate organizational change. The social forces include technological advances; the end of superpower conflict and military-model leadership; creation of new streamlined businesses; baby-boomer leadership styles; spiritually-oriented leadership; and changing workforce demographics.[36]

The diversity concerns driving change arose from major social institutions: religious, educational, philanthropic, and media-entertainment. Teachers unions and large foundations—notably Ford, Carnegie, MacArthur, and Pew Charitable Trusts— advanced the cause of multiculturalism in civic and community affairs and in the arts and education.[37]

The social forces and diversity concerns work to replace traditional command-and-control organizational leadership with its authoritarian ways by network leadership based upon collaboration and communication. Old rigid bureaucratic hierarchies are melting into fluid, shifting networks of relationships among employees, customers, suppliers, and allied competitors.[38]

As workforce demographics and social forces coalesce to change the nature of the work environment by channeling power and information to all individuals, organizations are forced to change their stances on how they handle their workforces and the diversities they contain.

Planning Change: The Blueprint   Band-aid or shotgun approaches will not effect sustained organizational change. Change efforts must be pervasive and systemic. Change involves new ways of thinking and acting. It must focus on the individual, not the group, because change affects all the roles people assume. Change efforts must also be adaptable to changing circumstances, and they must be continual. Last, but not least, communication is basic to initiation and maintenance of organizational change.[39]

Change Models   Frameworks for organizational change share a number of common threads:[40,41,42,43,44,45]

- Top management must be solidly behind the change effort.
- Frameworks are multidimensional, requiring change throughout the organization.
- A cultural audit is required to serve as a baseline against which to measure progress.
- CEOs and modelers alike agree that clear-cut goals are essential; progress can only be measured when goals are defined.
- Everyone in the organization must understand and be in agreement with the goals.
- Communication is basic to all change plans and procedures.
- Finally, change is not a quick fix. It is a process, usually a very long-term process.

Management Skills and Techniques

The finest policies, the best training programs, and the most comprehensive change plans will not work if managers lack the skills to effectively implement them. The management skills basic to all diversity engineering include (a) perceptual skills (for awareness recognition of differences); (b) cognitive skills (knowledge about diversity mixtures and related tensions); and (c) behavioral skills (ability to select appropriate responses)—skills that are wrapped up in communication.[46,47]

Much has been written about the awareness and knowledge skills, but relatively little has been said about the behavioral skills. Recognizing a situation is one thing; knowing what to do about it is another. One of the best schemas for deciding what response to make, what to say or do, is provided by Thomas and Woodruff, who adopt a framework devised by R. Roosevelt Thomas. This framework outlines eight general kinds of responses from which managers can choose:[48]

Responses That	Action
1. **Increase/decrease**	Increase or decrease amount of diversity, such as training sessions to increase diversity; excluding people to decrease diversity
2. **Deny**	Minimize diversity by ignoring it
3. **Assimilate**	Insist minorities conform to majority systems
4. **Suppress**	Don't discuss sensitive issues, e.g., religion
5. **Isolate**	Physically or socially isolate people
6. **Tolerate**	Benign live-and-let-live, while "limiting interactions . . . to superficial exchanges"
7. **Build future relationships**	Encouraging acceptance, e.g., training
8. **Foster mutual adaptation**	All parties adapt and adjust to get the job done.

Derived from Thomas and Woodruff

The best response is not the same in all situations. "The skill lies in being able to sort quickly through the possible options and choose the most effective one. Like most other skills, it is best learned through practice."[49]

Communication   There is universal recognition that communication is a singularly important managerial skill. It is becoming even more important as traditional managerial power structures give way to network and fluid structures and as international operations increase.[50,51,52,53,54]

Communication is more than just words. For many peoples, nonverbal communication is as important, if not more so, than spoken language. Nonverbal communication includes voice tone and inflection, phrasing, speech volume, gestures, eye contact and direction of gaze, posture and stance, facial expression, interpersonal distance and the person's status and history. South Koreans and Arabs, for example, consider body language, voice tone, and inflection to be especially important.[55]

Often overlooked is listening, yet listening is a key to effective communication in all cultures and critical in some. Asian communication is described as "listening-centered" and the importance of listening is openly recognized in some Native American cultures.[56] Stephen Covey underscores the value of listening when he recounts that he only learned the true art of communicating when he visited a Native American community to accept an award:

> This award was an "Indian Talking Stick," used when Elders gather in council to decide important matters or one could say, for conflict resolution. The stick works this way. Only the person holding the stick has the

right to talk, and he retains this right until everyone else in the circle can tell him what he is saying, from his (the speaker's) point of view.

RETOLD BY VIRGINIA MULLEN[57]

Another rarely recognized, but important form of communication is silence. For the Westerner, silence is uncomfortable, but not so for Asians, for whom silence is a tool of communication. It provides time to think about what has been communicated and to organize one's thoughts before giving voice to them. For Asians, "silence is not only comfortably tolerated, but is considered a desirable form of expression."[58]

The Impact of Diversity Initiatives: Outcomes

Do diversity initiatives really work? The answer is that little research has been done on the impact of training programs or of other diversity initiatives. It is difficult to obtain "hard data," as outcomes can be abstract and long term, goals are often nebulous, and individual and organizational outcomes are interwoven and interactive.[59,60]

The need for impact research is widely recognized. "Anecdotal evidence offers a potpourri of advice, suggesting that empirical examination [of diversity impact] must begin before problems are worsened rather than improved." [61]

What are the hoped-for advantages of diversity engineering? Desired outcomes include such intangibles as fresh outlooks, higher morale, increased flexibility, multiple perspectives, increased problem-solving skills, increased creativity, reduction in intergroup tensions, and improved market opportunities. Potential disadvantages include impasses in reaching agreements, miscommunication, confusion, ambiguity, fear, resistance and backlash from majority members, unrealistic expectations, high cost of litigation, and recruiting difficulties.

Outcomes Research   Anecdotal reports suggest there have been a whole range of outcomes: some were positive, some were negative, and some were neutral or inconclusive, but few were based on empirical measurement.

> . . . There is little systematic proof that the programs reduce intergroup tensions and increase productivity or creativity.
>
> The business case has yet to be established for more expansive, expensive organizational-change forms of diversity management.

—LYNCH[62]

Group Outcomes   One empirical study of three organizations found that diverse work groups had lower attachment among group members and lower organizational attachment than homogeneous groups. The effects were larger for the majority (whites and males) than for the minorities.[63]

Human dynamics with diverse teams should not be taken lightly. Many writers have reported that increasing diversity often has undesirable effects—as diverse teams tend to have a harder time working together, and tensions and conflicts can increase.[64,65,66,67] Robbins notes, " . . . diverse groups have more difficulty working together and solving problems, but *this dissipates with time*."[68]

The group findings should not be surprising in light of group dynamics. When groups get large, subgroups form; as diversity numbers increase within an organization, the diverse are apt to form their own affinity and caucus groups. Heterogeneous groups turn outward; attachment to the group and the organization lessens.[69]

Individual Outcomes The adjustments that employees make to an organization depend on the organization's tolerance for ambiguity, the value placed on cultural diversity, the demand for conformity, cultural fit, and any targeted acculturation.[70] According to Cox, individuals make one of four kinds of adjustments to an organization:[71]

Adjustments	
Assimilation	Adoption of the organization's culture
Separation	Alienation; individual doesn't adapt
Deculturation	Weak organization and individual cultures
Multiculturalism	Organization and individual both adapt; mutual appreciation

Derived from Cox

Just having diversity does not by itself guarantee greater business success nor does it guarantee qualitative social and creativity improvements. Too much diversity can be counterproductive, just as too much conformity can be stifling.

There has been no empirical evidence relating diversity programs to productivity or market share success. In noting this, T. J. Rogers, president and CEO of Cypress Semiconductor, commented: " . . . there has been no correlation between diversity programs and business success—wouldn't the great Japanese companies be in trouble if there *were* a correlation?"[72]

Few would argue the moral and fairness benefits of diversity. The jury is out, however, on how well current management frameworks, techniques, and training programs are working—at least in domestic organizations. In international ventures, the picture is more complicated. Diversity there is not an option; it is automatically part of the package, and some sort of diversity management framework is a necessity.

GLOBAL ORGANIZATIONS

> . . . The global community to which we belong consists of 6 billion people, more than 5,000 cultural and language groups, and a world of clashing civilizations and cultural and ethnic traditions.
>
> ANTHONY J. MARSELLA[73]

> Unless we become as global as foreign companies coming here, we're defining ourselves into a losing position.
>
> C. REYNOLDS[74]

International Cultures

More and more U.S. organizations are entering into joint ventures with organizations in other countries, setting up branches and factories, and even buying foreign companies. To manage such global enterprises necessitates knowing something about the character and values of the host or partner countries.

Managers and theorists have long been aware that the way organizations are managed in other cultures is not the same as in the United States and that cultural clashes easily occur in international ventures when values in other cultures are not understood. For several decades, attempts have been made to describe and classify world cultures on the assumption that foreign management practices reflect the values of their cultures.

Edward Hall classified cultures in terms of their communication patterns, using a continuum that ranged from very sensitive to nonverbal and situational cues **(high context cultures)** to not very sensitive to surrounding factors **(low context cultures).** Cultures low in context sensitivity respond more to actual words. Low-context cultures place a high value on individualism. Cultures high in context respond more to social factors and are more group-oriented, tending to "value harmony more than individual achievement." Establishing rapport and interpersonal relationships is important to communication in high context cultures.[75,76]

At the extreme with greatest sensitivity to context are Asian, Hispanic, American Indian, African-American, and Arabic cultures. Medium-context cultures are Southern European and Middle Eastern countries. Lowest in sensitivity to contextual cues are the Northern European, Germanic, and Scandinavian cultures.

Hall's model provides valuable keys to communication. Knowing that another culture is very sensitive to nonverbal cues opens the door to understanding how to communicate with that culture and also to understanding how that culture interprets your communications. For example, in some high-context cultures, a relationship of trust must be established before any business can be discussed.[77,78]

Probably the best-known system for evaluating other values was developed by Hofstede who, with colleagues at IBM, amassed over 72,000 questionnaires that provided descriptions of more than forty countries. In his system, indicators of cultural values are combined into five dimensions that reflect societal norms and are related to work behavior. Each of Hofstede's dimensions is expressed as a continuum with opposing values anchoring each end.[79,80]

China, for example, is characterized as having an extremely long-term orientation; West Africa is oriented to the short term. The Anglo cultures of the United States, Britain, Canada, and Australia are the most individualistic cultures and place a high value on autonomy and individual goals; Columbia, Peru, Venezuela, and Pakistan are the most collectivist and hold to strong group goals and group orientation.

The masculinity-femininity dimension indicates the extent to which biological differences translate into social roles. Defined social roles (masculinity) are strongest in Japan, Austria, Venezuela, and Italy; the least rigid sex roles (femininity) are found in Denmark, Norway, Sweden, and the Netherlands. Greece, Portugal, Belgium, and Japan show the greatest concern with uncertainty and the anxiety it creates, so people in these cultures often develop rules and rituals to minimize uncertainty. Sweden, Denmark, and Singapore are far more tolerant of ambiguity.

The power distance dimension is an indication of how strong status differences are in a culture. Rules and regulations and titles are used to maintain power distances in cultures with strong status hierarchies such as the Philippines, Mexico, Venezuela, and India. Cultures least concerned with maintaining social distances are New Zealand, Denmark, Israel, and Austria.[81]

	Continua	
Orientation		
	Long term (distant goals)	**Short term** (short-term goals)
Individualism		
	Individualism (autonomy) (individual advancement)	**Collectivism** (group goals) (group support)
Masculinity		
	Masculinity (traditional roles and jobs)	**Femininity** (flexible roles) (networking)
Uncertainty		
	Structured Avoidance (job security)	**Nonstructured preferences** (risk, fast-track advancement)
Power Distance		
	Equal Distance (consultative manager-worker)	**Unequal Distance** (teamwork with peers)

Derived from Hofstede

Although other international researchers also characterize cultures, most approaches are similar and use ratings made on continua.[82] There is a danger with this approach; it can easily lead to stereotyping entire cultures. If a culture is rated as highly individualistic, like the United States, then the tendency is to think of everyone in that culture as being highly individualistic. If a culture is characterized as having very defined gender roles, such as Austria, then all Austrians may be prejudged as reluctant or unwilling to work for a woman.

A more in-depth framework for describing cultures was developed by Ruhly, who adapted Hall's concepts. Ruhly's "culture iceberg" model describes three levels of a culture. This model is an important step forward because it recognizes that cultures have both visible and invisible layers and because it recognizes the differing communication implications of each layer.[83]

Cultural Level	*Visibility*	*Communication*
Technical	Visible	Little emotional content; straightforward communication
Formal	Partly visible	High emotional content; general social rules
Informal	Not visible	Intense emotional content; automatic learned behavior

Derived from Ruhly

At the technical level, "visible communication" includes such elements as the alphabet, numeric system, food-handling procedures, employer software packages, and information systems—accepted cultural features involving little emotion. As social rules prescribe what is done and not done, said and not said, in various situations however, communication becomes more emotional and less visible in a culture. For example, young people addressing older people or professionals by first name is offensive in many cultures. A boss publicly praising an employee from a culture where public boastfulness or standing out is not acceptable embarrasses the employee. A boss telling someone's personal problems to others is not only embarrassing, but is often viewed as an invasion of privacy.

The difficulty with understanding a culture through its cultural values and the behaviors they prescribe is that cultures, like people, don't follow rules of behavior perfectly. It is the paradoxes, the "exceptions to the rule," that make it so difficult to understand another culture. For example, the United States is a relatively egalitarian culture, but autocratic behavior is often tolerated in chief executives. In Latin America, status comes from one's class and family background except when it comes to professional soccer. In soccer, status is achieved and overrules class.[84] Paradoxes also occur as most people belong to multiple subcultures with different and sometimes clashing values that lead to behavior that does not mirror any one culture perfectly.[85,86]

A model to explain such exceptions and thereby provide a better understanding of culture is shown in Figure 1–3. This "cultural sense-making" model is a sequence that begins with making observations about a culture, then draws inferences and makes assumptions, and ends with choosing behaviors that take into account the values and history of the culture.[87]

Work Centrality   International cultures differ considerably on what work means in the lives of the people. A culture's view of work is reflected in worker behavior and expectations on the job. For example, in Thailand, work (*ngan*) means play and workdays have play periods; in Spain, work (*negocio*) indicates absence of leisure, a less positive outlook; and in work-oriented China, 7-day workweeks with long hours are not unusual. Understanding how a foreign workforce regards work is critical to the international manager. Failure to understand can lead to serious problems. In the case of Thailand, group cooperation is a value, and using individual merit can lower productivity as it runs counter to group values.

A group of researchers known as the MOW (Meaning of Work) International Research Team investigated the importance of work, its "centrality" to life, in eight different countries. Respondents indicated how satisfying they found work to be in terms of providing income, providing interest and satisfaction, providing contacts with others, facilitating service to society, keeping oneself occupied, and giving status and prestige. They found that in Japan, work was far more central to life than in

FIGURE 1-3 Cultural Sense-Making Model

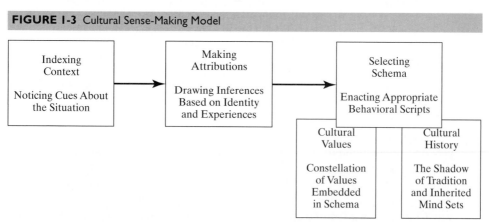

Source: Reprinted with permission of the Academy of Management from *Academy of Management Executive* (1991), Vol. 5, No. 3.

the other countries. Japan was followed by Yugoslavia and Israel. The United States was at the midpoint of the continuum, followed by Belgium, Netherlands, Germany, and Britain at the lowest centrality end.[88]

The MOW approach allows cultures to be compared, but more importantly for the global manager, gives insight into motivation and managing techniques. Knowing what the value of work is in a culture provides some clues about how to manage—how to motivate and what to expect from workers. For example, in Israel work is a source of interest and satisfaction, but not so for the Japanese. In the Netherlands and Japan, work is very low in satisfying status and prestige needs.[89]

Ronen and Shenkar combined findings from studies of work to group a number of societies on the basis of their job orientation and values. Their groupings of societies are presented as a "culture cake," with each grouping depicted as a "slice." Hickson and Pugh added two slices for a total of seven groupings (see Figure 1–4). Some, but not all, of the groupings are regional, that is, they are related by geographic proximity and/or language commonality.[90]

No one can know everything about the values in every culture, but there are similarities across cultural groupings. Using models such as these allows some educated guesses and suggests approaches based on those groupings.

International Organizations

The frameworks used by U.S. corporations to manage overseas ventures in part are based on whose cultural values the parent organization imposes. Moran and colleagues describe four different ways that world corporations set about to manage international operations:[91]

Global Management Orientations	
Ethnocentric	("home-country" centered) Key personnel are from home country and work in home country
Polycentric	("host-country" centered) Host country managers; loose federation of international operations
Regiocentric	(interdependent on a regional basis; focus on regional headquarters) Headquarters selects top management and sets corporate culture
Geocentric	(world-oriented "focus on both worldwide and local objectives") Goal is "integrated system" with worldwide approach

Derived from Moran, Harris, and Stripp

Ethnocentric management in which the home-country management style is imposed is often limited to entry modes such as exporting, licensing, and turnkey operations because management knows little about the host country, and what works at home "should work overseas." In **polycentric** management, the foreign market is "too hard to understand," so host-country managers are relatively free to manage their own way. Competition is focused on a market-by-market basis. One example of polycentric management is the original alliance between U.S. Air and British Overseas Airways

This diagram is derived from one by Ronen and Shenkar, 1985. These authors synthesized eight questionnaire studies by different researchers published between 1966 and 1980, chosen because each compared societies on job orientation and values. The most extensive was that by Hofstede. Ronen and Shenkar grouped nations by the cultural affinities they found in the research results. Two "slices" have been added, East-Central Europeans and Developing Countries for, although these do not have the same kind of internal cultural affinity as is apparent in the other slices, they complete the diagram so far as each slice is a chapter in this book.

The nations shown are self-evidently not complete listings. They exemplify the coverage of each of the Chapters 3 to 9. Those described in greater detail in each chapter as illustrative examples are italicized.

FIGURE 1-4 A Culture Cake

Source: From Hickson, David J. and Derick S. Pugh, *Management Worldwide*, Penguin Books, 1995, p. 44.

when each airline continued to operate fairly independently. Another example is Pepsi-Cola, with its large number of joint ventures around the world. It manages with a franchise system in which local managers are brought to the United States for training.

Parent organizations use **regiocentric** management when they feel that regional insiders can best coordinate operations within the region. For example, a Korean branch might manage Asian operations; a German company might coordinate European operations. Home-office functions include world strategy, country analyses, basic research and development, selection of top management, technology transfer and establishment of corporate culture.

Geocentric management is a highly interdependent system that speaks in terms of the global village. The focus is at once both worldwide and on local objectives.[92] Asea, Brown, Boveri, Inc. (ABB) is a "federation of national companies . . . [using] a matrix structure."[93] Some regional grouping is also used. Whirlpool global management is also geocentric in nature. Whirlpool recently designed a refrigerator that "used insulation technology from our European business, compressor technology from our Brazilian affiliates, and manufacturing and design expertise from our U.S. operation."[94]

These four management orientations are not mutually exclusive. Many organizations begin as ethnocentric or polycentric and gradually develop a more regiocentric or geocentric framework. The Bechtel Corporation, for instance, originally operated as two separate entities, one in the United States and one overseas, but now is highly integrated. ABB uses geocentric management with regiocentric groupings.

Specific Organizations   It is not enough for organizations to learn about the national values and management styles of their foreign affiliates. They must also understand the cultures of the specific organizations that they manage or with which they deal. Even within a national culture, there are organizational cultures. Organizations within a country share basic values originating from their national culture, but they also differ from each other in their own internal cultures

It is no easier to classify types of international organizations than it is to classify their national cultures, but there are themes.

> All the different types of organizations of the world cannot be pigeonholed into three (or any number of) limited classifications, . . . But general tendencies toward differences in organizational structure can be observed across countries, and these differences are most likely related to cultural differences.
>
> MATSUMOTO[95]

One way to describe the culture of an organization in another country is to look at the usual way they do things. Hickson and Pugh summarized the work of Hofstede, Neuijen, Ohayu, and Sanders to produce a set of "practices" that helps to define the culture of individual organizations.[96]

Another way to understand the culture of an organization in another country is by examining how the organization is structured, how jobs are designed, the delega-

Practices	*Focus*
1. **Process Orientation** versus **Results Orientation**	Means versus ends
2. **Employee Orientation** versus **Job Orientation**	Worker concern versus getting job done
3. **Parochial** versus **Professional**	Identification with organization versus professional identification
4. **Open System** versus **Closed System**	High newcomer acceptance and communication flow versus low
5. **Loose Control** versus **Tight Control**	Degree of strictness of work behavior code
6. **Normative** versus **Pragmatic**	Fixed system versus market-driven approach

Derived from Hickson and Pugh

tion of authority, and the assessment and control of performance. In **bureaucratic** cultures such as France and Japan, the management hierarchy tends to be pyramidal with stylized and rigid procedures. In **technical** cultures such as Germany and the United Kingdom, management is more likely to be paternalistic with controlled decision-making. **Managerial** cultures such as the Netherlands and Switzerland are more performance-oriented and tend to be adaptive and flexible with minimal organization.[97]

Research   Management issues become more complex in multinational organizations. Unfortunately, research does not always provide guidance for managers because it focuses primarily on organizational structure and rarely on corporate climate and because the scope differs from study to study. Studies may focus on single cultures, second cultures, multiple cultures, contrasting cultures, international management, or intercultural management.[98]

Not only does the concept of work differ across cultures, but so does the concept of management. Management styles are related to processes in society—family, school, politics, government, religion, and beliefs about science. "There is something in all countries called 'management,' but its meaning differs to a larger or smaller extent from one country to the other . . . ." American-style managers are missing in Germany, Japan, France, Holland, and China.[99]

An interesting illustration of how management practices differ among countries comes from a joint venture between Siemens AG (Germany), Toshiba Corp. (Japan), and IBM (United States). Siemens briefed its employees on the "American hamburger style of management" as follows:

> . . . American managers . . . prefer to criticize subordinates gently. They start with small talk: "How's the family?" That is the top of the hamburger bun. Then Americans slip in the meat—the criticism. And they exit with encouraging words—more bun. With Germans, . . . all you get is the meat. And with the Japanese, it's all the soft stuff—you have to *smell* the meat.
>
> NEW YORK TIMES[100]

In managing a global manufacturing corporation, Whirlpool CEO David Whitwam identifies three areas of similarity in the operations across countries that provide the common elements for a management framework:[101]

Technological	Many manufacturing processes are the same from one country to another.
Vision	Overseas branches must share a common mission.
Corporate values	Successful globalization is based on a clearly articulated and defined set of organizational values and core culture.

International Leadership

In today's period of globalism, corporate capital requires a multicultural, multinational management and labor force.

M. MARABLE[102]

Companies with overseas branches face staffing problems—particularly difficult is the selection of managers. What qualities and skills should global managers have? Are they the same as those for domestic managers? How should global managers be trained?

Several writers and CEOs have spoken to these issues:

> Clearly there is no single model for a global manager. Neither the old-line international specialist nor the more recent global generalist can cope with the complexities of cross-border strategies. Indeed, the dynamism of today's marketplace calls for managers with diverse skills.
>
> P. HARRIS AND R. MORAN[103]

> It is a simple and inescapable fact that the skills and capabilities required to manage a global company are different from those required for a domestic company.
>
> WHIRLPOOL CEO DAVID WHITWAM[104]

> Global managers are made, not born. . . . There is no substitute for line experience in three or four countries to create a global perspective. You also encourage people to work in mixed-nationality teams. You *force* them to create personal alliances across borders, which means that sometimes you interfere in hiring decisions.
>
> PRESIDENT AND CEO PERCY BARNEVIK
> ASEA BROWN BOVERI[105]

U.S. Global Leadership Different cultures have different expectations for the future and so select and train future executives differently. In spite of increasing international ventures, U.S. domestic corporations do not appear to focus very much on international concerns and, therefore, do not select or train CEOs along these lines. "A survey report of 1,500 top managers worldwide revealed that U.S. executives were too parochial and insular in their perspectives."[106] The survey, conducted by Korn/Ferry, predicted a shortage of global executives and revealed some interesting cultural differences in the qualities desired in future CEOs.

This study found that American leaders are focused on domestic competition and expect to compete in the twenty-first century primarily on price. In accordance with this market view, American CEOs select and groom their successors in marketing and finance and perhaps production technology. International experience is not viewed as being very important.

Japanese and European leaders, however, are focused on international competition, with "Europeans expecting more than half of their revenues to come from foreign markets." They expect to compete on product quality and innovation. These executives see technical and R&D skills as important, and they view international experience as crucial.[107]

No matter what their preparation or the model of global management the organization follows, its leadership must develop a strong corporate culture with a global mission and a set of core values and be able to communicate these to everyone in the organization. It is important that everyone share the vision and values.[108]

THE FUTURE

At least four trends can be expected to impact diversity initiatives in the future: organizations increasingly entering the international arena, continued growth of virtual organizations, continued decentralization of power within organizations, and changes in the ways that discrimination and prejudice are both expressed and received.

Trend 1: Internationalization

More and more organizations will "go global." Pressure will increase on U.S. organizations as they discover, as Whirlpool did, that their industries are going international whether or not they choose to do so. U. S. organizations already in the international arena will continue expansion of their overseas ventures. Motorola, for example, has already built 13 factories in nine countries and " . . . is pushing into practically every niche in Asia's booming telecom and semiconductor markets."[109] As U.S. organizations continue to expand internationally, other countries will also continue to expand their activities in the United States as well as elsewhere in the world. International business will become more interdependent and complex as regional trading blocs such as NAFTA and the European Union increase. The opening of new markets has already increased the number of cultures to understand. Interdependence becomes increasingly apparent as the actions of one country reverberate to others. The Mexican currency devaluation in 1995, for example, was felt around the world (especially in North America) and forced foreign firms to "immediately adjust their strategies."[110]

Internationalization means that organizations must not only learn to deal with foreign cultures, but they must also develop frameworks for managing foreign operations and for selecting and training international managers and overseas workforces. Major organizational change is in the future:

> For a company to become a truly global enterprise, employees will have to change the way they think and act, taking on progressively more responsibility and initiative until the company behaves globally in all its parts—without the CEO cracking the whip.
>
> D. WHITWAM[111]

Trend 2: Virtual Companies

Increasingly, companies such as Citicorp are becoming " . . . a web of informational relationships" where much of the work occurs electronically via computers, fax machines, videoconferencing, and car phones.[112] Most workers are in knowledge or service jobs; managers are facilitators relying on people skills. Emerging self-managed teams may include customers, suppliers, retailers, investors, and distributors; teams may change, may be scattered, may never meet. "The term headquarters is becoming immaterial. . . ."[113]

> The virtual corporation is built upon trust, collaboration, cooperation, and teamwork, but it also relies on individual achievement and the ability to be entrepreneurial, and therefore competitive, in outlook.
>
> CARR-RUFFINO[114]

The networks, peer relationships, and teamwork all require that diverse people work together. The entrepreneurial, competitive aspect of the virtual organization means harnessing the perspectives and contributions of diverse workers to maximize creativity and flexibility in order to be competitive.

Trend 3: Decentralization of Power

Technology is flattening layers of authority in manufacturing companies and in service industries. The downsizing and delayering of organizations goes hand in hand with virtual organizations. Like the virtual organizations, the impact of decentralization on diversity includes extensive networking and collaboration among diverse personnel and the development of self-managed teams.

Trend 4: Prejudice and Discrimination

Changes are appearing with regard to prejudice and discrimination in U.S. organizations. Discrimination still exists, but it is appearing more and more in altered forms such as social class and in exclusion from information and from informal networks. Blatant discrimination is giving way to more subtle forms that are more difficult to identify and prove. However, this discrimination is increasingly being challenged as more and more victims come forward and demand fair treatment.

Many now call for renewed educational efforts to deal with discrimination and diversity concerns, and these may well increase. Education per se may not be enough, however. Behavior change precedes attitude change. In this regard, Fraser's observation regarding racial prejudice may be applied to other forms of discrimination as well:

> It is believed by many that the key to overcoming racial hatred and prejudice is education. It is not! Education is very important but it's not the key. The key is close personal friendships.
>
> FRASER[115]

Future managers and change agents must be alert to these trends and to new and changing social forces. Organizational diversity efforts of the future must remain flexible to meet changing social circumstances.

Discussion Questions

1. a. Provide specific examples of Hofstede's dimensions translating into workplace behaviors. For example, a manager who is high on power distance might be overly critical of an employee who calls the boss by his first name and in general behaves casually in the workplace.
    b. Do the same for Hall's dimensions.
2. Referring to Bennett and Bennett's learning stages model, *honestly* assess your current stage. How could being in this stage negatively or positively impact your interactions in a diverse workplace?
3. This article says that management has to support change for diversity initiatives to succeed. What personal qualities do managers need to become effective leaders in diversity change initiatives? Why?

4. a. Which courses in your college program have contributed to preparing you to work in a diverse organization? Why?
   b. What life experiences have prepared you to work in a diverse organization? Why?
5. Have you worked for a company that has provided any type of diversity training to its employees? What level of employee was trained? What was the focus of the training (avoiding lawsuits, self-awareness, other)? Evaluate the effectiveness of the training program.
6. Go to the www.diversityinc.com Web site and find an example of a current news story that illustrates one of the stages of policy evaluation: assimilation, differentiation, or integration. Explain why this organization is operating in this stage.

Notes

1. Brown, G., Jr. (1994), "Our most serious problems are social problems for which there are no technical solutions, only human solutions." *The Chronicle of Higher Education*, p. B5.
2. Wong, F. (1990). "Commentary on Presumptions About Cultural Diversity." *WASC*.
3. Loden, M., and J. Rosener. (1991). *Workforce America: Managing Employee Diversity as a Vital Resource.* Homewood, Ill.: Business One Irwin, p. 18.
4. Thomas, R. R., Jr. (1992). "Teaching Diversity: Business Schools Search for Model Approaches." *AACSB, 23*, p. 3.
5. Simons, G., C. Vazquez, and P. Harris. (1993*). Transcultural Leadership: Empowering the Diverse Workforce.* Houston: Gulf Publishing.
6. Kessler-Harris, A. (1992). "Multiculturalism Can Strengthen, Not Undermine, a Common Culture." *The Chronicle of Higher Education*, Oct. 21, p. B3.
7. Samuels, W. (1991). "Dynamics of Cultural Change." *Society, 29*, p. 23–26.
8. Sowell, T. (1991). "A World View of Cultural Diversity." *Society, 29*, p. 38.
9. Locke, D. (1992). *Increasing Multicultural Understanding: A Comprehensive Model.* Newbury Park, Calif.: Sage, p. 6.
10. Thomas, R. R., Jr. *op. cit.*
11. Thomas, D., and R. Ely. (1996). "Making Differences Matter: A New Paradigm for Managing Diversity." *Harvard Business Review*, Sept–Oct, pp. 79–90.
12. Thomas, D., and R. Ely. *ibid.*
13. Thomas, D., and R. Ely. *ibid.*
14. Witherspoon, P., and K. Wohlert. (1996) "An Approach to Developing Communication Strategies for Enhancing Organizational Diversity." *The Journal of Business Communication, 33*, pp. 375–399.
15. Golembiewski, R. (1995). *Managing Diversity in Organizations.* Tuscaloosa: The University of Alabama Press.
16. Carr-Ruffino, N. (1996). *Managing Diversity: People Skills for a Multicultural Workplace.* Cincinnati, Ohio: International Thompson Publishing.
17. Lynch, F. (1997). *The Diversity Machine.* New York: The Free Press, p. 50.
18. Thomas, D., and R. Ely. *op. cit.*
19. Stranges, T. (1998). "Why White Males Hate Diversity Initiatives." *Managing Diversity, 7*, No. 12, pp. 1, 7.
20. Gormley, D. (1996). "Letters to the Editor: Managing Diversity." *Harvard Business Review*, Nov–Dec, p. 177.
21. Rogers, T. J. (1996). "Letters to the Editor: Managing Diversity." *Harvard Business Review*, Nov–Dec, pp. 177–178.
22. DeRosa, P. (1995). "Social Change or Status Quo? Implications of Diversity Training Models." *"The Fourth R" The Newsletter of the National Association for Mediation in Education, 56*, pp. 4–12.
23. Nemetz, P., and S. Christensen. (1996). "The Challenge of Cultural Diversity: Harnessing a Diversity of Views to Understand Multiculturalism." *Academy of Management Review, 21*, No. 2, pp. 434–462.

24. Markus, H.R., and D. Kitayama. (1991). "Culture and the Self: Implications for Cognition, Emotion, and Motivation." *Psychological Review, 98,* pp. 224–253.

25. Kennedy, J., and A. Everest. (1991). "Put Diversity in Context." *Personnel Journal,* pp. 50–54.

26. Matsumoto, D. (2000*). Culture and Psychology. People Around the World.* 2d. ed. Belmont, Calif.: Wadsworth.

27. Loden, M. (1996). *Implementing Diversity.* Chicago: Irwin.

28. Szapocznik, J., and W. Kurtines. (1993). "Family Psychology and Cultural Diversity: Opportunities for Theory, Research and Applications.*" American Psychologist, 48,* pp. 400–407.

29. Locke, D. (1998). *Increasing Multicultural Understanding.* Thousand Oaks, Calif.: Sage Publications.

30. Locke, D. *ibid.*

31. Bennett, M. (1986). "A Developmental Approach to Training for Intercultural Sensitivity." *International Journal of Intercultural Relations, 10,* pp. 179–196.

32. Carr-Ruffino, N. *op. cit.*

33. Thomas, P. (1995). "A Cultural Rapport Model." In Griggs L. and L. Louv (eds). *Valuing Diversity: New Tools for a New Reality.* New York: McGraw-Hill Inc., pp. 1–14.

34. Bennett, M., and J. Bennett. (1998). "Developing Intercultural Competence." Paper presented at Worcester State College, Worcester, Mass.

35. Witherspoon, P., and K. Wohlert. *op. cit.*

36. Fraser, G. (1998). "The Slight Edge: Valuing and Managing Diversity." *Vital Speeches of the Day,* Feb. 1, *64,* N. 8.

37. Lynch, F. (1997). *The Diversity Machine. The Drive to Change the "White Male Workplace."* New York: The Free Press.

38. Carr-Ruffino, N. *op. cit.,* p. 68

39. Witherspoon, P, and K. Wohlert. *op. cit.,* p. 378

40. Thomas, D., and R. Ely. *op. cit.*

41. Cox, T., Jr. (1993). *Cultural Diversity in Organizations: Theory, Research and Practice.* San Francisco: Berrett-Koehler.

42. Robinson-Easley, C. A. (2000). *Shaping Organizations for the Future Through the Effective Management of our Most Diverse Resources: Our People.* Unpublished manuscript.

43. Simons, G. et al. *op. cit.*

44. Simons, G. et al. *op. cit.*

45. Whitwam, D., in Maruca. R. (March-April 1994). "The Right Way to Go Global: An Interview with Whirlpool C.E.O. David Whitwam." *Harvard Business Review, 72,* No. 2, p. 72.

46. Gardenswartz, L., and A. Rowe. (1993). *Managing Diversity. A Complete Desk Reference and Planning Guide.* Business One Irwin/Pfeiffer Company.

47. Thomas, R., Jr., and M. Woodruff. (1999). *Building a House for Diversity. How a Fable About a Giraffe and an Elephant Offers New Strategies for Today's Workforce.* New York: AMACOM.

48. *Ibid.,* p. 20–21.

49. *Ibid.*

50. Bennett, M., and J. Bennett. (1995*). op. cit.*

51. Carr-Ruffino, N. *op. cit.*

52. Fiol, C. M. (1994). "Consensus, Diversity, and Learning in Organizations." *Organizational Science, 5,* No. 3. pp. 403–420.

53. Kennedy, J., and A. Everest. *op. cit.*

54. Witherspoon, P., and K. Wohlert. *op. cit.*

55. Deresky, H. (1997). *International Management.* 2d ed. Reading, Mass.: Addison-Wesley.

56. *Ibid.*

57. Covey, S. quoted in V. Mullen. (2000). "Lessons from the Field: Consulting in Third World Systems." Symposium paper presented at the American Psychological Association Annual Convention. Washington, D.C.

58. Deresky, H. *op. cit.*

59. Rossett, A., and T. Bickham. (1994). "Diversity Training. Hope, Faith and Cynicism." *Training,* Jan. pp. 41–46.

60. Nemetz, P., and S. Christensen. (1996). "The Challenge of Cultural Diversity: Harnessing a Diversity of Views to Understand Multiculturalism." *Academy of Management Review, 21* No. 2, pp. 434–462.

61. Rossett, A., and T. Bickham. *op. cit.*

62. Lynch, F. *op. cit.*

63. Tsui, A., Egan, R., and C. O'Reilly III. (1992). "Being Different: Relational Demography and Organizational Attachment.*" Administrative Science Quarterly,* pp. 549–579.

64. Thomas, D., and R. Ely. *op. cit.*
65. Cox, T. *op. cit.*
66. Nemetz, P., and S. Christensen. *op. cit.*
67. Robbins, S. (2001). *Organizational Behavior.* 9th ed. Upper Saddle River, N.J.: Prentice Hall.
68. Robbins, S. *ibid.*
69. Macionis, J. (2000). *Society. The Basics.* 5th ed. Upper Saddle River, N.J.: Prentice Hall.
70. Carr-Ruffino, N. *op. cit.*
71. Cox, T., and J. Finley-Nickerson. (1991). "Models of Acculturation for Intraorganizational Cultural Diversity." *Canadian Journal of Administrative Sciences, 8,* 2, pp. 90–100.
72. Rogers, T. *op. cit.*
73. Marsella, A. (2000). *Psychology International, 11,* 3, pp. 2–3.
74. Reynolds, C., Quoted in Solomon C. (1993). "HR Heads into The Global Age." *Personnel Journal, 76.*
75. Kennedy, J., and A. Everest. *op. cit.*
76. Matsumoto, D. *op. cit.*
77. Kennedy, J., and A. Everest. *op. cit.*
78. Matsumoto, D. *op. cit.*
79. Hofstede, G. (1998). "Cultural Constraints in Management Theories." In A. Francesco & B. Gold. *International Organizational Behavior: Text, Readings, Cases and Skills.* Upper Saddle River, N.J.: Prentice Hall.
80. Matsumoto, D. *op. cit.,* pp. 449–460.
81. Hofstede, G. (1998). *op. cit.*
82. Osland, J., and A. Bird. (2001). "Beyond Sophisticated Stereotyping: Cultural Sensemaking in Context." In Osland, J. D. Kolb, and I. Rubin (eds). *The Organizational Behavior Reader* 7th ed. Upper Saddle River, N.J.: Prentice Hall, pp. 356–370.
83. Thomas, P. *op. cit.*
84. Osland, J,. and A. Bird. *op. cit.*
85. Rokeach, M. (1993). *The Nature of Human Values.* New York: The Free Press.
86. Hofstede, G. (1994). *Cultures* and *Organizations: Intercultural Cooperation and Its Importance for Survival.* New York: McGraw Hill.
87. Osland, J., and A. Bird. *op. cit.*
88. Deresky, H. *op. cit.*
89. Deresky, H. *op. cit.*
90. Hickson, D., and D. Pugh. (1995). *Management Worldwide. The Impact of Societal Culture on Organizations around the Globe.* New York: Penguin.
91. Moran, R., P. Harris, and W. Stripp. (1993) *Developing the Global Organization: Strategies for Human Resource Professionals.* Houston: Gulf.
92. Harris, P., and R. Moran. (1996). *Managing Cultural Differences: Leadership Strategies for a New World of Business.* 4th ed. Houston: Gulf.
93. Solomon, C. (1993). "HR Heads into the Global Age." *Personnel Journal, 76,* p. 80.
94. Whitwam, D. *op. cit.,* pp. 135–146.
95. Matsumoto, D. *op. cit.,* p. 449.
96. Hickson, D., and D. Pugh. *op. cit.*
97. Hay Associates (1996). In Harris P. and R. Moran. *op.cit.*
98. Adler, N. (1983). "A Typology of Management Studies Involving Cultures." *Journal of International Business Studies,* pp. 29–46.
99. Hofstede, G. (1998). *op. cit.*
100. Siemens, A.G. (1994). Quoted in Browning E.S. "Computer Chip Project Brings Rivals Together, But the Cultures Clash." *New York Times,* May 3, pp. A1, A8.
101. Siemens, A.G. *op cit.*
102. Marable, M. (2000). "We Need New and Critical Study of Race and Ethnicity." *The Chronicle of Higher Education,* Feb 25, pp. B4–B7.
103. Harris, P,. and R. Moran. *op. cit.,* p. 8
104. Whitwam, D. *op. cit.*
105. Barnevik, P. Quoted in P. Harris and R. Moran. *op. cit.,* p. 8.
106. *Los Angeles Times,* January 15, 1989, pp. 5–6.
107. "Myopic High-Flyers," *The Economist,* June 17, 1989, p. 80.
108. Fraser, G. *op. cit.*
109. Deresky, H. *op. cit.*
110. Deresky, H. *op. cit.*
111. Whitwam, D. *op. cit.*
112. Deresky, H. *op. cit.*
113. Deresky, H. *op. cit.*
114. Carr-Ruffino, N. *op. cit.*
115. Fraser, G. *op. cit.*

Body Ritual Among the Nacirema

Horace Miner

The anthropologist has become so familiar with the diversity of ways in which different peoples behave in similar situations that he is not apt to be surprised by even the most exotic customs. In fact, if all of the logically possible combinations of behavior have not been found somewhere in the world, he is apt to suspect that they must be present in some yet undescribed tribe. This point has, in fact, been expressed with respect to clan organization by Murdock (1949:71). In this light, the magical beliefs and practices of the Nacirema present such unusual aspects that it seems desirable to describe them as an example of the extremes to which human behavior can go.

Professor Linton first brought the ritual of the Nacirema to the attention of anthropologists twenty years ago (1936:326), but the culture of this people is still very poorly understood. They are a North American group living in the territory between the Canadian Cree, the Yaqui and Tarahumare of Mexico, and the Carib and Arawak of the Antilles. Little is known of their origin, although tradition states that they came from the east. According to Nacirema mythology, their nation was originated by a culture hero, Notgnihsaw, who is otherwise known for two great feats of strength—the throwing of a piece of wampum across the river Pa-To-Mac and the chopping down of a cherry tree in which the Spirit of Truth resided.

Nacirema culture is characterized by a highly developed market economy which has evolved in a rich natural habitat. While much of the people's time is devoted to economic pursuits, a large part of the fruits of these labors and a considerable portion of the day are spent in ritual activity. The focus of this activity is the human body, the appearance and health of which loom as a dominant concern in the ethos of the people. While such concern is certainly not unusual, its ceremonial aspects and associated philosophy are unique.

The fundamental belief underlying the whole system appears to be that the human body is ugly and that its natural tendency is to debility and disease. Incarcerated in such a body, man's only hope is to avert these characteristics through the use of the powerful influences of ritual and ceremony. Every household has one or more shrines devoted to this purpose. The more powerful individuals in the society have several shrines in their houses and, in fact, the opulence of a house is often referred to in terms of the number of such ritual centers it possesses. Most houses are of wattle and daub construction, but the shrine rooms of the wealthy are walled with stone. Poorer families imitate the rich by applying pottery plaques to their shrine walls.

While each family has at least one shrine, the rituals associated with it are not family ceremonies but are private and secret. The rites are normally only discussed with children, and then only during the period when they are being initiated into these mysteries. I was able, however, to establish sufficient rapport with the natives to examine these shrines and to have the rituals described to me.

The focal point of the shrine is a box or chest, which is built into the wall. In this chest are kept the many charms and magical potions without which no native believes he could live.

These preparations are secured from a variety of specialized practitioners. The most powerful of these are the medicine men, whose assistance must be rewarded with substantial gifts. However, the medicine men do not provide the curative potions for their clients, but decide what the ingredients should be and then write them down in an ancient and secret language. This writing is understood only by the medicine men and by the herbalists who, for another gift, provide the required charm.

The charm is not disposed of after it has served its purpose, but is placed in the charm-box of the household shrine. As these magical materials are specific for certain ills, and the real or imagined maladies of the people are many, the charm-box is usually full to overflowing. The magical packets are so numerous that the people forget what their purposes were and fear to use them again. While the natives are very vague on this point, we can only assume that the idea in retaining all the old magical materials is that their presence in the charm-box, before which the body rituals are conducted, will in some way protect the worshipper.

Beneath the charm-box is a small font. Each day every member of the family, in succession, enters the shrine room, bows his head before the charm-box, mingles different sorts of holy waters in the font, and proceeds with a brief ritual of ablution. The holy waters are secured from the Water Temple of the community, where the priests conduct elaborate ceremonies to make the liquid ritually pure.

In the hierarchy of magical practitioners, and below the medicine men in prestige, are specialists whose designation is best translated "holy-mouth-men." The Nacirema have an almost pathological horror of and fascination with the mouth, the condition of which is believed to have a supernatural influence on all social relationships. Were it not for the rituals of the mouth, they believe that their teeth would fall out, their gums bleed, their jaws shrink, their friends desert them, and their lovers reject them. They also believe that a strong relationship exists between oral and moral characteristics. For example, there is a ritual ablution of the mouth for children which is supposed to improve their moral fiber.

The daily body ritual performed by everyone includes a mouth-rite. Despite the fact that these people are so punctilious about care of the mouth, this rite involves a practice which strikes the uninitiated stranger as revolting. It was reported to me that the ritual consists of inserting a magic bundle of hog hairs into the mouth, along with certain magical powder, and then moving the bundle in a highly formalized series of gestures.

In addition to the private mouth-rite, the people seek out the holy-mouth-man once or twice a year. These practitioners have an impressive set of paraphernalia, consisting of a variety of augers, awls, probes, and prods. The use of these objects in the exorcism of the evils of the mouth involves almost unbelievable ritual torture of the client. The holy-mouth-man opens the client's mouth and, using the above mentioned tools, enlarges any holes, which may have been created in the teeth. Magical materials are put into these holes. If there are no naturally occurring holes in the teeth, large sections of one or more teeth are gouged out so that the supernatural substance can be applied. In the client's view, the purpose of the ministrations is to arrest decay and to draw friends. The extremely sacred and traditional character of the rite is evident in the fact that the natives return to the holy-mouth-man, despite the fact that their teeth continue to decay.

It is to be hoped that, when a thorough study of the Nacirema is made, there will be careful inquiry into the personality structure of these people. One has but to watch the gleam in the eye of a holy-mouth-man, as he jabs an awl into an exposed nerve, to suspect that a certain amount of sadism is involved. If this can be established, a very interesting pattern emerges, for most of the population shows definite masochistic tendencies. It was to these that Professor Linton referred in discussing a distinctive part of the daily body ritual which was performed only by men. This part of the rite involves scraping and lacerating the surface of the face with a sharp instrument. Special women's rites are performed only four times during each lunar month, but what they lack in frequency is made up for in barbarity. As part of this ceremony, women bake their heads in small ovens for about an hour. The theoretically interesting point is that what seems to be a preponderantly masochistic people have developed sadistic specialists.

The medicine men have an imposing temple, or latipso, in every community of any size. The more elaborate ceremonies required to treat very sick patients can only be performed at this temple. These ceremonies involve not only the thaumaturge but a permanent group of vestal maidens who move sedately about the temple chambers in distinctive costume and headdress.

The latipso ceremonies are so harsh that it is phenomenal that a fair proportion of the really sick natives who enter the temple ever recover. Small children whose indoctrination is still incomplete have been known to resist attempts to take them to the temple because "that is where you go to die." Despite this fact, sick adults are not only willing but eager to undergo the protracted ritual purification, if they can afford to do so. No matter how ill the supplicant or how grave the emergency, the guardians of many temples will not admit a client if he cannot give a rich gift to the custodian. Even after one has gained admission and survived the ceremonies, the guardians will not permit the neophyte to leave until he makes still another gift.

The supplicant entering the temple is first stripped of all his or her clothes. In everyday life the Nacirema avoids exposure of his body and its natural functions. Bathing and excretory acts are performed only in secrecy of the household shrine, where they are ritualized as part of the body-rites. Psychological shock results from the fact that body secrecy is suddenly lost upon entry into the latipso. This sort of ceremonial treatment is necessitated by the fact that the excreta are used by a diviner to ascertain the course and nature of the client's sickness. Female clients, on the other hand, find their naked bodies are subjected to the scrutiny, manipulation, and prodding of the medicine men.

Few supplicants in the temple are well enough to do anything but lie on their hard beds. The daily ceremonies, like the rites of the holy-mouth-men, involve discomfort and torture. With ritual precision, the vestals awaken their miserable charges each dawn and roll them about on their beds of pain while performing ablutions, in the formal movements of which the maidens are highly trained. At other times they insert magic wands in the supplicant's mouth or force him to eat substances which are supposed to be healing. From time to time the medicine men come to their clients and jab magically treated needles into their flesh. The fact that these ceremonies may not cure, and may even kill the neophyte, in no way decreases the people's faith in the medicine men.

There remains one other kind of practitioner, known as a "listener." This witch-doctor has the power to exorcise the devils that lodge in the heads of people who have been bewitched. The Nacirema believe that parents bewitched their own children. Mothers are particularly suspected of putting a curse on children while teaching them the secret body rituals. The counter-magic of the witch-doctor is unusual in its lack of ritual. The patient simply tells the "listener" all his troubles and fears, beginning with the earliest difficulties he can remember. The memory displayed by the Nacirema in these exorcism sessions is truly remarkable. It is not uncommon for the patient to bemoan the rejection he felt upon being weaned as a babe, and a few individuals even see their troubles going back to the traumatic effects of their own birth.

In conclusion, mention must be made of certain practices which have their base in native esthetics but which depend upon the pervasive aversion to the natural body and its functions. There are ritual fasts to make fat people thin and ceremonial feasts to make thin people fat. Still other rites are used to make women's breasts larger if they are small, and smaller if they are large. General dissatisfaction with breast shape is symbolized in the fact that the ideal form is virtually outside the range of human variation. A few women afflicted with almost inhuman hypermammary development are so idolized that they make a handsome living by simply going from village to village and permitting the natives to stare at them for a fee.

Reference has already been made to the fact that excretory functions are ritualized, routinized, and relegated to secrecy. Natural reproduction functions are similarly distorted. Intercourse is taboo as a topic and scheduled as an act. Efforts are made to avoid pregnancy by the use of magical materials or by limiting intercourse to certain phases of the moon. Conception is actually very infrequent. When pregnant, women dress so as to hide their condition. Parturition takes place in secret, without friends or relatives to assist, and the majority of women do not nurse their infants.

Our review of the ritual life of the Nacirema has certainly shown them to be a magic-ridden people. It is hard to understand how they have managed to exist so long under the burdens which they have imposed upon themselves. But even such exotic customs as these take on real meaning when they are viewed with the insight provided by Malinowski when he wrote (1948:70).

> Looking from far and above, from our high places of safety in developed civilization, it is easy to see all the crudity and irrelevance of magic. But without its power and guidance, early man could not have advanced to the higher stages of civilization.

Discussion Questions

1. What general message do you think the author was trying to convey in this description of one aspect of American culture?
2. Why are some behaviors described as "magic"?
3. Why are some behaviors described as "rituals"? Do you think this is a fair label?
4. Does the humorous approach to our culture bother you? Do you feel that the description is belittling or sarcastic in tone?
5. Imagine that you are a member of the author's culture. What kinds of stereotypes could you have of the American culture and its people if this reading is your only source of information?

References

Linton, Ralph. (1936). *The Study of Man*. New York: D. Appleton-Century Co.

Malinowski, Bronislaw. (1948). *Magic, Science and Religion*. Glencoe: The Free Press.

Murdock, George P. (1949). *Social Structure*. New York: The MacMillan Co.

A World View of Cultural Diversity

Thomas Sowell

Diversity has become one of the most often used words of our time—and a word almost never defined. Diversity is invoked in discussions of everything from employment policy to curriculum reform and from entertainment to politics. Nor is the word merely a description of the long-known fact that the American population is made up of people from many countries, many races, and many cultural backgrounds. All this was well known long before the word "diversity" became an insistent part of our vocabulary, an invocation, an imperative, or a bludgeon in ideological conflicts.

The very motto of the country, *E. Pluribus Unum,* recognizes the diversity of the American people. For generations, this diversity has been celebrated, whether in comedies like *Abie's Irish Rose* (the famous play featuring a Jewish boy and an Irish girl) or in patriotic speeches on the Fourth of July. Yet one senses something very different in today's crusades for "diversity"; certainly not a patriotic celebration of America and often a sweeping criticism of the United States, or even a condemnation of Western civilization as a whole.

At the very least, we need to separate the issue of the general importance of cultural diversity—not only in the United States but in the world at large—from the more specific, more parochial, and more ideological agendas that have become associated with this word in recent years. I would like to talk about the worldwide importance of cultural diversity over centuries of human history before returning to the narrower issues of our time.

The entire history of the human race, the rise of man from the caves, has been remarked by transfers of cultural advances from one group to another and from one civilization to another. Paper and printing, for example, are today vital parts of Western civilization, but they originated in China centuries before they made their way to Europe. So did the magnetic compass, which made possible the great ages of exploration that put the Western hemisphere in touch with the rest of mankind. Mathematical concepts likewise migrated from one culture to another: Trigonometry from ancient Egypt, and the whole numbering system now used throughout the world originated among the Hindus of India, though Europeans called this system *Arabic numerals* because it was the Arabs who were the intermediaries through which these numbers reached medieval Europe. Indeed, much of the philosophy of ancient Greece first reached Western Europe in Arabic translations, which were then retranslated into Latin or into the vernacular languages of the West Europeans.

Reprinted with permission of Transaction Publishers from *Society,* Vol. 29, No. 1, 1991, pp. 37–44.

Much that became part of the culture of Western civilization originated outside that civilization, often in the Middle East or Asia. The game of chess came from India, gunpowder from China, and various mathematical concepts from the Islamic world, for example. The conquest of Spain by Moslems in the eighth century A.D. made Spain a center for the diffusion into Western Europe of the more advanced knowledge of the Mediterranean world and of the Orient in astronomy, medicine, optics, and geometry.

The later rise of Western Europe to world preeminence in science and technology built upon these foundations, and then the science and technology of European civilization began to spread around the world, not only to European offshoot societies such as the United States or Australia, but also to non-European cultures, of which Japan is perhaps the most striking example.

The historic sharing of cultural advances, until they became the common inheritance of the human race, implied much more than cultural diversity. It implied that some cultural features were not only different from others but better than others. The very fact that people—all people, whether Europeans, Africans, Asians, or others—have repeatedly chosen to abandon some feature of their own culture in order to replace it with something from another culture implies that the replacement served their purposes more effectively. Arabic numerals are not simply different from Roman numerals, they are better than Roman numerals. This is shown by their replacing Roman numerals in many countries whose own cultures derived from Rome, as well as in other countries whose respective numbering systems were likewise superseded by so-called Arabic numerals.

It is virtually inconceivable today that the distances in astronomy or the complexities of higher mathematics should be expressed in Roman numerals. Merely to express the year of the declaration of American independence as MDCCLXXVI requires more than twice as many Roman numerals as Arabic numerals. Moreover, Roman numerals offer more opportunities for errors, as the same digit may be either added or subtracted, depending on its place in sequence. Roman numerals are good for numbering kings or Super Bowls, but they cannot match the efficiency of Arabic numerals in most mathematical operations—and that is, after all, why we have numbers at all. Cultural features do not exist merely as badges of identity to which we have some emotional attachment. They exist to meet the necessities and to forward the purposes of human life. When they are surpassed by features of other cultures, they tend to fall by the wayside or to survive only as marginal curiosities, like Roman numerals today.

Not only concepts, information, products, and technologies transfer from one culture to another. The natural produce of the earth does the same. Malaysia is the world's leading grower of rubber trees—but those trees are indigenous to Brazil. Most of rice grown in Africa today originated in Asia, and its tobacco originated in the Western hemisphere. Even a great wheat-exporting nation like Argentina once imported wheat, which was not an indigenous crop to that country. Cultural diversity, viewed internationally and historically, is not a static picture of differentness but a dynamic picture of competition in which what serves human purposes more effectively survives while what does not tends to decline or disappear.

Manuscript scrolls once preserved the precious records, knowledge, and thought of European or Middle Eastern cultures. But once paper and printing from

China became known in these cultures, books were clearly far faster and cheaper to produce and drove scrolls virtually into extinction. Books were not simply different from scrolls; they were better than scrolls. The point that some cultural features are better than others must be insisted on today because so many among the intelligentsia either evade or deny this plain reality. The intelligentsia often use words like "perceptions" and "values" as they argue in effect that it is all a matter of how you choose to look at it.

They may have a point in such things as music, art, and literature from different cultures, but there are many human purposes common to peoples of all cultures. They want to live rather than die, for example. When Europeans first ventured into the arid interior of Australia, they often died of thirst or hunger in a land where the Australian aborigines had no trouble finding food or water, within that particular setting, at least, the aboriginal culture enabled people to do what both the aborigines and Europeans wanted to do—survive. A given culture may not be superior for all things in all settings, much less remain superior over time, but particular cultural features may nevertheless be clearly better for some purposes—not just different.

Why is there any such argument in the first place? Perhaps it is because we are still living in the long, grim shadow of the Nazi Holocaust and are, therefore, understandably reluctant to label anything or anyone "superior" or "inferior." But we do not need to. We need only recognize that particular products, skills, technologies, agricultural crops, or intellectual concepts accomplish particular purposes better than their alternatives. It is not necessary to rank one whole culture over another in all things, much less to claim that they remain in that same ranking throughout history. They do not.

Clearly, cultural leadership in various fields has changed hands many times. China was far in advance of any country in Europe in a large number of fields for at least a thousand years and, as late as the sixteenth century, had the highest standard of living in the world. Equally clearly, China today is one of the poorer nations of the world and is having great difficulty trying to catch up to the technological level of Japan and the West, with no real hope of regaining its former world preeminence in the foreseeable future.

Similar rises and falls of nations and empires have been common over long stretches of human history—for example, the rise and fall of the Roman Empire, the "golden age" of medieval Spain and its decline to the level of one of the poorest nations in Europe today, the centuries-long triumphs of the Ottoman Empire intellectually as well as on the battlefields of Europe and the Middle East, and then its long decline to become known as "the sick man of Europe." Yet, while cultural leadership has changed hands many times, that leadership had been real at given times, and much of what was achieved in the process has contributed enormously to our well-being and opportunities today. Cultural competition is not a zero-sum game. It is what advances the human race.

If nations and civilizations differ in their effectiveness in different fields of endeavor, so do social groups. Here is especially strong resistance to accepting the reality of different levels and kinds of skills, interests, habits, and orientations among different groups of people. One academic writer, for example, said that nineteenth-century Jewish immigrants to the United States were fortunate to arrive just as the garment industry in New York began to develop. I could not help thinking that

Hank Aaron was similarly fortunate that he often came to bat just as a home run was due to be hit. It might be possible to believe that these Jewish immigrants just happened to be in the right place at the right time if you restricted yourself to their history in the United States. But, again taking a world view, we find Jews prominent, often predominant, and usually prospering, in the apparel industry in medieval Spain, in the Ottoman Empire, in the Russian Empire, in Argentina, in Australia, and in Brazil. How surprised should we be to find them predominant in the same industry in America?

Other groups have excelled in other special occupations and industries. Indeed, virtually every group excels at something. Germans, for example, have been prominent as pioneers in the piano industry. American piano brands like Steinway and Knabe, not to mention the Wurlitzer organ, are signs of the long prominence of Germans in this industry, where they produced the first pianos in Colonial America. Germans also pioneered in piano-building in Czarist Russia, Australia, France, and England. Chinese immigrants have, at one period of history or another, run more than half the grocery stores in Kingston, Jamaica, and Panama City and conducted more than half of all retain trade in Malaysia, the Philippines, Vietnam, and Cambodia. Other groups have dominated the retail trade in other parts of the world—the Gujaratis from India in East Africa and in Fiji or the Lebanese in parts of West Africa, for example.

Nothing has been more common than for particular groups—often a minority—to dominate particular occupations or industries. Seldom do they have any ability to keep out others and certainly not to keep out the majority population. They are simply better at the particular skills required in that occupation or industry. Sometimes we can see why. When Italians have made wine in Italy for centuries, it is hardly surprising that they should become prominent among winemakers in Argentina and in California's Napa Valley. Similarly, when Germans in Germany have been for centuries renowned for their beermaking, how surprised should we be that in Argentina they became as prominent among brewers as Italians among winemakers? How surprised should we be that beermaking in the United States arose where there were concentrations of German immigrants in Milwaukee and St. Louis, for example? Or that the leading beer producers to this day have German names like Anheuser-Busch or Coors, among many other German names?

Just as cultural leadership in a particular field is not permanent for nations or civilizations, neither is it permanent for given racial, ethnic, or religious groups. By the time the Jews were expelled from Spain in 1492, Europe had overtaken the Islamic world in medical science, so that Jewish physicians who sought refuge in the Ottoman Empire found themselves in great demand in that Moslem country. By the early sixteenth century, the sultan of the Ottoman Empire had on his palace medical staff 42 Jewish physicians and 21 Moslem physicians.

With the passage of time, however, the source of the Jews' advantage—their knowledge of Western medicine—eroded as successive generations of Ottoman Jews lost contact with the West and its further progress. Christian minorities within the Ottoman Empire began to replace the Jews, not only in medicine but also in international trade and even in the theater, once dominated by Jews. The difference was that these Christian minorities—notably Greeks and Armenians—maintained their ties in Christian Europe and often sent their sons there to be educated. It was not race or ethnicity as such that was crucial but maintaining contacts with the ongoing progress of Western civilization. By contrast, the Ottoman Jews became a declining people in a declining empire. Many, if not most, were Sephardic Jews from Spain, once the elite of the world Jewry. But by the time the state of Israel was formed in the twentieth century, those Sephardic Jews who had settled for centuries in the Islamic world now lagged painfully behind the Ashkenazic Jews of the Western world—notably in income and education. To get some idea what a historic reversal that has been in the relative positions of Sephardic Jews and Ashkenazic Jews, one need only note that Sephardic Jews in colonial America sometimes disinherited their own children for marrying Ashkenazic Jews.

Why do some groups, subgroups, nations, or whole civilizations excel in some particular fields rather than others? All too often, the answer to this question must be: Nobody really knows. It is an unanswered question largely because it is an unasked question. There is an uphill struggle merely to get acceptance of the fact that large differences exist among peoples, not just in specific skills in the narrow sense (computer science, basketball, or brewing beer) but more fundamentally in different interests, orientations, and values that determine which particular skills they seek to develop and with what degree of success. Merely to suggest that these internal cultural factors play a significant role in various economic, educational, or social outcomes is to invite charges of "blaming the victim." It is much more widely acceptable to blame surrounding social conditions or institutional policies.

But if we look at cultural diversity internationally and historically, there is a more basic question than whether blame is the real issue. Surely, no human being should be blamed for the way his culture evolved for centuries before he was born. Blame has nothing to do with it. Another explanation that has had varying amounts of acceptance at different times and places is the biological or genetic theory of differences among peoples. I have argued against this theory in many places but will not take the time to go into these lengthy arguments here. A world view of cultural differences over the centuries undermines the genetic theory as well. Europeans and Chinese, for example, are clearly genetically different. Equally clearly, China was a more advanced civilization than Europe in many ways, scientific, technological, and organizational, for at least a thousand years. Yet over the past few centuries, Europe has moved ahead of China in many of these same ways. If those cultural differences were due to genes, how could these two races have changed positions so radically from one epoch in history to another?

All explanations of differences between groups can be broken down into heredity and environment. Yet a world view of the history of cultural diversity seems, on the surface at least, to deny both. One reason for this is that we have thought of environment too narrowly, as the immediate surrounding circumstances or differing institutional policies toward different groups. Environment in that narrow sense may explain some group differences, but the histories of many groups completely contradict that particular version of environment as an explanation. Let us take just two examples out of many that are available.

Jewish immigrants from Eastern Europe and Italian immigrants from southern Italy began arriving in the United States in large numbers at about the same time in the late nineteenth century, and their large-scale immigration also ended at the same time, when restrictive immigration laws were passed in the 1920s. The two groups arrived here in virtually the same economic condition—namely, destitute. They often lived in the same neighborhoods and their children attended the same schools, sitting side by side in the same classrooms. Their environments, in the narrow sense in which the term is commonly used, were virtually identical. Yet their social histories in the United States have been very different.

Over the generations, both groups rose, but they rose at different rates, through different means, and in a very different mixture of occupations and industries. Even wealthy Jews and wealthy Italians tended to become rich in different sectors of the economy. The California wine industry, for example, is full of Italian names like Mondavi, Gallo, and Rossi but the only prominent Jewish winemaker, Manishewitz, makes an entirely different kind of wine, and no one would compare Jewish winemakers with Italian winemakers in the United States. When we look at Jews and Italians in the very different environmental setting of Argentina, we see the same general pattern of differences between them. The same is true if we look at the differences between Jews and Italians in Australia, or Canada, or Western Europe.

Jews are not Italians and Italians are not Jews. Anyone familiar with their very different histories over many centuries should not be surprised. Their fate in America was not determined solely by their surrounding social conditions in America or by how they were treated by American society. They were different before they got on the boats to cross the ocean, and those differences crossed the ocean with them.

We can take it a step further. Even Ashkenazic Jews, those originating in Eastern Europe, have had significantly different economic and social histories from those originating in Germanic Central Europe, including Austria as well as Germany itself. These differences have persisted among their descendents not only in New York and Chicago but as far away as Melbourne and Sydney. In Australia, Jews from Eastern Europe have tended to cluster in and around Melbourne, while Germanic Jews have settled in and around Sydney. They even have a saying among themselves that Melbourne is a cold city with warm Jews while Sydney is a warm city with cold Jews.

A second and very different example of persistent cultural differences involves immigrants from Japan. As everyone knows, many Japanese-Americans were interned during the Second World War. What is less well known is that there is and has been an even larger Japanese population in Brazil than in the United States. These Japanese, incidentally, own approximately three-quarters as much land in Brazil as there is in Japan. (The Japanese almost certainly own more agricultural land in Brazil than in Japan.) In any event, very few Japanese in Brazil were interned during the Second World War. Moreover, the Japanese in Brazil were never subjected to the discrimination suffered by Japanese-Americans in the decades before the Second World War.

Yet, during the war, Japanese-Americans overwhelmingly remained loyal to the United States and Japanese-American soldiers won more than their share of medals in combat. But in Brazil, the Japanese were overwhelmingly and even fanatically loyal to Japan. You cannot explain the difference by anything in the environment of the United States or the environment of Brazil. But if you know something about the history of those Japanese who settled in these two countries, you know that they were culturally different in Japan before they ever got on the boats to take them across the Pacific Ocean and they were still different decades later. These two groups of immigrants left Japan during very different periods in the cultural evolution of Japan itself. A modern Japanese scholar has said: "If you want to see Japan of the Meiji era, go to the United States. If you want to see Japan of the Taisho era, go to Brazil." The Meiji era was a more cosmopolitan, pro-American era; the Taisho era was one of fanatical Japanese nationalism.

If the narrow concept of environment fails to explain many profound differences between groups and subgroups, it likewise fails to explain many very large differences in the economic and social performances of nations and civilizations. An eighteenth-century writer in Chile described that country's many natural advantages in climate, soil, and natural resources and then asked in complete bewilderment why it was such a poverty-stricken country. The same question could be asked of many countries today.

Conversely, we could ask why Japan and Switzerland are so prosperous when they are both almost totally lacking in natural resources. Both are rich in what economists call "human capital"—the skills of their people. No doubt there is a long and complicated history behind the different skill levels of different peoples and nations. The point here is that the immediate environment—whether social or geographic—is only part of the story.

Geography may well have a significant role in the history of peoples, but perhaps not simply by presenting them with more or less natural resources. Geography shapes or limits peoples' opportunities for cultural interaction and the mutual development that comes out of this. Small, isolated islands in the sea have seldom been sources of new scientific advances of technological breakthroughs, regardless of where such islands were located and regardless of the race of people on these islands. There are islands on land as well. Where soil, fertile enough to support human life, exists only in isolated patches, widely separated, there tend to be isolate cultures (often with different languages or dialects) in a culturally fragmented region. Isolated highlands often produce insular cultures, lagging in many ways behind the cultures of the lowlanders of the same race—whether we are talking about medieval Scotland, colonial Ceylon, or the contemporary montagnards of Vietnam.

With geographical environments as with social environments, we are talking about long-run effects not simply the effects, of immediate surroundings. When Scottish highlanders, for example, immigrated to North Carolina in colonial times, they had a very different history from that of Scottish lowlanders who settled in North Carolina. For one thing, the lowlanders spoke English while the highlanders spoke Gaelic on into the nineteenth century. Obviously, speaking only Gaelic in an English-speaking country affects a group's whole economic and social progress.

Geographical conditions vary as radically in terms of how well they facilitate or impede large-scale cultural interactions as they do in their distribution of natural resources. We are not even close to being able to explain how all these geographical influences have operated throughout history. This too is an unanswered question largely because it is an unasked question, and it is an unasked question because many are seeking answers in terms of immediate social environment or are vehemently insistent that they have already found the answer in those terms.

How radically do geographic environments differ, not just in terms of tropical versus arctic climates, but also in the very configuration of the land and how this helps or hinders large-scale interactions among peoples? Consider one statistic:

Africa is more than twice the size of Europe, and yet Africa has a shorter coastline than Europe. This seems almost impossible. But the reason is that Europe's coastline is far more convoluted, with many harbors and inlets being formed all around the continent. Much of the coastline of Africa is smooth, which is to say, lacking in the harbors that make large-scale maritime trade possible by sheltering the ships at anchor from the rough waters of the open sea.

Waterways of all sorts have played a major role in the evolution of cultures and nations around the world. Harbors on the sea are not the only waterways. Rivers are also very important. Virtually every major city on earth is located either on a river or a harbor. Whether it is such great harbors as those in Sydney, Singapore, or San Francisco; or London on the Thames, Paris on the Seine, or numerous other European cities on the Danube—waterways have been the lifeblood of urban centers for centuries. Only very recently has man-made, self-powered transportation, like automobiles and airplanes, made it possible to produce an exception to the rule like Los Angeles. (There is a Los Angeles River, but you do not have to be Moses to walk across it in the summertime.) New York has both a long and deep river and a huge sheltered harbor.

None of these geographical features in themselves create a great city or develop an urban culture. Human beings do that. But geography sets the limits within which people can operate and in some places it sets those limits much wider than in others. Returning to our comparison of the continents of Europe and Africa, we find that they differ as radically in rivers as they do in harbors. There are entire nations in Africa without a single navigable river—Libya and South Africa, for example.

"Navigable" is the crucial word. Some African rivers are navigable only during the rainy season. Some are navigable only between numerous cataracts and waterfalls. Even the Zaire River, which is longer than any river in North America and carries a larger volume of water, has too many waterfalls too close to the ocean for it to become a major artery of international commerce. Such commerce is facilitated in Europe not only by numerous navigable rivers but also by the fact that no spot on the continent, outside of Russia, is more than 500 miles from the sea. Many places in Africa are more than 500 miles from the sea, including the entire nation of Uganda.

Against this background, how surprised should we be to find that Europe is the most urbanized of all inhabited continents and Africa the least urbanized? Urbanization is not the be-all and end-all of life, but certainly an urban culture is bound to differ substantially from non-urban cultures, and the skills peculiar to an urban culture are far more likely to be found among groups from an urban civilization. Conversely, an interesting history could be written about the failures of urbanized groups in agricultural settlements.

Looking within Africa, the influence of geography seems equally clear. The most famous ancient civilization on the continent arose within a few miles on either side of Africa's longest navigable river, the Nile, and even today the two largest cities on the continent, Cairo and Alexandria, are on that river. The great West African kingdoms in the region served by the Niger River and the long-flourishing East African economy based around the great natural harbor on the island of Zanzibar are further evidences of the role of geography. Again, geography is not all-determining—the economy of Zanzibar has been ruined by government policy in recent decades—but nevertheless, geography is an important long-run influence on the shaping of cultures as well as in narrow economic terms.

What are the implications of a world view of cultural diversity on the narrower issues being debated under that label in the United States today? Although "diversity" is used in so many different ways in so many different contexts that it seems to mean all things to all people, there are a few themes that appear again and again. One of these broad themes is that diversity implies organized efforts at the preservation of cultural differences, perhaps governmental efforts, perhaps government subsidies to various programs run by the advocates of diversity.

This approach raises questions as to what the purpose of culture is. If what is important about cultures is that they are emotionally symbolic, and if differentness is cherished for the sake of differentness, then this particular version of cultural diversity might make some sense. But cultures exist even in isolated societies where there are no other cultures around—where there is no one else and nothing else from which to be different. Cultures exist to serve the vital, practical requirements of human life—to structure a society so as to perpetuate the species, to pass on the hard-earned knowledge and experience of generations past and centuries past to the young and inexperienced in order to spare the next generation the costly and dangerous process of learning everything all over again from scratch through trial and error—including fatal errors. Cultures exist so that people can know how to get food and put a roof over their head, how to cure the sick, how to cope with the death of loved ones, and how to get along with the living. Cultures are not bumper stickers. They are living, changing ways of doing all the things that have to be done in life.

Every culture discards over time the things that no longer do the job or which do not do the job as well as things borrowed from other cultures. Each individual does this, consciously or not, on a day-to-day basis. Languages take words from other languages, so that Spanish as spoken in Spain includes words taken from Arabic, and Spanish as spoken in Argentina has Italian words taken from the large Italian immigrant population there. People eat Kentucky Fried Chicken in Singapore and stay in Hilton Hotels in Cairo. This is not what some of the advocates of diversity have in mind. They seem to want to preserve cultures in their purity, almost like butterflies preserved in amber. Decisions about change, if any, seem to be regarded as collective decisions, political decisions. But this is not how cultures have arrived where they are. Individuals have decided for themselves how much of the old they wished to retain, how much of the new they found useful in their own lives.

In this way, cultures have enriched each other in all the great civilizations of the world. In this way, great port cities and other crossroads of cultures have become centers of progress all across the planet. No culture has grown great in isolation—but a number of cultures have made historic and even astonishing advances when their isolation was ended, usually by events beyond their control.

Japan was a classic example in the nineteenth century, but a similar story could be told of Scotland in an earlier era, when a country where once even the nobility were illiterate became, within a short time as history is measured, a country that produced world pioneers in field after field: David Hume in philosophy, Adam Smith in economics, Joseph Black in chemistry, Robert Adam in architecture, and James Watt, whose steam engine revolutionized modern industry and transport. In the process, the Scots lost their language but gained world preeminence in many fields. Then a whole society moved to higher standards of living than anyone ever dreamed of in their poverty-stricken past.

There were higher standards in other ways as well. As late as the eighteenth century, it was considered noteworthy that pedestrians in Edinburgh no longer had to be on the alert for sewage being thrown out the windows of people's homes or apartments. The more considerate Scots yelled a warning, but they threw out the sewage anyway. Perhaps it was worth losing a little of the indigenous culture to be rid of that problem. Those who use the term "cultural diversity" to promote a multiplicity of segregated ethnic enclaves are doing an enormous harm to the people in those enclaves. However they live socially, the people in those enclaves are going to have to compete economically for a livelihood. Even if they were not disadvantaged before, they will be very disadvantaged if their competitors from the general population are free to tap the knowledge, skills, and analytical techniques Western civilization has drawn from all the other civilizations of the world, while those in the enclaves are restricted to what exists in the subculture immediately around them.

We need also to recognize that many great thinkers of the past—whether in medicine or philosophy, science or economics—labored not simply to advance whatever particular group they happened to have come from but to advance the human race. Their legacies, whether cures for deadly diseases or dramatic increases in crop yields to fight the scourge of hunger, belong to all people—and all people need to claim that legacy, not seal themselves off in a dead-end of tribalism or in an emotional orgy of cultural vanity.

Discussion Questions

1. Most Americans have grown up with the United States leading the world in many areas such as technology, standard of living, medicine, and education. Is it important that we always lead in these areas? How can diversity in the workforce help us advance? Have we made good use of our people power resources in the past? Why or why not?

2. The United States regularly exchanges scientists, business and industry leaders, and technology with countries all over the world. Would the author think this is a good idea, or will this just help other countries get ahead of us?

3. In America, the management of workers by "assimilation into the workforce" is being replaced by the "integration of diversity." How would the author explain this shift in approach?

4. The author states that "What serves human purposes more effectively survives, while what does not, tends to decline or disappear." What aspects of American culture in general do you think may decline? What aspects of American business culture may decline?

5. List objects that we have now or the ways things are done now that differ markedly from your parents' generation.

6. It has been said that English is the international language of business; Italian is the international language of music; French is the international language of diplomacy. What explanation would the author give for this? Might this change?

SECTION TWO

Perspectives on Organizations and Diversity

Managing Cultural Diversity: Implications for Organizational Competitiveness

Taylor H. Cox
Stacy Blake
University of Michigan

OVERVIEW

The recent business trends of globalization and increasing ethnic and gender diversity are turning managers' attention to the management of cultural differences. The management literature has suggested that organizations should value diversity to enhance organizational effectiveness. However, the specific link between managing diversity and organizational competitiveness is rarely made explicit and no article has reviewed actual research data supporting such a link.

This article reviews arguments and research data on how managing diversity can create a competitive advantage. We address cost, attraction of human resources, marketing success, creativity and innovation, problem-solving quality, and organizational flexibility as six dimensions of business performance directly impacted by the management of cultural diversity. We then offer suggestions for improving organizational capability to manage this diversity.

Workforce demographics for the United States and many other nations of the world indicate that managing diversity will be on the agendas of organizational leaders throughout the 1990s. For example, a recent report of the workforces of 21 nations shows that nearly all of the growth in labor force between now and 2000 will occur in nations with predominately non-Caucasian populations. Behind these statistics are vastly different age and fertility rates for people of different racio-ethnic groups. In the United States for example, the average white female is 33 years old and has (or will have) 1.7 children. Corresponding figures for blacks are 28 and 2.4, and for Mexican-Americans, 26 and 2.9.[1]

Leading consultants, academics, and business leaders have advocated that organizations respond to these trends with a "valuing diversity" approach. They point

Reprinted with permission of Academy of Management from *Academy of Management Executive* (1991, Vol. 5, No. 3).

out that a well-managed, diverse workforce holds potential competitive advantages for organizations.[2] However, the logic of valuing diversity argument is rarely made explicit, and we are aware of no article that reviews actual data supporting the linkage of managing diversity and organizational competitiveness. This article reviews the arguments and research data on this link, and offers suggestions on improving organizational capability for managing cultural diversity. As shown in Figure 2-1, the term *managing diversity* refers to a variety of management issues and activities related to hiring and effective utilization of personnel from different cultural backgrounds.

DIVERSITY AS A COMPETITIVE ADVANTAGE

Social responsibility goals of organizations is only one area that benefits from the management of diversity. We will focus on six other areas where sound management can create a competitive advantage: (1) cost, (2) resource acquisition, (3) mar-

FIGURE 2-1 Spheres of Activity in the Management of Cultural Diversity

Organization Culture
• Valuing Differences
• Prevailing Value System
• Cultural Inclusion

Mind-Sets About Diversity
• Problem or Opportunity?
• Challenge Met or Barely Addressed?
• Level of Majority-Culture Buy-In (Resistance or Support)

HR Management Systems (Bias Free)
• Recruitment
• Training and Development
• Performance Appraisal
• Compensation and Benefits
• Promotion

Management of Cultural Diversity

Cultural Differences
• Promoting Knowledge and Acceptance
• Taking Advantage of the Opportunities that Diversity Provides

Higher Career Involvement of Women
• Dual-Career Couples
• Sexes and Sexual Harassment
• Work-Family Conflict

Education Programs
• Improve Public Schools
• Educate Management on Valuing Differences

Heterogeneity in Race/Ethnicity/Nationality
• Effect on Cohesiveness, Communication, Conflict, Morale
• Effects of Group Identity on Interactions (e.g., Stereotyping)
• Prejudice (Racism, Ethnocentrism)

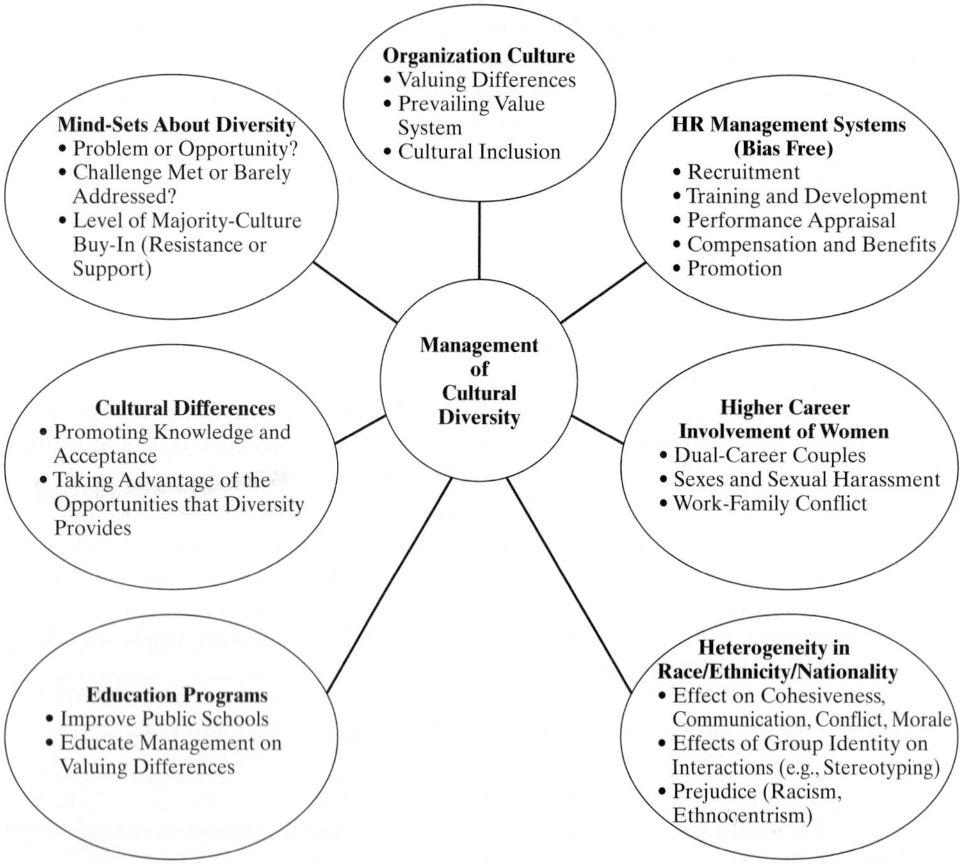

keting, (4) creativity, (5) problem-solving, (6) organizational flexibility.[3] Table 2-1 briefly explains their relationship to diversity management.

The first two items of the table, the cost and resource acquisition arguments, are what we call the "inevitability-of-diversity" issues. Competitiveness is affected by the need (because of national and cross-national workforce demographic trends) to hire more women, minorities, and foreign nationals. The marketing, creativity, problem-solving, and system flexibility arguments are derived from what we call the value-in-diversity hypothesis—that diversity brings net-added value to organization processes.

Cost

Organizations have not been as successful in managing women and racioethnic minorities (racially and/or ethnically different from the white/Anglo majority) as white males. Data show that turnover and absenteeism are often higher among

TABLE 2-1   Managing Cultural Diversity Can Provide Competitive Advantage

1. Cost Argument	As organizations become more diverse, the cost of a poor job in integrating workers will increase. Those who handle this well will thus create cost advantages over those who don't.
2. Resource-Acquisition Argument	Companies develop reputations on favorability as prospective employers of women and ethnic minorities. Those with the best reputations for managing diversity will win the competition for the best personnel. As the labor pool shrinks and changes composition, this edge will become increasingly important.
3. Marketing Argument	For multinational organizations, the insight and cultural sensitivity that members with roots in other countries bring to the marketing effort should improve these efforts in important ways. The same rationale applies to marketing to subpopulations within domestic operations.
4. Creativity Argument	Diversity of perspectives and less emphasis on conformity to norms of the past (which characterize the modern approach to management of diversity) should improve the level of creativity.
5. Problem-Solving Argument	Heterogeneity in decision-and problem-solving groups potentially produces better decisions through a wider range of perspectives and more thorough critical analysis of issues.
6. System Flexibilty Argument	An implication of the multicultural model for managing diversity is that the system will become less determinant, less standardized, and therefore more fluid. The increased fluidity should create greater flexibility to react to environmental changes (i.e., reactions should be faster and at less cost).

women and racioethnic minorities than for white males. For example, one study reported that the overall turnover rate for blacks in the United States workforce is 40 percent higher than for whites. Also, Corning Glass recently reported that between 1980–87, turnover among women in professional jobs was double that of men, and the rates for blacks were 2.5 times those of whites. A two-to-one ratio for women/men turnover was also cited by Felice Schwartz in her article on multiple career tracks for women in management.[4]

Job satisfaction levels are also often lower for minorities. A recent study that measured job satisfaction among black and white MBAs revealed that blacks were significantly less satisfied with their overall careers and advancement than whites.[5]

Frustration over career growth and cultural conflict with the dominant, white-male culture may be the major factor behind the different satisfaction levels. Two recent surveys of male and female managers in large American companies found that although women expressed a much higher probability of leaving their current employer than men, and had higher actual turnover rates, their primary reasons for quitting were lack of career growth opportunity or dissatisfaction with rates of progress. One of the surveys also discovered that women have higher actual turnover rates at all ages, and not just during the child-bearing and child-rearing years.[6]

Organizations that fail to make appropriate changes to more successfully use and keep employees from different backgrounds can expect to suffer a significant competitive disadvantage compared to those that do. Alternatively, organizations quick to create an environment where all personnel can thrive should gain a competitive cost advantage over nonresponsive or slowly responding companies.

Cost implications in managing diversity also occur in benefits and work schedules. In one study, companies were assigned an "accommodation score" based on the adoption of four benefit-liberalization changes associated with pregnant workers. Analysis revealed that the higher the company's accommodation score, the lower the number of sick days taken by pregnant workers and the more willing they were to work overtime during pregnancy.[7]

Two other studies investigated the effect of company investment in day care on human resource cost variables. In one study, turnover and absenteeism rates for working mothers using a company-sponsored child development center were compared to those who either had no children or had no company assistance. Absenteeism for the day care users versus the other groups was 38 percent lower and the turnover rate was less than 2 percent compared to more than 6 percent for the non-benefit groups. The second study showed that in a company that initiated an in-house child care facility, worker attitudes improved on six measures including organizational commitment and job satisfaction. In addition, turnover declined by 63 percent.[8]

Greater use of flextime work scheduling is another type of organizational accommodation to diversity. A recent field experiment assessing the impact of flextime use on absenteeism and worker performance found that both short- and long-term absence declined significantly. Three out of four worker efficiency measures also increased significantly.[9]

Cost savings of organizational changes must be judged against the investment. Nevertheless, the data strongly suggest that managing diversity efforts have reduced absenteeism and turnover costs, as cited earlier.

Research evidence relevant to cost implications of managing diversity on some dimensions other than benefit and work-schedule changes come from a UCLA study of the productivity of culturally heterogeneous and culturally homogeneous work teams. Among the heterogeneous teams, some were more and some were less productive than the homogeneous teams.[10] This research suggests that if work teams "manage" the diversity well, they can make diversity an asset to performance. For example, all members should have ample opportunity to contribute and potential communications, group cohesiveness, and interpersonal conflict issues need to be successfully addressed. Alternatively, if diversity is ignored or mishandled, it may detract from performance.

Actual cost savings from improving the management of diversity are difficult to determine. It is, however, possible to estimate those related to turnover. For example, let us assume an organization has 10,000 employees in which 35 percent of personnel are either women or racioethnic minorities. Let us also assume a white male turnover rate of 10 percent. Using the previous data on differential turnover rates for women and racioethnic minorities of roughly double the rate for white males, we can estimate a loss of 350 additional employees from the former groups. If we further assume that half of the turnover rate difference can be eliminated with better management, and that total turnover cost averages $20,000 per employee, the potential annual cost savings is $3.5 million. This example only addresses turnover, and additional savings may be realized from other changes such as higher productivity levels.

Although accurate dollar cost savings figures from managing diversity initiatives of specific companies are rarely published, Ortho Pharmaceuticals has calculated its savings to date at $500,000, mainly from lower turnover among women and ethnic minorities.[11]

Resource Acquisition

Attracting and retaining excellent employees from different demographic groups is the second "inevitability" -related competitiveness issue. As women and racioethnic minorities increase in proportional representation in the labor pool, organizations must compete to hire and retain workers from these groups. Recently published accounts of the "best companies" for women and for blacks have made public and highlighted organizations which are leaders in organizational change efforts to effectively manage diversity.[12] In addition to listing the best companies, the publications also discuss why certain companies were excluded from the list.

The impact of these publications on recruitment of quality personnel has already begun to surface. Merck, Xerox, Syntex, Hoffman-La Roche, and Hewlett-Packard have been aggressively using favorable publicity to recruit women and racioethnic minorities. According to company representatives, the recognitions are, in fact, boosting recruiting efforts. For example, Merck cites its identification as one of the 10 best companies for working mothers as instrumental in recent increases in applications.[13]

As these reputations grow, and the supply of white males in the labor market shrinks, the significance of the resource acquisition issue for organizational competitiveness will be magnified.

Marketing

Markets are becoming as diverse as the workforce. Selling goods and services is facilitated by a representational workforce in several ways. First, companies with good reputations have correspondingly favorable public relations. Just as people, especially women and racioethnic minorities, may prefer to work for an employer who values diversity, they may also prefer to buy from such organizations.

Second, there is evidence that culture has a significant effect on consumer behavior. For example, in the Chinese culture, values such as tradition of thrift, and teenagers' deference to their parent's wishes in making purchases, have been identified as affecting consumer behavior.[14] While much of the research on cross-cultural differences in consumer behavior has focused on cross-national comparisions, this research is also relevant to intra-country ethnic group differences.

> Immigration from Latin America and Asia will continue to be high in the 90s. This represents a large influx of first-generation Americans having strong ties to their root cultures. Acculturation patterns among Asian and Hispanic Americans indicates that substantial identity with the root cultures remains even after three or more generations of United States citizenship. This implies that firms may gain competitive advantage by using employee insight to understand culture effects on buying decisions and map strategies to respond to them.

USA Today provides a good example. Nancy Woodhull, president of Gannett News Media, maintains that the newspaper's marketing success is largely attributable to the presence of people from a wide variety of cultural backgrounds in daily news meetings. Group diversity was planned and led to a representation of different viewpoints because people of different genders and racioethnic backgrounds have different experiences shaped by group identities.

Avon Corporation used cultural diversity to turn around low profitability in its inner-city markets. Avon made personnel changes to give black and Hispanic managers substantial authority over these markets. These formerly unprofitable sectors improved to the point where they are now among Avon's most productive U.S. markets. Avon President Jim Preston commented that members of a given cultural group are uniquely qualfied to understand certain aspects of the world view of persons from that group.

In some cases, people from a minority culture are more likely to give patronage to a representative of their own group. For at least some products and services, a multicultural sales force may facilitate sales to members of minority culture groups.

Cultural diversification of markets is not limited to U.S. companies. Globalization is forcing major companies from many nations to address cultural difference among consumers. The fact that the United States contains one of the most culturally heterogeneous populations in the world represents a possible advantage in "national" competitiveness. Just having diversity, however, is not sufficient to produce benefits. We must also manage it.

Creativity

Advocates of the value-in-diversity hypothesis suggest that work team heterogeneity promotes creativity and innovation (see Note 1). Research tends to support this relationship. Kanter's study of innovation in organizations revealed that the most innovative companies deliberately establish heterogeneous teams to "create a marketplace of ideas, recognizing that a multiplicity of points of view need to be brought to bear on a problem" (p. 167). Kanter also specifically noted that companies high on innovation had done a better job than most on eradicating racism, sexism, and classism and tended to employ more women and racioethnic minorities than less innovative companies.[15]

Research by Charlene Nemeth found that minority views can stimulate consideration of non-obvious alternatives in task groups. In a series of experiments, participants were asked to form as many words as possible from a string of 10 letters. Individual approaches to the task were determined and then groups formed that were either majority (all members subscribed to the strategy for forming letters advocated by the majority of participants) or minority (non-majority individuals were present in the groups). Nemeth found that the "minority" groups adopted multiple strategies and identified more solutions than the "majority" groups. She concluded that the groups exposed to minority views were more creative than the more homogeneous, majority groups. She further concluded that persistent exposure to minority viewpoints stimulates creative thought processes.

Another experiment compared the creativity of teams that were homogeneous on a series of attitude measures against teams with heterogeneous attitudes. Problem solution creativity was judged on originality and practicality. Results indicated that as long as the team members had similar ability levels, the heterogeneous teams were more creative than the homogeneous ones.[16] If people from different gender, nationality, and racioethnic groups hold different attitudes and perspectives on issues, then cultural diversity should increase team creativity and innovation.

> Attitudes, cognitive functioning, and beliefs are not randomly distributed in the population but tend to vary systematically with demographic valuable such as age, race, and gender.[17] Thus, an expected consequence of increased cultural diversity in organizations is the presence of different perspectives for problem solving, decision making, and creative tasks.

Specific steps must be taken, however, to realize this benefit. The research shows that in order to obtain the performance benefits, it was necessary for heterogeneous team members to have awareness of the attitudinal differences of other members. Similarly, diversity needs to be managed in part by informing workgroup members of their cultural differences. In recognition of this, cultural awareness training has become a standard element of organization change projects focusing on managing diversity.

Problem Solving

Diverse groups have a broader and richer base of experience from which to approach a problem. Thus, managing diversity also has the potential to improve problem solving and decision making.

In the 1960s, several University of Michigan studies discovered that heterogeneous groups produced better quality solutions to assigned problems than homogeneous groups. Dimensions of group diversity included personality measures and gender. In one study, 65 percent of heterogeneous groups produced high quality solutions (solutions that provided either new, modified, or integrative approaches to the problem) compared to only 21 percent of the homogeneous groups. This difference was statistically significant. The researchers noted that "mixing sexes and personalities appears to have freed these groups from the restraints of the solutions given in the problem."[18]

Later studies also confirmed the effects of heterogeneity on group decision quality. The same conclusion is indirectly indicated by research on the "groupthink" phenomenon—the absence of critical thinking in groups caused partly by excessive preoccupation with maintaining cohesiveness. Most of the examples of groupthink cited in the literature, such as the decision of the Kennedy administration to invade Cuba in 1961, portray decision processes as producing disastrous results. Because group cohesiveness is directly related to degrees of homogeneity, and groupthink only occurs in highly cohesive groups, the presence of cultural diversity in groups should reduce its probability.[19]

Decision quality is best when neither excessive diversity nor excessive homogeneity are present. This point has been well summarized by Sheppard: "Similarity is an aid to developing cohesion; cohesion in turn, is related to the success of a group. Homogeneity, however, can be detrimental if it results in the absence of stimulation. If all members are alike, they may have little to talk about, they may compete with each other, or they may all commit the same mistake. Variety is the spice of life in a group, so long as there is a basic core of similarity."[20]

A core of similarity among group members is desirable. This theme is similar to the "core value" concept advocated in the organization culture literature.[21] Our interpretation is that all members must share some common values and norms to promote coherent actions on organizational goals. The need for heterogeneity, to promote problem solving and innovation, must be balanced with the need for organizational coherence and unity of action.

Additional support for the superior problem solving of diverse workgroups comes from the work of Nemeth cited earlier. In a series of studies, she found that the level of critical analysis of decision issues and alternatives was higher in groups subjected to minority views than in those which were not. The presence of minority views improved the quality of the decision process regardless of whether or not the minority view ultimately prevailed. A larger number of alternatives were considered and there was a more thorough examination of assumptions and implications of alternative scenarios.[22]

In sum, culturally diverse workforces create competitive advantage through better decisions. A variety of perspectives brought to the issue, higher levels of critical analysis of alternatives through minority-influence effects, and lower probability of groupthink all contribute.

System Flexibility

Managing diversity enhances organizational flexibility. There are two primary bases for this assertion. First, there is some evidence that women and racioethnic minorities tend to have especially flexible cognitive structures. For example, research has shown that women tend to have higher tolerance for ambiguity than men. Tolerance for ambiguity, in turn, has been linked to a number of factors related to flexibility such as cognitive complexity, and the ability to excel in performing ambiguous tasks.[23]

Studies on bilingual versus monolingual sub-populations from several nations show that compared to monolinguals, bilinguals have higher levels of divergent thinking and of cognitive flexibility.[24] Since the incidence of bilingualism is much greater among minority culture groups (especially Hispanics and Asians) than the majority-white Anglo group, this research strongly supports the notion that cognitive flexibility is enhanced by the inclusion of these groups in predominantly Anglo workforces.

The second way that managing cultural diversity may enhance organizational flexibility is that as policies and procedures are broadened and operating methods become less standardized, the organization becomes more fluid and adaptable. The tolerance for different cultural viewpoints should lead to greater openness to new ideas in general. Most important of all, if organizations are successful in overcoming resistance to change in the difficult area of accepting diversity, it should be well positioned to handle resistance to other types of change.

SUGGESTIONS FOR ORGANIZATION CHANGE

We have reviewed six ways in which the presence of cultural diversity and its effective management can yield a competitive advantage. Organizations wishing to maximize the benefits and minimize the drawbacks of diversity, in terms of work-group cohesiveness, interpersonal conflict, turnover, and coherent action on major organizational goals, must create "multicultural" organizations. The typical organization of the past has been either monolithic (homogeneous membership with a culture dominated by one cultural group) or plural (ostensibly diverse membership but still culturally monolithic and without valuing and using differences to benefit the organization). By contrast, the multicultural organization is one where members of nontraditional backgrounds can contribute and achieve to their fullest potential.

The multicultural organization's specific features are as follows: (1) Pluralism: reciprocal acculturation where all cultural groups respect, value, and learn from one another; (2) full structural integration of all cultural groups so that they are well represented at all levels of the organization; (3) full integration of minority culture-group members in the informal networks of the organization; (4) an absence of prejudice and discrimination; (5) equal identification of minority- and majority-group members with the goals of the organization, and with opportunity for alignment of organizational and personal career goal achievement; (6) a minimum of inter-group conflict which is based on race, gender, nationality, and other identity groups of organization members.[25]

Five key components are needed to transform traditional organizations into multicultural ones.

1. Leadership
2. Training
3. Research
4. Analysis and change of cultural and human resource management systems
5. Follow up

Each of these is briefly discussed.

Leadership

Top management's support and for genuine commitment to cultural diversity are crucial. Champions for diversity are needed—people who will take strong personal stands on the need for change, role model the behaviors required for change, and assist with the work of moving the organization forward. Commitment must go beyond sloganism. For example, are human, financial, and technical resources being provided? Is this item prominently featured in the corporate strategy and consistently made a part of senior level staff meetings? Is there a willingness to change human resource management systems such as performance appraisal and executive bonuses? Is there a willingness to keep mental energy and financial support focused on this for a period of years, not months or weeks? If the answer to all of these questions is yes, the organization has genuine commitment; if not, then a potential problem with leadership is indicated.

Top management commitment is crucial but not sufficient. Champions are also needed at lower organizational levels, especially key line managers. Many organizations are addressing the leadership requirement by the formation of task forces or advisory committees on diversity, often headed by a senior manager. Some companies also have a designated manager for diversity who oversees the work company-wide (examples include Corning Inc. and Allstate Insurance). We advise using the manager of diversity in addition to, rather than as a substitute for, a broader involvement team such as a diversity task force. This is especially important in the early stages of work.

Training

Managing and valuing diversity (MVD) training is the most prevalent starting point for managing diversity. Two types of training are popular: awareness training and skill-building training. Awareness training focuses on creating an understanding of the need for, and meaning of, managing and valuing diversity. It is also meant to increase participants' self-awareness on diversity related issues such as stereotyping and cross-cultural differences and how to respond to differences in the workplace. Often the two types are combined. Avon, Ortho Pharmaceuticals, Procter and Gamble, and Hewlett-Packard are examples of companies with extensive experience with training programs.

Training is a crucial first step. However, it has limitations as an organization change tool and should not be used in isolation. It is also important to treat training as an on-going education process rather than a one-shot seminar.

Research

Collection of information about diversity-related issues is the third key component. Many types of data are needed including traditional equal-opportunity profile data, analysis of attitudes and perceptions of employees, and data which highlights the career experiences of different cultural groups (e.g., are mentors equally accessible to all members).

Research has several important uses. First, it is often helpful for identifying issues to be addressed in the education process. For example, data indicating differences of opinion about the value in diversity based on culture group can be used as a launching point for mixed-culture discussion groups in training sessions. Second, research helps identify areas where changes are needed and provides clues about how to make them. Third, research is necessary to evaluate the change effort. Baseline data on key indicators of the valuing diversity environment needs to be gathered and periodically updated to assess progress.

Culture and Management Systems Audit

A comprehensive analysis of the organization culture and human resource systems such as recruitment, performance appraisal, potential assessment and promotion, and compensation should be undertaken. The primary objectives of this audit are (1) to uncover sources of potential bias unfavorable to members of certain cultural groups, and (2) to identify ways that corporate culture may inadvertently put some members at a disadvantage.

It is important to look beyond surface data in auditing systems. For example, research that we reviewed or conducted indicated that even when average performance ratings for majority versus minority culture members are essentially the same, there may be differences in the relative priority placed on individual performance criteria, the distribution of the highest ratings, or the relationship between performance ratings and promotion.[26] The audit must be an in-depth analysis, and the assistance of an external cultural diversity expert is strongly advised.

To identify ways that corporate culture may put some members at a disadvantage, consider a scenario where a prominent value in the organization culture is "aggressiveness." Such a value may place certain groups at a disadvantage if the norms of their secondary or alternative culture discouraged this behavior. This is indeed the case for many Asians and for women in many countries including the United States. While it is conceivable that the preservation of this value may be central to organizational effectiveness (in which case the solution may be to acknowledge the differential burden of conformity that some members must bear and to give assistance to them in learning the required behaviors), it may also be that the organizational values need to change so that other styles of accomplishing work are acceptable and perhaps even preferred. The point is that the prevailing values and norms must be identified and then examined critically in light of the diversity of the workforce.

Follow-up

The final component, follow-up, consists of monitoring change, evaluating the results, and ultimately institutionalizing the changes as part of the organization's regular ongoing processes. Like other management efforts, there is a need for accountability and control for work on diversity. Accountability for overseeing the change process might initially be assigned to the diversity task force, or if available, manager of diversity. Ultimately, however, accountability for preserving the changes must be established with every manager. Changes in the performance appraisal and reward processes are often needed to accomplish this.

Follow-up activities should include additional training, repetition of the systems audit, and use of focus groups for ongoing discussions about diversity issues.[27]

> The results of the audit must be translated into an agenda for specific changes in the organization culture and systems which management must then work to implement.

CONCLUSION

Organizations' ability to attract, retain, and motivate people from diverse cultural backgrounds may lead to competitive advantages in cost structures and through maintaining the highest quality human resources. Further capitalizing on the potential benefits of cultural diversity in work groups, organizations may gain a competitive advantage in creativity, problem solving, and flexible adaptation to change. We have identified steps that organizations can take toward accomplishing this.

While this article has reviewed a significant amount of relevant research, additional work clearly needs to be done, especially on the "value-in-diversity" issues. Nevertheless the arguments, data, and suggestions presented here should be useful to organizations to build commitment and promote action for managing diversity efforts in the 1990s and beyond.

Discussion Questions

1. This article discusses the benefits of worker diversity in terms of gender and race/ethnicity. Do you think the same benefits can occur with diversity of physical disability? Age? Sexual orientation? Explain why or why not.
2. Why is excessive heterogeneity (diversity) not recommended in the article? How do you avoid this?
3. List some of the possible reasons that women and minorities are often less satisfied with their jobs than are white men.

4. How does an organization's failure to manage women and minorities effectively translate into unnecessary costs? How can more effective management of these groups lead to competitive advantages?
5. If some managers do not seem to be handling the diversity of their personnel well, how might the performance appraisal and reward process be used to encourage them to improve?

Notes

1. See Johnston, and William B. "Global Work Force 2000." *Harvard Business Review.* March/April 1991, and "Middle-Age at 26." *The Wall Street Journal,* April 10, 1990.
2. For examples of the competitive advantage argument, see Thomas, Jr., R. Roosevelt. "From Affirmative Action to Affirming Diversity." *Harvard Business Review,* 2, March/April 1990, pp. 107–117; Copeland, Lennie. "Learning to Manage a Multicultural Workforce." *Training,* May 1988, pp. 48–56; Mandrell, Barbara and Susan Kohler-Gray. "Management Development That Values Diversity." *Personnel,* 67, March 1990, pp. 41–47; Etsy, Katherine. "Diversity Is Good for Business." *Executive Excellence,* 5, 1988, pp. 5–6; and Sodano, A. G. and S. G. Baler. "Accommodation to Contrast: Being Different in the Organization." *New Directions in Mental Health,* 20, 1983, pp. 25–36.
3. This focus is not intended to undermine the importance of social, moral, and legal reasons for attention to diversity. We have chosen to address its relevance for other types of goals, such as worker productivity and quality of decision making, because the impact of diversity in these areas has received relatively little attention in the past compared to the equal-opportunity related goals.
4. See the following sources for details on the turnover data: Bergmann, B. R. and W. R. Krause. "Evaluating and Forecasting Progress in Racial Integration of Employment." *Industrial and Labor Relations Review,* 1968, pp. 399–409; Hymowitz, Carol. "One Firm's Bid to Keep Blacks, Women." *The Wall Street Journal,* February 16, 1989, Sec. B, 1; Schwartz, Felice. "Management,

Women, and the New Facts of Life." *Harvard Business Review,* January/February 1989, pp. 65–76.
5. Cox, Jr., Taylor and Stella Nkomo. "A Race and Gender Group Analysis of the Early Career Experience of MBA." *Work and Occupations,* 1991.
6. These surveys were reviewed by Trost, Cathy. "Women Managers Quit Not for Family But to Advance Their Corporate Climb." *The Wall Street Journal,* May 2, 1990. For additional evidence on this point, including discussions of the cultural-conflict issue, see Schwartz, Endnote 3; Morrison, A. M., R. P. White, and E. Van Velsor. "Executive Women: Substance Plus Style." *Psychology Today,* August 1987, pp. 18–25; and DeGeorge, Gail. "Corporate Women: They're About to Break Through to the Top." *Business Week,* June 22, 1987, pp. 72–77.
7. "Helping Pregnant Workers Pays Off." *USA Today,* December 2, 1987.
8. Youngblood, Stewart A. and Kimberly Chambers-Cook. "Child Care Assistance Can Improve Employee Attitudes and Behavior." *Personnel Administrator,* February 1984, pp. 93–95+.
9. Kim, Jay S. and Anthony F. Campagna. "Effects of Flextime on Employee Attendance and Performance: A Field Experiment." *Academy of Management Journal,* December 14, 1981, pp. 729–741.
10. Reported in Adler, Nancy. *International Dimensions of Organizational Behavior.* Boston: Kent Publishing Co., 1986, p. 111.
11. The figure of $20,000 is based on computations of Michael Mercer for turnover costs of a computer programmer. Readers may wish to consult one of the following

sources for turnover cost formulas and then use their own job structure to determine cost factors for the actual turnover costs: Michael Mercer. "Turnover: Reducing the Costs." *Personnel*, Vol. 5, 1988, pp. 36–42; Darmon, Rene. "Identifying Sources of Turnover Costs." *Journal of Marketing*, 1990, Vol. 54, pp. 46–56. The data on Ortho is provided in Bailey, Juliane. "How to Be Different but Equal." *Savvy Woman*, November, 1989, p. 47+.

12. Examples of these publications include Zeitz, Baila and Lorraine Dusky. *Best Companies for Women*. New York: Simon and Schuster, 1988; and "The 50 Best Places for Blacks to Work." *Black Enterprise*, February 1989, pp. 73–91.

13. Feinstein, Selwyn. "Being the Best on Somebody's List Does Attract Talent." *The Wall Street Journal*, October 10, 1989. For other examples supporting the resource acquisition argument, see Dreyfuss, Joel. "Get Ready for the New Work Force." *Fortune*, April 23, 1990, pp. 165–181.

14. Redding, S. G. "Cultural Effects on the Marketing Process in Southeast Asia." *Journal of Market Research Society*, Vol. 24, 19, pp. 98–114.

15. Moss Kanter, Rosabeth. *The Change Masters*. New York: Simon and Schuster, 1983.

16. For details on the research in this section, readers should see Nemeth, Charlan Jeanne. "Differential Contributions of Majority and Minority Influence." *Psychological Review*, 93, 1986, pp. 23–32 and Triandis, H. C., E. R. Hall, and R. B. Ewen. "Member Homogeneity and Dyadic Creativity." *Human Relations*, 19, 1965, pp. 33–54.

17. Jackson, Susan E. "Team Composition in Organizational Settings: Issues in Managing a Diverse Workforce." in *Group Process and Productivity*. J. Simpson, S. Warchel, and W. Woods (eds.). Beverly Hills, Calif.: Sage Publications, 1989.

18. Hoffman, L. Richard and Norman R. F. Maier, "Quality and Acceptance of Problem Solving by Members of Homogeneous and Heterogenous Groups." *Journal of Abnormal and Social Psychology*, 62, 1961, pp. 401–407. The quote in the text is from page 404.

19. For reviews of research on the effect of group heterogeneity on problem solving, see Shaw, M. E. *Group Dynamics: The Psychology of Small Group Behavior*. New York: McGraw Hill, 1981; McGrath, J. E. *Groups: Interaction and Performance*. Upper Saddle River, N.J.: Prentice Hall, 1984; and Janis, Irving. *Victims of Groupthink*. Boston: Houghton Mifflin Co., 1972.

20. Shepard, C. R. *Small Groups*. San Francisco: Chandler Publishing Co., 1964, p. 118.

21. See Schein, Ed. "Organizational Socialization and the Profession of Management." In Kolb, D. A., I. M. Rubin, and J. M. McIntyre (eds.). *Organizational Psychology*, Upper Saddle River, N.J.: Prentice Hall, 1984, pp. 7–21; and Weiner, Y. "Forms of Value Systems: A Focus on Organizational Effectiveness and Cultural Change and Maintenance." *Academy of Management Review*, 13, 1988, pp. 534–545.

22. See Nemeth, Charlan Jeanne. "Dissent, Group Process, and Creativity." *Advances in Group Processes*, 2, 1985, pp. 57–75; and Nemeth, Charlan Jeanne and Joel Wachter. "Creative Problem Solving as a Result of Majority Versus Minority Influence." *European Journal of Social Psychology*, 13, 1983, pp. 45–55.

23. See G. Rotter, Naomi and Agnes N. O'Connell. "The Relationships Among Sex-Role Orientation, Cognitive Complexity, and Tolerance for Ambiguity." *Sex Roles*, 8(12), 1982, pp. 1209–1220; and Shaffer, David R. et al. "Interactive Effects of Ambiguity Tolerance and Task Effort on Dissonance Reduction." *Journal of Personality*, 41(2), June 1973, pp. 224–233.

24. These research studies are reviewed by Lambert, Wallace. "The Effects of Bilingualism on the Individual: Cognitive and Sociocultural Consequences." in A. Hurnbey, Peter (ed.). *Bilingualism: Psychological, Social, and Educational Implications*. New York: Academic Press, 1977, pp. 15–27.

25. This discussion of traditional versus multicultural organizations is based on Taylor Cox's article, "The Multicultural Organization," which appeared in the May 1991 issue of *The Executive*.

26. For a specific example of race differences in priorities of performance rating criteria, see Cox, Taylor and Stella Nkomo. "Differential Performance Appraisal Criteria." *Group and Organizational Studies*, 11, 1986, pp. 101–119. For an example of subtle bias in performance rating distributors see Asya Pazy's article: "The Persistence of Pro-Male Bias." *Organization Behavior and Human Decision Processes*, 38, 1986, pp. 366–377.

27. For additional discussion of organization change processes to manage diversity including specific examples of what pioneering companies are doing in this area, please see Taylor Cox's article, "The Multicultural Organization." (Note 25).

Strategies for Managing Human Resource Diversity: From Resistance to Learning

Parshotam Dass
Barbara Parker

Most writing on the subject suggests there is one best way to manage workforce diversity in organizations. We argue that there is no single best way but that the organization's approach depends on the degree of pressure for diversity, the type of diversity in question, and managerial attitudes. Strategic responses for managing diversity are presented in a framework of proactive, accommodative, defensive, and reactive modes. These responses are discussed in terms of episodic, freestanding, and systemic implementation practices.

Does diversity by race, gender, ethnicity, or anything else improve organizational performance?[1] Finding reliable answers to this question is difficult because people define diversity in different, even conflicting ways. Consequently, an increasingly diverse workforce is variously viewed as opportunity, threat, problem, fad, or even nonissue. These disparate views lead people to manage workforce diversity in distinct ways, resulting in different costs and benefits. Despite the claim by some that there is one best way to manage a diverse workforce, there is little agreement on what it is.

THE FRAMEWORK

This article proposes a framework that links executives' perspectives and priorities to managing workforce diversity, organizational conditions, and performance. Figure 2-2 presents an outline of the general framework, which shows that different steps in the process of managing diversity are related and can occur simultaneously. In practice, most U.S. organizations have assembled a more diverse workforce in response to external and/or internal pressures. For example, customers, suppliers, civil liberties groups, or others representing social, legal, economic, and other imperatives might exert external pressures to hire more people of color. At the same time, diversity champions, employee groups, or change managers might apply internal pressures for diversity in organizational hiring. The unique set of pressures brought to bear on a single organization combine to influence managers' perspectives, priorities, and strategic responses. Other managers may assemble more di-

Reprinted with permission of the Academy of Management from *Academy of Management Executive* (1999, Vol. 13, No. 2).

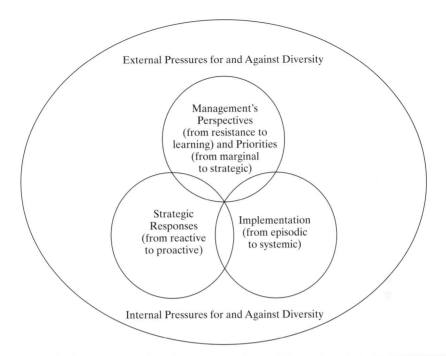

FIGURE 2-2 General Framework for Managing Diversity

verse workforces even when there are few pressures to do so. Their choices affect strategic responses and implementation, which, in turn, alter pressures for diversity.

While some pressures have usually favored greater organizational diversity, other pressures also arise to reduce it.[2] Some firms, for example, have been lobbied to eliminate same-sex benefits policies. A fit or match among diversity pressures, perspectives, and strategic responses is likely to improve organizational performance, whereas a mismatch is likely to entail economic and noneconomic costs. Managers who acknowledge they face strong legal and social mandates for diversity may conclude that accommodating racial diversity provides a better fit with organizational circumstances than resisting it. This implies that the best approach to diversity management is particular rather than universal. Because pressures for diversity can vary and even conflict, matches made within an organization may also differ, producing different initiatives on sexual orientation, gender, ethnicity, or other types of human difference.

DIVERSITY PERSPECTIVES AND ASSOCIATED STRATEGIC RESPONSES

In the United States, affirmative action and equal employment opportunity regulations have helped to make organizations more diverse in race, gender, and national origin.

Yet, as several writers have observed, diversity can be viewed through lenses other than legal or ethical,[3] and diversity has been defined, studied, and approached in quite different ways.[4] Researchers examining how organizations manage workforce diversity have identified three different perspectives:[5] the discrimination and fairness paradigm, the access and legitimacy paradigm, and the learning and effectiveness paradigm. Since we believe that different perspectives can be effective under some circumstances,[6] we call the third paradigm *learning*. We also have identified a fourth perspective: resistance (see Table 2-2).

RESISTANCE PERSPECTIVE AND REACTIVE STRATEGIC RESPONSE

Resistance to diversity occurred during the pre-civil rights movement in the United States and the postcolonial era in Europe, when there were fairly clear lines between racial and ethnic groups and few pressures for workforce diversity. As the pressures increased in the 1980s, concerns that minorities might displace the established majorities became an important reason to resist diversity. Individuals embodying some visible form of difference—nationality, color, or gender—were seen as not like the homogeneous insiders in business organizations. Growing pressures for diversity are likely to be perceived as threats.

By some accounts, the resistance perspective is alive and well in some organizations.[7] Videotapes showed that Texaco executives used racial epithets and planned to destroy evidence of discriminatory practices. Both Mitsubishi Motor Manufacturing of America and Astra Pharmaceuticals were accused of sexual harassment, suits were filed, and managers were subsequently fired or reassigned.

Many other organizations worldwide face discrimination claims from immigrants, ethnic groups, gays, lesbians, aging employees, and women. The dominant response for the resistance perspective is reactive,[8] characterized by denial, avoidance, defiance, or manipulation.[9] Although it was traditional for male agents and their regional managers to hire male relatives, State Farm Insurance avoided change and denied any alleged effects in a 9-year gender-bias suit that the company lost.

TABLE 2-2 Diversity Perspectives and Associated Strategic Responses

Diversity Perspectives	Problem Statement	Internal Definition	Prescription	Desired Outcome	Strategic Response
Resistance Perspective	Diversity as nonissue or threat	Not "us"	Sustain homogeneity	Protect the status quo	Reactive
Discrimination and Fairness Perspective	Differences cause problems	Protected groups	Assimilate individuals	Level the playing field for members	Defensive
Access and Legitimacy Perspective	Differences create opportunities	All differences	Celebrate differences	Access to employees and consumers	Accommodative
Learning Perspective	Differences and similarities offer opportunities and bear costs	Important differences and similarities	Acculturate; pluralism	Individual and organizational learning for long-term effect	Proactive

Demands for organizational change can be deflected by defiant assertions that changes are inefficient or unacceptable to shareholders because they increase costs and reduce profits. When Shoney's then-CEO J. Mitchell Boyd organized sensitivity sessions for the 60 top managers, the board fought the sessions on the basis of their cost. An organization under court order to hire more minorities and women used manipulation tactics when it counted the same person three times in the same compliance report because one parent was black, the other Asian, and she was female. Such responses may be found in monolithic organizations[10] where bias in human resources and other systems is ubiquitous.

A reactive strategic response may be appropriate when pressure for a particular type of diversity is low. A women's sports league might make hiring of male athletes a nonissue; religious entities are likely to resist hiring priests from other religions to preserve the nature and character of their organizations; and multinational organizations that otherwise hire from a diverse workforce may be less diverse in homogeneous nations.

DISCRIMINATION AND FAIRNESS PERSPECTIVE AND DEFENSIVE STRATEGIC RESPONSE

The discrimination and fairness paradigm is adopted most in U.S. organizations facing moderate pressures to incorporate diversity. This perspective assumes that prejudice has kept members of certain groups out of organizations, but that with equal access and fair treatment under the law [there] are available remedies. This perspective is based primarily on legal decisions, particularly on affirmative action policies and equal employment opportunity legislation.

The discrimination and fairness perspective perceives diversity as an organizational problem to be solved.[11] It focuses on members of historically disadvantaged groups[12] more than on individuals or on the organization as a whole. Employees may be encouraged to view people of different color, gender, or national origin as the same and thus be pressured to "make sure that differences among them do not count."[13]

This perspective gives rise to a defensive strategic response that includes such tactics as negotiating with, balancing, and pacifying different interest groups. Organizations may seek to pacify a minority group by selecting the director of affirmative action from that group. Similarly, many colleges and universities advertise their positions in minority publications, and many businesses include minority and female vendors among their suppliers. In practice, these actions may improve equity and fairness, providing economic resources as well as role models for members of historically disadvantaged groups. However, these actions can have negative effects, as well, if there is confusion about what diversity or legal compliance means. When organizational leaders allow or encourage employees to view affirmative action as a barrier to their own advancement, the result may be defensive employees who feel the leaders are unfair to them in order to be more fair to others.

Similarly, enforcing quotas can create backlash if unqualified people are hired. Another challenge occurs when surface-level forms of diversity are mistaken for deep-level diversity.[14] For example, Thurgood Marshal's Supreme Court seat was filled by Clarence Thomas, an African-American, but many felt Thomas identified more with Caucasians than with other African-Americans. Such a view can generate homogeneity, assimilation, colonization, and control rather than diversity.[15]

ACCESS AND LEGITIMACY PERSPECTIVE AND ACCOMMODATIVE STRATEGIC RESPONSE

Workforce 2000, a widely cited landmark study, predicted that more women, minorities, older workers, and immigrants would join the U.S. workforce.[16] Such demographic changes in Europe and the United States, as well as growing competitive pressures worldwide, created the context for the access and legitimacy perspective, which can emphasize access or legitimacy or both. For example, 44 percent of managers in 34 multinational firms believed that the most compelling reason to implement diversity programs was to tap diverse markets and customers.[17] Legitimacy may be sought by IBM managers who believe it is important for customers to look inside the company and see people like themselves,[18] but Alpine Bank sought access when it recruited bilingual employees to attract Spanish-speaking customers. Some organizations often advocate acceptance and even celebration of differences based on a perception that differences create opportunities (see Table 2-2).

Companies operating from the access and legitimacy perspective tend to emphasize bottom-line reasons for incorporating diversity. To leaders like Pitney Bowes CEO Michael Critelli, diversity "is a business necessity."[19] Bottom-line objectives can include cost reductions, reduced turnover, enhanced profitability resulting from improved morale or team spirit, or improved market value. Leaders may refer to studies that demonstrate links between diversity initiatives and annual returns or stock market values.[20]

This perspective typically defines diversity in broad terms that affirm differences throughout the workforce whether they are legally protected or not. Among these differences are a propensity for risk-taking, birth order, family relationships, nationality, sexual orientation, and values. Pillsbury defines diversity as "all those ways in which we differ."[21] An organization operating from this perspective often draws on concepts of inclusion to manage the many differences it endorses. While the discrimination and fairness perspective is typically adopted because of social or legal mandates, organizations following the access and legitimacy perspective usually do so by choice. This perspective not only recognizes differences but also values them. While improved performance may be one result of feeling valued, diverse communities may also feel they are being used to serve interests of a dominant class.[22] Valuing all differences equally may seem to ultimately value none. Celebrations of diversity can normalize differences and mask homogeneous values and practices.[23]

The access and legitimacy perspective is likely to be associated with an accommodative strategic response. Rather than tolerate diversity until people can be assimilated, this perspective promotes greater diversity in the workplace. Organizations with an accommodative response are likely to reflect a higher level of heterogeneity and inclusion than those with a defensive one. Their perspective is often guided by demographic pressures. Tyson Foods hired hundreds of Mexican immigrants in its poultry processing plants because of labor market shortages, presumably caused by low wage rates in the industry. Similarly, long-distance telephone companies in the United States often select sales representatives from immigrant groups because they may attract immigrant users. The restaurant and hospitality industries recognized that diverse consumers and employees stimulate industry growth.[24]

LEARNING PERSPECTIVE AND PROACTIVE STRATEGIC RESPONSE

Three characteristics distinguish the learning perspective from other perspectives on diversity: (1) It sees similarities and differences as dual aspects of workforce diversity; (2) it seeks multiple objectives from diversity, including efficiency, innovation, customer satisfaction, employee development, and social responsibility; (3) it views diversity as having long-term as well as short-term ramifications.

The learning perspective encourages legal compliance and training, but encourages active participation in finding better, faster, or more efficient ways of compliance beyond those legally mandated. Learning motivations might also include a desire to gain access to employees and new customer groups, with the purpose of learning from employees' different perspectives. Its focus is on identifying important similarities and differences[25] and managing them in the interests of long-term learning. Its emphasis on the unity-in-diversity less evident in other perspectives could be described as multiculturalism. IBM's slogan that "none of us is as strong as all of us" expresses the synergy it seeks.

The learning perspective is primarily associated with active strategic initiatives. Organizations that take this perspective are often early adopters of diversity policies. These policies seek to nurture homogeneity and diversity, and to address core issues of race, ethnicity, and gender along with other similarities and differences important to the organization. Creativity is necessary to generate a sense of similarity among cultural, functional, and hierarchical groups accustomed to differences, and is essential for identifying options when downsizing and diversity clash. AT&T believed downsizing would reduce diversity, but a new leave policy enabled redundant employees to travel or study. As openings occurred, these employees returned to AT&T, restoring diversity and bringing enhanced skills and experience.

Organizational leaders who act strategically to manage diversity usually recognize the important role that conflict and debate can play in creating a common sense of vision and beliefs within an organization. Honest expression of differences can lead to a synthesis of conflicting perspectives,[26] but destructive conflict also can emerge to prevent synergies.

IMPLEMENTING THREE USEFUL STRATEGIC RESPONSES

Pressures for diversity range in intensity and can vary and even conflict. In the United States, some pressures favor immigrant hiring, while other pressures oppose it. The implementation of diversity initiatives depends not only on these pressures, perspectives, and responses, but also on where managers place diversity on their lists of organizational priorities. One manager might view all forms of diversity as strategic, while another sees gender diversity as marginal and ethnic diversity as strategic. In either case, these priorities and pressures combine to yield three general approaches to implementation. These are shown in the diagonal cells of Figure 2-3, which managers can use as a diagnostic tool to gauge the match between pressures and their own priorities for managing diversity. The options described on the diagonal suggest the best fit as measured by past and current conditions, but there are other options.

Of the three general approaches to implementation, two were suggested by DeLuca and McDowell,[27] who view diversity initiatives as either programmatic (what we call *freestanding*) or nonprogrammatic (what we call *systemic*). We believe a third episodic approach to implementation exists. These three approaches to implementation are more or less integrated with core organizational activities: The episodic approach represents the lowest level of integration; the systemic approach, the highest.

The Episodic Approach

This approach is usually dominant when there are few pressures for diversity and managers view diversity as a marginal issue. The diversity initiatives of these managers tend to be isolated, disjointed, and separate from core organizational activities. They may make it difficult to identify, understand, or connect various diversity issues and pressures. Denny's Restaurant leaders dismissed racial problems in

FIGURE 2-3 Implementation of Strategic Responses for Managing Diversity

Priorities for Managing Diversity

		Marginal	Significant	Strategic
Pressures for Diversity	Low	Episodic Structure: Ad hoc, isolated Controls: Vary Rewards: Vary		
	Moderate		Freestanding Structure: Ongoing Stand alone Controls: Staff positions Rewards: Negative	
	High			Systemic Structure: Ongoing integrated Controls: Line positions Rewards: Positive and negative

west coast U.S. stores as isolated misunderstandings[28] rather than as signals of a widespread problem. Organizations may also use an episodic approach to experiment with new ideas. Goodyear sent upper-level managers to a week-long seminar on diversity and race relations to learn if that was a good way for them to improve managerial understanding of diversity. Except when it is used to experiment, the episodic approach usually results in few changes in organizational policies or practices.

The Freestanding Approach

Executives who experience moderate pressures for diversity and think of it as a significant but side issues are likely to formalize diversity initiatives, but without integrating them fully with core activities. R. B. Donnelly sponsors an exchange program where counterparts in two nations swap positions for several weeks to learn about each other's countries and customs. When such programs are independent of each other and core activities, the organization can easily add or drop them as circumstances change.

This approach can create a plethora of unrelated programs and generate more sanctions than rewards, as when ombudsman offices focus exclusively on compliance failures. If multiple freestanding programs and projects are introduced serially, diversity may be viewed as serving political expediency more than organizational plans. Some of these challenges may be avoided if it is clear that individual freestanding programs are consistent with pressures for diversity.

The Systemic Approach

Executives who experience high pressures for diversity and view diversity as a strategic issue are most likely to adopt a systemic approach to diversity. This approach involves linking diversity initiatives with existing systems and core activities of the organization. Responsibilities for monitoring and managing diversity are typically assigned to line organizational positions and are coupled with positive rewards and with sanctions. Although a systemic approach is expected to be comprehensive, it also incorporates simplicity and flexibility. When an audit showed units were defining diversity in different ways, GTE responded by asking a multi-unit group to create a definition of diversity broad enough to apply to the whole, but flexible enough to permit unit adaptations. S. Kirk Kinsell, Apple South's president, believes diversity management is successful only when it is "integrated fully—that is, made a part of all customer, vendor and employee programs."[29]

Although both the freestanding and systemic approaches may involve such diversity initiatives as work and family issues or veterans' affairs, only systemic approaches would integrate programs with one another and with structural mechanisms. At Motorola, diversity progress includes training programs to hire and develop from diverse groups, but retention and promotion then become part of every manager's appraisal and compensation package. Deep systemic change necessarily takes time and may create challenges when diversity pressures call for immediate or demonstrable change.

PULLING IT ALL TOGETHER

The twelve cells shown in Figure 2-4 pull together the four perspectives, the associated strategic responses toward diversity depicted in Table 2-2, and the three general approaches to implementing them shown in Figure 2-3. The following section describes diversity initiatives typical for each of the 12 cells.

IMPLEMENTING REACTIVE STRATEGIC RESPONSE

Episodic Approaches—Cell 1

Episodic approaches for implementing a reactive strategic response could include denial and projection. According to employees, Denny's chairman Raymond Danner "sometimes ordered managers to fire blacks if they were too visible to white customers,"[31] and managers rearranged work shifts to ensure that Danner did not see black employees during scheduled visits. Similarly, when CEO J. Mitchell Boyd tried to change Shoney's culture, the board resisted and ignored warnings of a pending discrimination lawsuit.[32] Projection occurred when North American managers

FIGURE 2-4 Strategic Responses for Managing Diversity and Their Implementation

Implementation

	Episodic	Freestanding	Systemic	
Reactive	Denying a European assignment to an African-American	Legal department to fight equal employment opportunity programs	Hiring and firing based on stereotypes	Low
	1	2	3	
Defensive	Training workshops for minorities: Learn the ropes and succeed	Affirmative action for women and minorities	Socialization of minorities to assimilate in the dominant culture	
	4	5	6	Pressure for Diversity
Accommodative	Diversity awareness for managers: Be sensitive to your new employees	Diversity caucus and communication committee to improve interpersonal relationships	Appraisal systems that establish diversity as a managerial goal at every level	
	7	8	9	
Proactive	Unity-in-diversity workshops for all	Director of multicultural affairs to coordinate relevant functions	Structural and cultural transformation to integrate diversity with other activities of the organization	
	10	11	12	High

Strategic Responses for Managing Diversity

Marginal ◄————————————————► Strategic

Priorities for Managing Diversity

concluded that Japanese businessmen would not like working with women,[33] and when a small company refused to expatriate an African-American because it believed he would not be well received in Europe.[34]

Freestanding Approaches—Cell 2

Managers can purposefully design programs and policies to avoid diversity, such as creating a legal defense fund to fight rather than follow affirmative action mandates. One organization instructed human resource employees to use secret codes on application forms so black applicants would not be called for interviews. Freestanding resistance also can be unintentional. Robert E. Flynn, CEO of Nutra-Sweet, reported that some executives had an unconscious yet ongoing program of filling key positions with individuals similar to themselves without posting the jobs for females, minorities, or others.[34]

Systemic Approaches—Cell 3

Organizations often resist diversity in a systemic manner. Selecting or rejecting employees based on stereotypes, for example, may be an unconscious yet systemic way of excluding diversity. Most existing systems were designed to screen out variation, which makes it difficult to incorporate greater diversity in organizations.[35] Efforts to maintain the status quo also result from malice, the degree of difficulty involved with change, or perceptions that other demands are more immediate. Shoney's culture, for example, showed systemic opposition to diversity because it had neither discussed nor implemented affirmative action at any level by 1988.[37] Even while expressing a desire to incorporate greater diversity, some managers claim they cannot do so because other demands, such as global competition, are more pressing.

Another tactic to resist diversity is deflection. Claims that diversity in hiring and promotion conflict with existing merit or seniority systems may be valid, but they also deflect further diversity. For firms facing few legal or social mandates for diversity, a primary mode of organizational resistance may be as passive or evasive as keeping a low public profile. Still another systemic approach to resisting diversity may involve manipulation. Some organizations sponsor research to show why the organization or industry should or cannot accommodate diversity, and others mount public relations campaigns to discredit those who champion diversity or highlight failures of diversity programs in other settings.

IMPLEMENTING DEFENSIVE STRATEGIC RESPONSE

Episodic Approaches—Cell 4

Following a discriminatory event, organizations may assume a defensive posture by launching an investigation to disarm public concern, but little change occurs when investigations continue for months or even years. Some organizations may provide suggestion boxes, toll-free telephone lines, or counseling sessions to keep pressures from building. Organizations also may respond with explanations, apologies, or cosmetic changes, particularly when such incidents invite public scrutiny. Mitsubishi Motor Manufacturing of America claimed that sexual harassment complaints in its Illinois plant were not widespread and said subsequent changes in top management were unrelated. Organizations often tend to focus on symptoms without seeing the bigger picture. Although a Navy tribunal found fault with high-ranking officers in the Tailhook incident, subsequent discriminatory behavior in other branches of the U.S. armed forces suggests that the hearings fostered little awareness of the overall problem.

Freestanding Approaches—Cell 5

Organizations pursuing this approach may shape diversity parameters, perhaps emphasizing do's and don'ts of affirmative action compliance or avoiding sexual harassment claims. They may also set up separate interest groups for women, African-Americans, and others. For example, Sun Microsystems initially formed five focus groups to help recruit, hire, and develop new employees from particular groups. Other organizations may emphasize concrete affirmative action programs that usually concentrate on objectively measurable goals. An advantage of this approach is to specify organizational intentions and set measurable standards. Disadvantages are that managers may be encouraged to set low goals or to adopt quotas that objectify people or prevent hiring good candidates from nonprescribed categories.

Systemic Approaches—Cell 6

Organizations may assimilate members of diverse groups via socialization. In the late 1980s, GE Silicone asked minority and women employees to meet informally to discuss why they were not assimilating effectively into the dominant culture. Organizations may institutionalize like-to-like mentoring relationships—for instance, Hispanic mentors for Hispanic mentees—to reduce gaps between affirmative action targets and results. In addition, organizations may design systems for continuous evaluation and control of their diversity efforts. American Express institutionalized a process to implement and measure the effectiveness of diversity initiatives.

IMPLEMENTING ACCOMMODATIVE STRATEGIC RESPONSE

Episodic Approaches—Cell 7

Many organizations offer diversity awareness sessions. At a U.S. Tyson Foods plant, managers organized diversity-training sessions for supervisors to help them understand how cultural values of Hispanics in the workplace differed from dominant U.S. culture. Likewise, when faced by pressures for diversity, organizations may review existing practices. *The Seattle Times* conducted a content audit to count the number of news stories covering different constituent activities.

Freestanding Approaches—Cell 8

According to a Conference Board survey of 131 organizations, 60 percent located diversity positions at the director or vice presidential level.[37] This is one way to place more emphasis on diversity initiatives. Other organizations may institute diversity caucuses and communication committees to improve interpersonal relationships among diverse individuals and groups. Still other organizations may establish independent diversity departments with the objectives of matching internal diversity with external diversity. These departments may organize a celebration of diversity week, as at Rockwell. Such initiatives are likely to have an impact on external constituencies, as well. Gannett's diversity goal is to assemble a workforce that reflects the communities where the company does business.[38] Hoechst Celanese set a 2001 target to hire 34 percent women and minorities to mirror the anticipated workforce.[39] Stereotyped or blanket celebration of diversity may divert attention from important historical discrimination issues and generate backlash.

A Workways consultant described a bank that featured an unsuccessful Black History Month celebration featuring watermelon and collard greens as the lunch offering.

Systemic Approaches—Cell 9

Organizations may alter existing systems to accommodate diversity. Harris Bank and John Hancock Financial Services both use standard forms for employees who want flexible work hours[40] to encourage a systemic approach to flexible scheduling. This approach incorporates the kind of counting required for affirmative action reports and results in altered evaluation systems to accommodate changing needs of new parents, caregivers for elderly parents, or disabled employees. Hoechst Celanese conducts regular salary reviews to identify and adjust pay differentials between white males and other employees. It also uses a computerized succession review plan to show where high-potential women or minority employees encounter roadblocks. General Mills has designed a mentoring system that leads to an individual development plan meant to identify actions that enhance personal growth and effectiveness. This formal aspect of mentoring is supplemented by informal ones to nurture employee networks and forums.

Organizational socialization may encourage values exploration to help individuals recognize their own stereotypes and implicit assumptions. A focus on inclusion is evident in Honeywell's belief that each individual is unique and valuable. At Gannett, diversity involves recognition of all the differences among workers and the variety of perspectives and values that are part of each person.

IMPLEMENTING PROACTIVE STRATEGIC RESPONSE

While the essential point in the systemic approach is full integration with organizational core activities, an organization does not have to fully integrate diversity in its system to learn from it. The organization can also learn from taking action on an occasional basis or in an ongoing program.

Episodic Approaches—Cell 10

Some diversity trainers suggest that organizational leaders may use the episodic approach to test the waters in their own organizations, using an introductory workshop to explore the topic's continuing relevance to the workforce. At AT&T, a 1989 workshop on "Homophobia in the Workplace" proved successful and subsequently became an offering in the regular diversity curriculum.[41] Recognizing that organizations must be dynamic, managers may occasionally organize informal discussions to monitor emerging diversity issues. Subsequent support for grassroots organizing helps constituents learn which among many diversity issues are central to their long-term interests and can be incorporated in organizational processes. Digital Equipment Corporation's core groups have evolved over the years to include similarities as well as differences.

Freestanding Approaches—Cell 11

Motorola requires that employees enroll in 40 hours of training per year. Any employee can enroll in courses covering diversity as a competitive advantage, the spirit of diversity, or transition to diversity, but other courses target specific audiences. There are 2-day courses for senior managers, special workshops on sexual harassment and diversity awareness for other managers, and diversity awareness and interviewing for managers and directors. Sears became a model for Americans with Disabilities compliance by benchmarking other firms' practices and then shaping them for their workforce. Sara Lee defined diversity in terms of women because they consider them the critical constituency to represent in the organization. American Express created a new program called "Diversity Learning Labs" to focus on diverse market segments, such as the women's market, to improve learning about specialized groups and to identify learning generalizable to other groups. From these groups, American Express learned that leaders of diverse client acquisition efforts also need strong project management experience. Vendors or suppliers operating from different perspectives sometimes frustrated US West's diversity goals. They and other firms, therefore, externalized diversity programs to encourage vendors and suppliers to learn about diversity and help them meet their diversity objectives.

Systemic Approaches—Cell 12

Systemic approaches to incorporating diversity may lead to more diverse structures and processes as well as to more diverse people in the organization. Resulting realignments often entail mutual learning and adjustment. Business units as well as top managers identify and develop the diverse skills and competencies that Hewlett-Packard will need in the next millennium. Safeco institutionalized a process to rehire promising minority candidates during university vacations to nurture long-term learning opportunities for employees and employers. Coopers and Lybrand framed child care, elder care, and work/life balance issues as relevant for the entire workforce, not just women. The firm then developed an ongoing process by which the field units could propose, experiment, evaluate, and share relevant common solutions.[42]

Organizations use different methods to incorporate a systemic approach to learning from diversity, including organization development, transition management, transformational leadership, team entrepreneurship, action research, reengineering, total quality management, and team learning. However, a diverse group of top managers who embody the change desired may be the best catalyst for this transformation. Thomas and Ely suggest other preconditions they believe would apply.[43] However, systemic changes may be easier to describe than to achieve. In particular, learning is most likely to be oriented toward management's interests, and a possible result may be increased managerial control instead of employee buy-in or stakeholder interests. In other words, the learning perspective on diversity entails opportunities and costs, just as does any other perspective.

Some writers suggest a normative pattern of organizational approaches to diversity.[44] However, we think that while some organizations may evolve from episodic to freestanding to systemic, others can successfully follow different patterns when they are congruent with pressures for diversity and managers' priorities for managing different types of diversity. Further, whether an organization can achieve commitment to any particular strategic response depends on external pressures (e.g., government, community, supplier, customer, societal), internal pressures (e.g., employees, stakeholders, internal consultants, change managers), and managerial perspectives, as outlined in Figure 2-2 and detailed in Figures 2-3 and 2-4.

IMPLEMENTATION IN COMPLEX SITUATIONS

In practice, diversity initiatives usually will not be organized in the mutually exclusive categories shown in the figures. On the contrary, diversity management in many organizations may seem more a potpourri of ideas, programs, and pet projects. Perspectives on diversity have evolved over time, and thinking consistent with different time periods is likely to be embedded in diversity practices. Although top executives usually select the organization's strategy for managing workforce diversity, it is up to middle- and lower-level managers to implement them and to employees to operationalize them, often according to personal perspectives and priorities. Every variety of resistance, discrimination, fairness, access, legitimacy, and learning operates today within, as much as between, organizations.

Growing pressures for diversity have led many executives to revise their perspectives and priorities for managing diversity and to introduce many diversity initiatives. But these initiatives occur in a specific context. For example, the founder of Denny's Restaurants became a champion for diversity after decades of documented resistance to it, but implementation may be made difficult by the organization's past.

Although our proposed framework represents ideal rather than actual types, it has practical merit. Executives can use Figure 2-2 to examine current pressures for and against diversity and anticipate future ones. The figure also suggests that managing diversity can be approached in a step-by-step manner or as a process requiring simultaneous consideration of pressures, perspectives, and strategic responses. The categories shown in Table 2-2 provide a checklist to assess any organization's dominant perspective on diversity and establish a beginning point for assessing actual or intended matches with internal definitions, strategic responses, and initiatives related to managing diversity. Inconsistencies or gaps can be used to align the organization with present or future conditions and to develop a more purposeful and cohesive approach to managing diversity.

Organizational responses to strategic issues such as diversity have an important impact on organizational performance.[45] Most theorists and practitioners believe that matching internal resources and external opportunities can yield strategic advantages, and this argument for fit should encourage leaders to carefully choose their strategic response to managing diversity with regard for the type of diversity under consideration. Organizational leaders also need to examine their internal and external environments to adopt an approach to implementation that matches their particular context[46] or with a context they believe will emerge. Consequently, research examining the relationship between diversity and performance needs to consider the perspectives and priorities adopted, as well as the organization's strategic response, its approach to implementation, and the type of diversity under consideration.

Organizations operating on the diagonal in Figure 2-3 where current pressures and perceptions match probably experience the fewest costs and the most benefits from their approach to managing diversity. If diversity pressures are low, then efficiency may best be served with a low involvement approach, like that practiced by domestic firms operating in homogeneous nations. Similarly, high pressures for diversity are best met with recognition that diversity is a core issue calling for a systemic approach. This approach to thinking about diversity management suggests opportunities for achieving fit, but it also is an argument for purposefully choosing an approach to managing diversity. Random acts of kindness may be enough in some cases, whereas systemic acts of engagement may be essential in others. Either choice entails opportunities and costs. Executives who become champions for organizational diversity, even when pressures for it are low, may confront stockholder alarm, internal resistance, or criticism when their efforts raise unfulfilled aspirations.

Similarly, those who resist high pressures for diversity risk public censure. Yet, there may be reasons for operating outside the box. Becoming a champion may be appropriate for an organizational leader who foresees industry or demographic change, and resistance can be appropriate when pressures for a particular type of diversity are perceived to be transitory or to entail more costs than benefits. The important point is that ideas presented in this article provide executives with a framework that can help them systematically consider approaches to managing diversity, choose appropriate ones, and establish priorities. A review of diversity initiatives throughout the organization should help executives organize and act on what may appear to be chaotic or disorganized behavior. Fragmented and freestanding diversity programs resulting from good intentions at different points in time represent a different challenge than fragmented programs that arose because leaders changed firm directions. Efforts and good intentions may become the glue for a revised, more cohesive set of diversity initiatives, but employees may be cynical and adept at resisting changes in the name of diversity. In either case, consistency between perspectives and action is certain to reduce employee confusion about roles they are expected to play in managing diversity.

Our examples throughout this paper have come primarily from U.S., European, and Japanese firms that operate in multiple domestic and increasingly global environments, where social, legal, cultural, and competitive pressures combine and seem to require greater diversity in personnel and organizational structures and processes. Ideal transnational firms will be those whose strategic capabilities include global competitiveness, flexibility, and worldwide learning,[47] capabilities that are enhanced by high degrees of human diversity in organizations.

Confusion, wariness, and cynicism may be produced by conflicting pressures and approaches to managing diversity. However, executives who reflect on their own perspectives and diversity practices may become more aware of available alternatives and uncover unspoken assumptions and biases that guide their practices and theories. Such awareness may raise challenging new questions about managing workforce diversity.

ACKNOWLEDGMENT

An earlier version of this article was published in Kossek, E. E., and Lobel, S. A. (Eds.). 1966. *Managing Diversity: Human Resource Strategies for Transforming the Workplace*. Cambridge, Mass.: Blackwell Business.

Discussion Questions

1. Select an organization that you are familiar with, such as your college or your workplace. Analyze this organization's current pressures for and against diversity.
2. How could the diversity perspectives cited in this article influence the types of diversity training that an organization provides for its employees?
3. Go to www.diversityinc.com and find an organization that exemplifies each of the types of organizational responses to diversity cited by the authors.

Notes

1. Deadrick, D., and T. Kochan. (1997). "A Call for Research on Diversity and Organizational Effectiveness." A session at the Academy of Management meeting in Boston, Mass.; Glick, W., C. Miller, and G. Huber. (1993). "The Impact of Upper Echelon Diversity on Organizational Performance." In Huber, G., and W. Glick (eds.). *Organizational Change and Redesign*. New York: Oxford University Press, pp. 176–214; Watson, W. E., K. Kumar, and L. K. Michaelsen. (1993). "Cultural Diversity's Impact on Interaction Process and Performance: Comparing Homogeneous and Diverse Task Groups." *Academy of Management Journal*, 36, pp. 590–602; Wright, P., S. Ferris, J. Hiller, and M. Kroll. (1995). "Competitiveness Through Management of Diversity: Effects on Stock Price Valuation." *Academy of Management Journal*, 38, pp. 272–287.

2. Ginsberg, A. (1988). "Measuring and Modeling Changes in Strategy: Theoretical Foundations and Empirical Directions." *Strategic Management Journal*, 9, pp. 559–575.

3. Thomas, R. H. (1991). "Beyond Race and Gender: Unleashing the Power of Your Total Workforce by Managing Diversity." New York: AMACOM; Herriot, P., and C. Pemberton. (1995). *Competitive Advantage Through Diversity*. London: Sage Publications.

4. For example, Nkomo and Cox identified six major bodies of research contributing to diverse identities and social relations in organizations. Nkomo, Stella M., and Taylor H. Cox, Jr. (1996). "Diverse Identities in Organizations." In Stewart Clegg, Cynthia Hardy, and Walter Nord (eds.). *Handbook of Organization Studies*. London: Sage, pp. 338–356.

5. Thomas, D., and H. Ely. (1996). "Making Differences Matter. A New Paradigm for Managing Diversity." *Harvard Business Review*, pp. 79–90.

6. Bowens, H., I. Merenivitch, L. P. Johnson, A. H. James, and D. J. McFadden-Bryant. (1993). "Managing Cutural Diversity Toward True Multiculturalism: Some Knowledge from the Black Perspective." In H. H.

Sims and R. F. Dennehy (eds.). *Diversity and Differences in Organizations.* Westport, Conn.: Quorum Books, pp. 33–45; Thomas and Ely. *op. cit.*

7. Nkomo and Cox. *op. cit.*

8. For more details on the reactive, defensive, accommodative, and proactive strategic responses and their performance implications, see Clarkson, M. B. E. (1995). "A Stakeholder Framework for Analyzing and Evaluating Corporate Social Performance." *Academy of Management Review,* 20, pp. 92–117.

9. Oliver, C. (1991)." Strategic Responses to Institutional Processes." *Academy of Management Review,*16, pp. 145–79.

10. Cox, T. (1993). *Cultural Diversity in Organizations: Theory, Research, and Practice.* San Francisco: Berrett-Koehler.

11. Nemetz, P., and S. L. Christensen. (1996). "The Challenge of Cultural Diversity: Harnessing a Diversity of Views to Understand Multiculturalism." *Academy of Management Review,* 21(2), pp. 434–482.

12. For a thorough review of individual and group identity issues, see Nkomo and Cox. *op. cit.*

13. Thomas and Ely. *op. cit.*

14. Harrison, D. A., K. H. Price, and M. P. Bell. (1998). "Beyond Relational Demography: Time and the Effects of Surface- and Deep-Level Diversity on Work Group Cohesion," *Academy of Management Journal,* 41, pp. 96–107; Jackson, S. E., K. E. May, and Whitney, K. (1995). "Understanding the Dynamics of Diversity in Decision-Making Teams." In R. A. Guzzo and E. Salas (eds.). *Team Decision-Making Effectiveness in Organizations.* San Francisco, Jossey-Bass, pp. 204–261; Milliken, F. J., and L. I. Martins. (1996). "Searching for Common Threads: Understanding the Multiple Effects of Diversity in Organizational Groups." *Academy of Management Review,* 21, pp. 402–433.

15. Humphries, M., and S. Grice. (1995). "Equal Employment Opportunity and the Management of Diversity: A Global Discourse of Assimilation?" *Journal of Organizational Change Management,* 8, (5), pp. 17–32.

16. Johnston, B. William, and Arnold E. Packer. (1987). *Workforce 2000.* Indianapolis, IN: Hudson Institute.

17. "Diversity: Making the Business Case." *Business Week,* Dec. 9, 1996. Special advertising section.

18. *Ibid.*

19. Cox, T. H., Jr., and S. Blake. (1991). "Managing Cultural Diversity: Implications for Organizational Competitiveness." *Academy of Management Executive,* 5, pp. 45–56.

20. Koretz, G. (1991). "An Acid Test of Job Discrimination in the Real World." *Business Week,* p 23; Covenant Investment Management. (1993). "Equal Opportunity, Stock Performance Linked." Press Release, Chicago, Ill.; Wright, Ferris, Hiller, and Kroll. *op. cit.*

21. *Business Week. op. cit.*

22. Calas, M., and L. Smircich. (1993). "Dangerous Liaisons: The 'feminine-in-management' meets 'globalization.'" *Business Horizons,* March–April, pp. 71–82.

23. Humphries and Grice. *op. cit.*

24. Hayes, J., and M. Prewilt. (1998). "Operators Explore Diversity at 1st Multicultural Conference." *Nation's Restaurant News,* 32 (34), 3, p. 127.

25. Ofori-Dankwa, J., and C. L. Ortega Sysak. (1994). "DiverSimilarity: The Reengineering of Diversity Training." In *DiverSimilarity: The Paradigm for Workforce 2000* (1–25). Conference Readings, May 12–13. Saginaw Valley State University, Saginaw, Mich.

26. Ofori-Dankwa, and Ortega Sysak. *op. cit.;* Thomas. (1991). *op. cit.*

27. DeLuca, J. M., and H. N. McDowell. (1992). "Managing Diversity: A Strategic 'Grassroots' Approach." In S. E. Jackson and Associates (eds.). *Diversity in the Workplace: Human Resources Initiatives.* New York: Guilford Press, pp. 227–247.

28. Rice, Faye. (1994). "How to Make Diversity Pay." *Fortune,* Aug. 8, pp. 78–86.

29. Hayes and Prewitt. *op. cit.*

30. "Eating Crow: How Shoney's, Belted by a Lawsuit, Found the Path to Diversity." *The Wall Street Journal,* April 16, 1996, pp. A1, A11.

31. Gaiter. *op. cit.*

32. Adler, N. J. (1987). "Pacific Basin Managers: A *Gaijin*, Not a Woman." *Human Resource Management*, 26, pp. 169–191.

33. Gentile, M. C. (1994). "The Case of the Unequal Opportunity." In M. C. Gentile (ed.). *Differences That Work—Organizational Excellence Through Diversity*. Boston: Harvard Business School Press, pp. 223–238.

34. "White, Male, and Worried." *Business Week*, Jan. 31, 1994, pp. 50–55.

35. Milliken and Martins. *op. cit.*

36. Gaiter. *op. cit.*

37. Wheeler, Michael L. (1994). *Diversity Training*. New York: Conference Board, pp. 1083–94-RR.

38. Jennings. *op. cit.*

39. Rice. *op. cit.*

40. "How Accommodating Workers' Lives Can Be a Business Liability." *The Wall Street Journal*, Jan. 4, 1995, p. B1.

41. "AT&T Class Teaches an Open Workplace Is Profitably Correct." *The Wall Street Journal,* Nov. 10, 1995, p. B1; "Denny's Changes Its Spots." *Fortune*, May 13, 1996, pp. 133–142.

42. Deluca and McDowell. (1992). *op. cit.*

43. Thomas and Ely. (1996). *op. cit.*

44. Bowens et al. *op. cit.*

45. Ansoff, H. I. (1980). "Strategic Issue Management." *Strategic Management Journal*, 1, 131–148; Mintzberg, H., D. Raisinghani, and A. Theoret. (1976). "The Structure of Unstructured Decision Processes." *Administrative Science Quarterly*, 21, pp. 246–275.

46. Micklethwait, J., and A. Wooldridge. (1997). *The Witch Doctors: Making Sense of the Management Gurus*. Heinemann, U. K.

47. Bartlett, C. A., and S. Ghoshal. (1989). *Managing Across Borders: The Transnational Solution*. Boston: Harvard Business School Press.

The Emotional Connection of Distinguishing Differences and Conflict

Carole G. Parker
Frostburg State University

In recent years, diversity in organizations has been an exciting, stimulating and intriguing topic. What happens in organizations to influence either the discounting or appreciation of individual differences? Is there a way to appreciate diversity and yet value differences? Smart managers today realize the importance of balance in work groups and are moving to incorporate (diversity) differences—age, gender, race, culture, sexual preference, styles of being—in their organizations to capitalize on the potential that diversity offers. In order to manage differences, the interest, energy, and commitment of the various parties involved must be shared. Because differences among people are not inherently good or bad, there is no "right" way to deal with differences. Although differences are sometimes disruptive, they can also lead to very important benefits, both to individuals and organizations.

HOW DIFFERENCES ARE OFTEN MANAGED

What action and factors must be uppermost in selecting the most appropriate approach to addressing differences? Differences are often managed by avoidance or repression. The avoidance of differences too often takes the form of associating mostly with individuals with similar backgrounds, experiences, beliefs, and values. Usually this allows an environment of mutual support and predictability. Another avoidance strategy is to separate individuals who create sparks between each other.

The repression of differences occurs when an individual refuses to allow disagreements to emerge. This happens frequently in team activities or by emphasizing behavior focusing on cooperation, collaboration, and loyalty.

Repression is quite costly. Resistances develop that have both organizational and individual consequences. The process of blocking strong feelings and repressing differences may result in desensitization and a loss of productivity. When individuals with differences come together, managers must exert self-control to reduce unnecessary conflict.

There are both appropriate times and dangers associated with the use of avoidance and repression in managing differences. Teams or work groups faced with tight deadlines may want to limit the number and type of ideas generated. Avoidance may be an appropriate interim strategy for dealing with differences by enabling an individual to learn more about a person or situation before declaring a stance. The challenge to management is to decide when to use these approaches. Avoidance of difference can lead to "groupthink," which occurs when everyone in a group agrees with everyone else, although there are different opinions, values, beliefs, and perceptions. Groupthink is the result of a lack of challenge for ideas, opinions, values, or beliefs. The more diversity an organization has, the more likely there will be a variety of ideas, opinions, values, beliefs, and perceptions.

Still another danger in avoiding differences is overcompatibility. When overcompatibility exists in an organization, it may be due to a strong need for support, reassurance, security, or a need to reduce a threat. In an organization, this can severely hamper new ideas, productivity, growth, and development. Avoidance and repression of differences are not viable solutions. When differences are present, they must be expressed and worked through. If not, conflict will result.

POSITIVE ASPECTS OF DIFFERENCES

1. Difference can be regarded as an opportunity. "Two heads are better than one" because they often represent a richer set of experiences, and the variability of these combined may lead to a more creative approach than could be achieved independently.

2. Differences can be used to test the strength of a position. Have all the aspects been considered, all loops carefully closed? When developing policy or organizational processes, it is important to cover all the bases.

A healthy interaction among differences (gender, age, race, or culture, etc.) could address these concerns. Two factors influence the treatment of differences: first, the needs, wants, and goals of the individual; second, the value placed on the relationship. People are often motivated by the desire to meet their needs and satisfy their wants and desires. The stronger the motivation, the greater the likelihood of addressing differences. Furthermore, when the persons involved are important to each other, or valued, the tendency to manage the difference increases to preserve the relationship. The reverse is likely when there is no value in the relationship. Once these factors have been assessed, it becomes necessary to recognize behavior and attitudes that will be helpful in managing the differences.

Differences are not problems to be solved; they are dilemmas to be managed. Successful managers of difference reduce their judgments and accept the difference as legitimate. Clear boundaries between self and others, a willingness and interest in being influenced, and an awareness of choice with the ability to make choices are also helpful. Furthermore, using strong language such as *must, should, will, ought, cannot, necessary, impossible, requirement, or mandate,* will diminish success.

Differences are experienced from interacting with others who are dissimilar. A range of experiences and success in interpersonal relationships support the ability to deal with differences. Individuals who have traveled or have had unusual experiences tend to develop an appreciation for differences. Managing differences is not an individual process; it is interactive among individuals. When only one individual is attempting to deal with the difference, the result is coping behavior. Dealing with differences evokes emotion. A range of emotions for human interaction that leads to awareness of difference is necessary. These emotions can lead to conflict but conflict is not a prerequisite to managing differences.

Differences evoke emotions at different levels, ranging from small or minor to large or major. An inverted triangle graphically shows the escalating intensity in each level as differences are heightened (see Figure 2-5).

The first level involves an awareness of the difference. Here the parties are exploring each other—what is similar, what is not—and discomfort may result. When the differences appear to be greater than the similarities, annoyance occurs. The parties are not able to appreciate how their differences may be beneficial to each other. Irritation, on the next level, may result from continued exploration, possibly through the dialectic process. Tension is heightened as more contact occurs; there is an overlay of fear. The boundaries of self may be threatened (What will happen to me if I continue with this encounter?) and anger develops. After anger, open disagreements follow, and the dispute solidifies. Each party has developed a firm stance reflecting his/her position. The final level is conflict or war, where each party works hard to repress or neutralize the other. In Figure 2-5, we suggest that an individual may, depending on the situation, traverse through each of these emotional levels in addressing differences. This is not necessarily a linear process. Emotions run deep on various issues and could erupt immediately from awareness to hostility or anger or any other step on the triangle.

Conflict may result or emerge from differences. There are many publications defining conflict. For our purposes, conflict is briefly defined based on the experiences of par-

FIGURE 2-5 The Escalation of Differences into Conflict

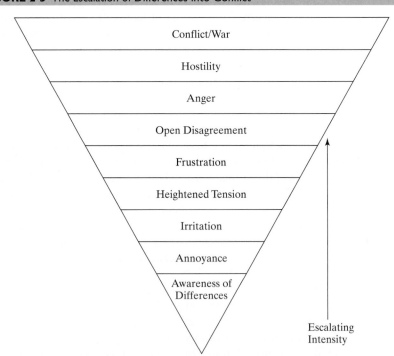

ticipants in the Transcendus Exercise found in this text (page 263). From the moment Earthling groups come together to figure out how to explain conflict to their visitors, students often find themselves confronting substantial differences with respect to both their ways of defining conflict and the positive and negative values attached to it. Listed here are typical examples of definitions generated by Earthling groups about conflict:

1. Conflict exists when two or more parties want the same thing or their wants are incompatible in some way.
2. Conflict must involve emotionality; it is a disturbing emotion within ourselves and may involve feelings of anger and frustration.
3. The higher the stakes, the greater the conflict; one must care to have conflict.
4. Conflict can be within: oneself, a group, between groups. Conflict involves competition of wants and of viewpoints.
5. Conflict can be enjoyable.

It is important to distinguish conflict from difference. Difference and conflict are both important and necessary ingredients in human interaction and, if valued, can lead to opportunity, creativity, and appreciation. Difference is a component of diversity, which is a constant in our environment. Managers and the workforce are beginning to grapple with this constant and are learning that appreciating or valuing differences opens the door to new and creative ways of addressing organizational challenges. For example, when a group of salaried and union personnel from the automotive industry were invited to identify adjectives they associate with conflict, most of the language was highly charged, emotional, and violent. The list generated for differences was dramatically broader, more varied, less emotionally charged, and contained a language of hope (see Table 2-3).

The autoworkers pointed out that differences can lead to conflict and cited examples including the inability to motivate employees to complete their assigned jobs, poor communication, pressures concerning time, inequity in work assignments, differences of opinions, and methods for getting work done. They further

TABLE 2-3   Distinguishing Difference and Conflict

Conflict	*Difference*
Anger	Opinions
War	Ideas
Tension	Options
Frustration	Methods
Kill	Skills
Hostility	Race
Shouting	Gender
	Jobs
	Age
	Interpretation
	Values
	Environment

pointed out how important it is for people to listen to each other and pay attention to the difference, incorporating the difference in the process of solving a problem or completing a task, not just engaging in conflict as a result of the difference. It was believed that when a diverse team worked together, there was greater creativity and innovation, a sense of connectedness, more risk-taking, less boredom, higher productivity and greater cooperation. On the other hand, mismanaging differences or engaging in conflicting behavior in the organization would most likely lead to higher stress, individual withdrawal, limited learning, less risk-taking, overcompatibility, interpersonal tension, and decreased communication.

THE EMOTIONAL CONNECTION

Emotional intelligence is one key to developing the ability to manage and appreciate differences. Emotional intelligence is the ability of an individual to be aware of information about oneself as it relates to interactions with others. It involves one's ability to be aware of, name, and manage individual experiences of emotions. The triangle in Figure 2-5 illustrates the escalating intensity of emotion when differences are mismanaged or misunderstood and develop into conflict. Managers must recognize that it is the diversity in styles of interacting and the particular way a person or group makes meaning of their experience that create the experience of difference. Difference enables choice and opportunity as much as it may create tension and insecurity; this also enables the organization to achieve its objectives.

The answer to understanding the emotional impact of encountering difference (diversity) may come with knowledge of three major transitions occurring in contemporary society. Fritzof Capra suggests that a paradigm shift in the thoughts, perceptions, and values that form a particular view of reality is essential if the world is to survive. This is a pattern or paradigm shift involving moving from certainty to uncertainty, closed to open systems, truth to no truth, and a realization that there are multiple realities that coexist in a complex society. Recognition and mastery of this paradigm shift may prove to be a foundation for developing the emotional skills necessary to valuing diversity and managing differences. Historically, it has not been acceptable for professionals to lose control, demonstrate emotions, or otherwise display behaviors that create discomfort for others. One way to manage emotions is to be aware of our emotions and factors that trigger an emotional response. Developing healthy ways to acknowledge and respond to these emotions increases our ability to not only manage ourselves but also to manage others as we encounter diversity and differences in workplace settings.

Discussion Questions

1. How can one distinguish difference from conflict?
2. What are some of the dangers of avoiding and repressing differences?
3. Think of an experience in an organization or social setting that you have had involving the avoidance or repression of differences. What was the outcome?
4. What are some of the positive aspects of difference?

5. Can you think of any examples of difference other than those already mentioned in the reading?
6. How can differences be managed while minimizing the risk of conflict?
7. What role do emotions play in our ability to manage differences?
8. How can we develop the skills needed to increase our emotional intelligence? See www.feel.org/articles/index.html

Carole G. Parker, Ph.D., teaches in the MBA department of the College of Business at Frostburg State University in Frostburg, Maryland. She is responsible for teaching courses in leadership (with a focus on intrapersonal and interpersonal growth of the leader), management, and organizational behavior. She also functions as a management consultant to business and nonprofit organizations and specializes in executive coaching. Among the organizations for which Dr. Parker has served as consultant or trainer are such firms as General Electric Co.; General Motors Corporation; Touch Ross, Canada; University Hospital of Cleveland; EG&G Idaho, Inc.; Mt. Sinai Medical Center; and Evangelical Health Systems. She has also served as member of the visiting staff of the Gestalt Institute of Cleveland and is a member of NTL Institute for Applied Behavioral Science.

The Diversimilarity Approach to Diversity Management: A Primer and Strategies for Future Managers

Joseph C. Ofori-Dankwa
Scott D. Julian
Saginaw Valley State University

Over the last several decades, there has been an increased emphasis on diversity in the workplace. To some extent, this change was brought about by the civil rights movement and the resulting legislation and regulation. The emphasis on diversity has also been bolstered by the realization that workplace diversity can bring with it many benefits. Workplace diversity can increase creativity and problem-solving ability, enhance the effectiveness of marketing efforts toward minority niche markets, enlarge the pool of potential applicants from which to hire, and improve a firm's image and reputation in the eyes of various stakeholders (Cox and Blake, 1993).

However, accompanying these benefits has been an increase in workplace tensions and conflicts that some writers have described (Mobley and Payne, 1992; Karp and Sutton, 1993). Members of majority groups can feel threatened and diminished, creating a backlash. This backlash then causes members of minority groups to feel cut off from the interpersonal networks and mentoring resources so important for a successful career; this leads to alienation.

Increased diversity can thus prove to be a mixed blessing for managers who fail to manage it adequately. The question, therefore, is to identify strategies that future managers can learn in order to take advantage of the benefits of diversity while avoiding its pitfalls. We propose three interrelated strategies.

STRATEGY ONE: THINK DIVERSIMILARITY

One possible solution lies in maintaining the increased emphasis on workplace diversity while also emphasizing the importance of similarities between individuals and groups. It may be that a singular focus on interpersonal and intergroup differences, while not diminishing the potential benefits of workplace diversity, can at the same time magnify the negative potential of those differences. Focusing on differences alone can lead to a diminished realization of the things that individuals have in common, their similarities. Thus, a focus on differences alone can lead to hostile defensiveness, alienation, increased social distance, diminished comfort levels, restricted intergroup communication, and ultimately to intergroup and interpersonal conflict. Furthermore, if we only look for differences, we are likely to find only differences (Ofori-Dankwa and Ricks, 2000).

The concept of diversimilarity is a different way to look at workplace diversity issues that simultaneously considers the differences *and* the similarities between individuals, and one that considers both to be equally important (Loden and Rosener, 1991; Ofori-Dankwa, 1996; Ofori-Dankwa and Bonner, 1998). Diversimilarity suggests that diversity can be better managed if people are simultaneously made aware of the differences and similarities that exist between them. While recognizing that differences do clearly exist across various groups, the concept of diversimilarity also stresses the importance of finding similarities across ethnicity, religion, sex, age, social status, or levels of education.

STRATEGY TWO: CONSIDER DIVERSIMILARITY PRINCIPLES

Diversimilarity is based on the idea that either/or thinking is too simplistic to adequately address complex organizational problems (Quinn, 1988): *either* different *or* similar, for example. Rather, the reality of individuals and their interactions with one another can best be captured with a both/and perspective: *both* different *and* similar at the same time. This dual focus on potentially opposite perspectives is called the *competing values* approach, which Professor Quinn of the University of Michigan has proposed. The recognition that people are similar in some ways while at the same time being different in others is an important element in educating people to value and benefits from diversity (Loden and Rosener, 1991). Once individuals recognize the commonalities that exist between them, workplace conflict associated with diversity can be reduced because people now have common points of reference around which to interact.

Ofori-Dankwa and Bonner (1998) summarized the diversimilarity viewpoint using five principles: (1) creativity and adversity in diversity; (2) conformity and compatibility in similarity; (3) diversity within diversity; (4) similarity across diversity; and (5) managing diversity by managing diversimilarity.

The creativity and adversity in diversity principle recognizes the inherent trade-off of increased workplace diversity. When people of diverse backgrounds and viewpoints are brought together, creativity and innovation are often increased. Previously unrecognized points of view can broaden and enrich any group's capacity for thinking in new ways and in finding novel solutions to long-standing problems. Conversely, bringing together people of different backgrounds and viewpoints can also increase interpersonal conflict. The ways in which individuals are different can easily become points of controversy and conflict. This can happen over time even in an environment that was initially open to new ways of thinking.

The conformity and compatibility in similarity principle recognizes the inherent trade-off of stressing similarities across different groups of individuals. Once people understand the many ways in which they are similar, compatibility between them will increase because they can access common frames of reference for understanding the world about them. On the other hand, these common frames of reference can prove stifling to creativity, leading to a numbing conformity in both thinking and acting. Though individuals from different groups may indeed be different in important ways, when together they focus on and cluster about their similarities and lose the ability to think creatively.

The diversity within diversity principle recognizes that there is a significant amount of variation even within categories such as ethnicity and sex that are sometimes viewed as homogenous. Knowing a few categories into which an individual can be placed does not tell one all the information about a person. Personality, political view, hobbies, and religious beliefs, to name a few things, can vary greatly between members of supposed monolithic groups.

The similarity across diversity principle stresses that important similarities exist between individuals in different demographic groups. Ofori-Dankwa and Bonner (1998) use as an example the universality of entrepreneurship across sex, ethnicity, nationality, and culture. Basic motivations such as the need for achievement or a desire for self-esteem show up frequently in different demographic groups, but are manifested differently. Thus, although people may be diverse in outward and obvious demographic characteristics, for example, they may have numerous similarities that may not be obvious to a casual observer.

The managing diversity by managing diversimilarity principle recognizes that people are simultaneously different and similar, not alike but yet alike. When the stress is put upon how individuals between demographic groups differ from one another, the many similarities that exist between members of these groups can be, and often are, overlooked. Thus, the diversimilarity approach becomes important when conducting diversity training and engaging in day-to-day management activities. Although it is important to affirm and exploit diversity (the ways in which we are different), it is also important not to forget about similarity (the ways in which we are the same).

STRATEGY THREE: ACT DIVERSIMILARITY

At the individual level, managers should focus on training employees to not only be aware of, and appreciate, differences but to also be on the lookout for similarities between themselves and those who, at least initially, may appear to be quite different. An exclusive focus on diversity may end up asking too much of employees: They must accept people whom they perceive to be entirely different from themselves when, in fact, these others are not so different as may be supposed. Training employees to recognize similarities between themselves and others as well as differences can make it easier to achieve higher levels of workplace diversity without suffering the potential negative side effects.

At the group and organizational levels, Ofori-Dankwa and Bonner (1998) recommend a more elaborate approach of managers emphasizing demographic diversity, demographic simulation, mental diversity, and organizational simulation.

First, managers should be aware of the benefits of demographic diversity and should continue, or seek, to maintain workplace diversity at levels that deliver diversity's benefits. This diversity goal should exist simultaneously with respecting each individual's rights to equal access and employment opportunity. Although industry has made progress in various areas with respect to equal opportunity and enhancing workplace diversity, managers should be ever vigilant to areas still in need of improvement.

Second, managers must seek demographic similation, meaning to help individuals in different demographic groups realize the things they have in common with members of other demographic groups. The goal here is *not* to assimilate, which would entail changing the interests and cultural predispositions of those from differing groups, but rather to leave these differences alone while recognizing and highlighting the many areas of commonality across groups. For many, someone being different from them is acceptable if there are many other ways that this individual can be seen as being similar. To some extent, the similarities can legitimate the differences that exist between individuals and groups and make them acceptable (Goldstein and Leopold, 1990).

Third, managers should seek intellectual/mental diversity. Group members should be encouraged to be independent and out-of-the-box thinkers. Uniformity in thinking and acting on the part of group or organization members can lead to subpar decision making and vulnerability to changes in the business environment. Hiring procedures that emphasize bringing in people who think like others in the organization are likely to be efficient in the short run (easier to fit the person in with the corporate culture, for example) but are not likely to be effective in the long run (due to a reduced capacity to think creatively or to innovate).

An important point to make here is that demographic diversity should not be confused with intellectual/mental diversity: The two are often related, but are not the same thing. Thus, achieving demographic diversity may not ensure that a group or organization will achieve intellectual/mental diversity. This is particularly true if an organization has a strong, assimilationist culture.

Fourth, and finally, managers should seek group/organizational similation, meaning that different individuals and groups within the organization must be made to realize the common elements and interests that bind them together. Emphasizing the importance and primacy of the organization's mission, goals, and strategies is one way to do this. Also, cultivating a common culture and creating a set of values that define how the organization will conduct its business are also important steps toward group and organizational similation. These efforts must not be pushed too far in such a way as to squelch the diversity that managers within the organization have tried hard to achieve.

CONCLUSION

Many executives and managers within industry have now accepted, at least with lip service if not with actions, the idea that workplace diversity is not only the morally correct course, but also one that can significantly benefit their organization, as well. This increased emphasis on differences between people may obscure the many similarities that exist between individuals from different demographic groups and make it more difficult for firms to achieve the full potential of diversity. By paying attention to both differences and similarities, the diversimilarity approach offers future managers an important perspective they can use to build on the gains in workplace diversity that have taken place, and enable them to capture the complete potential of the workers.

Discussion Questions

Assign students to groups of three, ensuring that at least one person in each group is of a different gender or ethnic group. Give each group 10 minutes to discuss the following questions.

1. Define in your own words what the concept of "diversimilarity" means and identify the advantages and disadvantages of such an approach.
2. Carefully distinguish between similation and assimilation.
3. Explain in your own words the diversimilarity principles of "diversity within diversities" and explain why these principles are important.

References

Cox, T. H., and S. Blake. (1993). "Managing Cultural Diversity: Implications for Organizational Competitiveness." *Academy of Management Executive*, 5(3), pp. 45–46.

Goldstein, J., and M. Leopold. "Corporate Culture Versus Ethnic Culture," *Personnel Journal*, Nov. 1990, 69(11), pp. 82–89.

Karp, H. B., and N. Sutton. (1993). "Where Diversity Training Goes Wrong." *Training*, July, pp. 30–34.

Loden, M., and J. B. Rosener. (1991). *Workforce America: Managing Employee Diversity as a Vital Resource*. Homewood, Ill.: Business One Irwin.

Mobely, M., and T. Payne. (1992). "Backlash! The Challenge to Diversity Training." *Training and Development*, December, pp. 45–52.

Ofori-Dankwa, J. (1996). "From Diversity to Diversimilarity: Shifting Paradigms to Match Global and National Realities." In K. Robers and M. Wilson (eds.), *Policy Choices: Nafta and Michigan's Future*. East Lansing: Michigan State University Press, pp. 271–287.

Ofori-Dankwa, J., and R. Bonner. (1996). "From Affirming Diversity to Affirming Diversimilarity: A New Look at Corporate Diversity Training and Management." *Multicultural Review*, 7:3, pp. 40–43, 54.

Ofori-Dankwa, J., and D. Ricks. (2000). "Research Emphases on Cultural Differences and/or Similarities: Are We Asking the Right Questions?" *Journal of International Management*, 6, pp. 173–186.

Quinn, R. (1988). *Beyond Rational Management: Managing the Paradoxes and Competing Demand of High Performance*. San Francisco: Jossey-Bass.

Joseph Ofori-Dankwa (Ph.D., Michigan State University) is a professor of management at Saginaw Valley State University. He has presented seminars and written extensively on the diversimilarity concept of diversity management. He has published in journals such as the *Academy of Management Review*, *Human Relations*, *Journal of International Management*, and *Public Administration Quarterly*.

Scott D. Julian (Ph.D., Louisiana State University) is an assistant professor of management at Saginaw Valley State University. He has published in the *Journal of Small Business Management*, *European Management Journal*, and *I.E.E.E. Transactions*. His current research interests include strategic control, strategic issue management, diversimilarity, and research on time.

How Canada Promotes Workplace Diversity

Marc S. Mentzer
University of Saskatchewan

When an American visits Canada, at first glance Canada is just like the United States, except it is a bit colder and has money with funny colors. Even though Canada is outwardly similar to the United States, there are deeply-rooted differences in history and in society's values that are not immediately evident to the visitor.

To begin to comprehend the differences between the two countries, we must go back to the time of the American Revolution. The American revolutionaries expected that present-day Canada would join them in the fight against the English king; however, the area that makes up present-day Canada stayed loyal to the king and continued under British rule until Canada became independent in 1867. As a result, Canadians have a faith in government that is very different from the usual skepticism and suspicion toward government that one sees in the United States.

Another key difference is that the Canadian federal government has less power than the U.S. government, especially where employment regulation is concerned. Canadian government law on employment issues affects only those industries that are federally regulated according to the Canadian constitution. These are broadcasting, telecommunications, banking, railroads, airlines, shipping, other transport across provincial boundaries, uranium mining, and crown corporations. (A crown corporation is a company in which the government owns all the stock, such as Canada Post or the Canadian Broadcasting Corporation.) All other businesses are beyond the jurisdiction of the Canadian government and are affected only by laws passed by the province in which they operate.

As an example, consider Sears, the department store chain. In the United States, Sears must obey the U.S. federal law regarding nondiscrimination, minimum wage, and so on. Each state has its own laws, but with some exceptions, a company as large as Sears can ignore the state laws because these laws are overridden by U.S. federal law.

In Canada, Sears also has stores throughout the country; however, retailing is not federally regulated under the Canadian constitution. Therefore, Sears in Canada must obey the laws of each province in which it operates. A Sears store in Ontario must obey Ontario laws; a store in Quebec must obey Quebec laws; and so on. Overall, this makes the task of obeying the law much more complicated for Sears in Canada than it is for Sears in the United States.

THE CANADIAN HUMAN RIGHTS ACT

In 1977, the Parliament passed the Canadian Human Rights Act, which forbids discrimination on the basis of race, gender, and certain other grounds. This act prohibits systemic (indirect) discrimination—as when an employer asks an applicant about her childbearing plans or engages in sexual harassment—as well as direct discrimination, when an employer says women will not be considered for a job. Instead of complaints being heard in court, as is the U.S. practice, discrimination complaints are made to the Canadian Human Rights Commission. This allows victims to have a hearing without having to hire a lawyer, although monetary damages tend to be much lower than they would be in a U.S. court. In severe cases of discrimination by an employer, the Commission has the power to impose a hiring quota. In 1984, Canadian National Railways was ordered to hire women for at least one-fourth of all the new hires for its blue-collar jobs. This power is rarely used by the Commission, but it remains in the background as a powerful tool for punishing employers who are the worst offenders.

Another feature of the Canadian Human Rights Act is that it requires comparable worth in pay policies known in Canada as pay equity. Every covered employer must ensure that predominantly female occupations are paid the same as predominantly male occupations of equal importance or difficulty in the same organization. For example, secretaries working for a railroad might claim that their job is of equal importance or difficulty as that of a track maintenance worker, and thus they could demand that their pay be the same. Pay equity or comparable worth is a type of law that does not exist in the U.S. at the federal level because it is seen as interfering with market forces. However, pay equity is a fact of life for organizations under the jurisdiction of the Canadian federal government. At the provincial level, Ontario and Quebec also have pay equity laws that cover employers, and most other provinces have pay equity laws limited to public-sector organizations such as universities and hospitals.

EMPLOYMENT EQUITY LEGISLATION

Initially it was hoped that the Canadian Human Rights Act would be sufficient to break down the barriers in the labor market that prevented the economic progress of women and minorities. However, with the passage of time, it became apparent that simply forbidding discrimination was not enough. Thus, in 1983 Parliament created a one-person commission headed by Judge Rosalie Abella to investigate what additional legislation would be desirable. Judge Abella's investigation concluded that it would be appropriate to have a law pushing employers to take proactive or aggressive measures to increase the numbers of women and minority employees (Canada, 1984). However, Judge Abella saw the U.S. experience with affirmative action as a divisive policy that actually hurt the cause of human rights; in her view, it pits men against women and whites against minorities. Thus, to avoid the ill will surrounding the term *affirmative action,* she proposed a new term, *employment equity,* to cover such proactive measures as aggressive recruiting among women and minorities, providing child care facilities, accommodating the needs of people with disabilities, and so on. Judge Abella's report became the basis of the Canadian Employment Equity Act of 1986. Covered employers submit their data to the federal government, which then assigns grades (A, B, and so forth) to each employer. The act was mainly symbolic, relying on persuasion and embarrassment so that employers would be more serious about creating workplaces that value diversity. A later version of the law, the Canadian Employment Equity Act of 1995, put in place modest fines (up to $50,000) for employers not meeting their targets, although in practice these fines are rarely if ever imposed.

THE FOUR PROTECTED GROUPS

In the United States, initially, the main thrust of civil rights legislation was to end discrimination against blacks. This has never been the burning issue in Canada that it is in the United States, because blacks comprise only 2 percent of the Canadian population, versus 13 percent in the United States. Similarly, Hispanics comprise only 1 percent of the Canadian population, compared to 12 percent in the United States. Therefore, when Canada introduced employment equity legislation, there was some question as to which groups should be chosen for special protection. In the end, the government designated four protected groups:

1.) Women. As in the United States, Canadian women lag behind men in income and representation in high-paying jobs. Thus, women were identified as one of the groups to be targeted under employment equity.

2.) Native peoples. This group includes Indians, Inuit (the aboriginal people of the far north), and Métis (those of mixed French–Indian ancestry in western Canada). Canadian natives constitute 3 percent of the Canadian population, compared to only 1 percent in the United States The plight of Canadian natives is of deep concern in Canadian society. Many natives live in poverty in isolated villages or remote reservations; others have moved to the cities but still have difficulty entering the economic mainstream.

3.) People with disabilities. Both Canada and the United States define disabilities to include psychological conditions such as mental illness, as well as physical conditions such as blindness or use of a wheelchair.

4.) Visible minorities. This is the most interesting, and most controversial, of the four protected groups under Canadian law, and it has no exact equivalent in United States law. Visible minorities refer to those of black, Asian, Arab, Pacific Islander, or Latin American ancestry. Chinese Canadians, comprising 3 percent of the Canadian population, are the largest of the ethnic groups in this category. The visible minority category includes some groups, such as Japanese Canadians, that have very high income levels today, but had historically been the target of discrimination. Visible minorities include other groups, such as Pacific Islander Canadians or Southeast Asian Canadians, that are very recent arrivals in Canada, with high unemployment rates and, on average, very low incomes. In short, the category of visible minorities is quite an assortment of ethnic groups that have very little in common with one another.

Because so many unrelated ethnic groups have been lumped together, there could be the temptation to load up on one visible minority ethnic group while neglecting certain others. Altogether, visible minorities make up 11 percent of the

Canadian population. In percentage terms, people of black or Hispanic ancestry are more numerous in the United States than in Canada; there is a larger percentage of people of Asian ancestry in Canada than in the United States.

Some other minorities sought to be included as protected groups under the Employment Equity Act, but they were excluded, although their rights are protected elsewhere under Canadian law. For example, note that lesbians and gays are not a protected group. Also, French-speaking people in predominantly English-speaking areas wanted to be treated as a protected group, but were not. (One-fourth of the population speaks French as their first language. In some areas, they feel they are at a disadvantage in an English-language-dominated society.) Because these minority groups are covered by the Human Rights Act, it is still illegal to discriminate against someone on the basis of their sexual orientation or whether they learned French before English. Employers are not required to engage in proactive or aggressive actions to increase their representation in the workforce.

There have been some problems with employment equity, however. An employee cannot be counted as a member of a minority group unless he or she identifies as such on a questionnaire administered by the employer. For example, Toronto-Dominion Bank has complained that employees of native ancestry often do not complete the questionnaire because they want to blend in and do not want special treatment (Canada, 1990). However, the bank cannot count them in their employment equity statistics unless they self-identify on their questionnaires. On the other hand, some banks have been accused of padding their statistics by encouraging nondisabled employees to check the disabled box on their questionnaires (Fine, 1990).

In the United States, some white individuals have won lawsuits claiming reverse discrimination, which has caused the unraveling of some of the U.S. affirmative action initiatives. A claim of reverse discrimination cannot be made in the Canadian legal system. Section 15 of the Charter of Rights and Freedoms, which is part of the Canadian constitution, states that discrimination is illegal. It then goes on to state that policies to improve the situation of disadvantaged groups are an allowable exception to the antidiscrimination clause. This is a key difference between the U.S. and Canadian constitutions, with far-ranging implications for affirmative action and employment equity policies in the two countries.

EMPLOYMENT EQUITY IN ACTION

Employment equity, when properly implemented, goes far beyond merely increasing the number of women and minority employees. Instead, the focus of employment equity should be to encourage flexibility and inclusion of people of all backgrounds.

For example, Canada's largest bank, the Royal Bank, is highly regarded for its outreach toward people with disabilities. Making arrangements for employees with disabilities can involve substantial expenses; hence, Royal Bank has created a central fund for these, so that individual managers do not have to worry about such expenses coming out of their departmental budgets (Young, 2000a).

When properly implemented, employment equity aims to change the organization's internal culture to one where people will be accepting of diversity in all its forms, unlike the old-fashioned approach of expecting all employees to come out of the same mold.

CANADA'S PROVINCES AND TERRITORIES

Canada is divided into 10 provinces and three territories, each of which has its own legislature and each of which passes whatever antidiscrimination legislation it wishes. Each of the 10 provinces and three territories has its own human rights laws forbidding discrimination. These laws also include provisions for imposing hiring quotas on employers who are chronic offenders, similar to the features of the Canadian Human Rights Act, although the provisions for punitive hiring quotas are rarely used. Although each province and territory forbids discrimination, none of them have any laws that require employers to engage in proactive measures in the spirit of employment equity or affirmative action.

Thus, only those employers in federally regulated industries are required by legislation to have employment equity programs. Such household names as Wal-Mart, McDonald's, or General Motors are not in federally regulated industries and, therefore, are not covered by the Canadian Employment Equity Act, although they certainly may create *voluntary* employment equity plans if they wish. In addition, such companies must obey the antidiscrimination laws of the provinces and territories in which they operate.

Thus, we see how executives of companies operating in both the United States and Canada face a particular challenge, because they must be knowledgeable about two countries' sets of laws and, in some instances, the laws of Canada's 10 provinces and three territories as well. In many instances, a human resource policy that is legal in the United States will be illegal in Canada, and such companies have to obey the laws of the jurisdiction in which they operate. Two countries, similar in so many ways, have entirely different legal structures to address the issue of increasing diversity in the workplace.

Note: U.S. demographic statistics are based on estimates for 2000 as reported by the U.S. Census Bureau (www.census.gov, accessed September 2000). Canadian demographic statistics are based on the 1996 census, as reported by Statistics Canada (www.statcan.ca, accessed September 2000).

Discussion Questions

1. Is the power of the Canadian federal government similar in relation to the provinces, as the power of the U.S. federal government in relation to the states? Why or why not?
2. If a U.S.-based retail chain has stores throughout Canada, which laws apply: those of the United States, those of the Canadian federal government, or those of each province?
3. What is the difference between employment equity and pay equity?

4. Which minority groups are of most interest in Canada? How does this differ from the U.S. situation?
5. How does the Canadian constitution affect affirmative-action-type programs?
6. Is it easier for employers to comply with diversity legislation in Canada or in the United States?

References

Canada. Minister of Supply and Services. (1984). *Report of the Commission on Equality in Employment.* Judge Rosalie Silberman Abella, Commissioner. Ottawa.

Canada. Minister of Supply and Services and Canada. (1990). *Employment Equity Act: 1990: Annual Report for the Year Ending December 1989: Toronto-Dominion Bank: # 5323.* Ottawa. [Issued by Employment and Immigration Canada.]

Fine, S. (1990). "Employers Pad Lists, Disabled Contend." *Globe and Mail,* Toronto, November 5, p. A1–A2.

Young, Lesley. (2000a). "Leveraging Diversity at Royal Bank Financial Group." *Canadian HR Reporter,* 13(6), March 27, p. 9.

Young, Lesley. (2000b). "Mentoring Program Is One Diversity Step in a Series at Rogers." *Canadian HR Reporter,* 13(6), March 27, p. 8.

Marc S. Mentzer is Associate Professor of Industrial Relations and Organizational Behaviour at the University of Saskatchewan. His degrees include an MBA from McGill University and a Ph.D. from Indiana University. Marc's research has appeared in such journals as *Canadian Journal of Administrative Sciences, Canadian Review of Sociology and Anthropology, Organization Studies,* and *Ethnic Groups.*

Innovative Work Models for Older Workers

Carol P. Harvey
Assumption College

Pamela D. Sherer
Providence College

Due to large numbers of baby boomers and increased life expectancies, people over 65 will represent 20 percent of the United States population by 2030 (Committee for Economic Development, 1999). Today, a fifty-five-year-old male can expect to live another 23 years and a female of the same age, 27 years (National Center for Health Statistics, 2001; Public Health Service, 1996). Unlike their parents and grandparents, who often made full retirement a life goal, a recent survey of baby boomers revealed that 70 percent of them expect to continue to work at least part-time after retirement (AARP, 1998).

Because the baby boomers are reaching traditional retirement ages at the same time that the United States is faced with a severe shortage of skilled and experienced labor, these economic, social, and demographic changes would seem to support the development of innovative programs to employ older workers. However, extensive research reveals that few organizations actually have programs in place that capitalize on the advantages of retaining or hiring older workers.

> American businesses do not yet regard the aging of the workforce as a compelling business issue. This lack of concern is further indicated by the small number of companies that have implemented programs or policies that could help employers fully utilize older employees. (AARP, 2000)

Most retirees who want or need to work have found it necessary to seek their own solutions. Typically, these jobs have taken the form of underemployment in low-level part-time service industries, like McDonald's, where 7% of the workforce is age sixty or older; seasonal employment; occasional consultant projects; or short-term placements through temporary work agencies.

Stereotypes about age still have considerable influence on workplace decisions. In a national survey, finding and keeping skilled employees was identified as the most important issue for human resource managers. They scored this item 8.9 on a 10-point scale. In the same survey, the respondents perceived older workers as having all but one of the top seven most desirable employee qualities. Older workers were identified as functioning well in a crisis; loyal; solid performers; experienced; having basic skills in reading, writing, and arithmetic; and possessing the ability to get along with coworkers. The only negative characteristic associated with older workers was their willingness to be flexible about performing different tasks, which scored a low mean rating of 4.5 (AARP, 2000).

"Age Works" author Beverly Goldberg warns corporate America that they must change their attitudes toward older workers or face the consequences of a shortage of skilled labor.

> As early as 2005, when some boomers begin retiring early, a sharp increase in the number of workers over 55 will be needed to maintain the percentage of the population that is employed . . . . A lot of companies will have to scramble to retain or hire older workers, many of whom are sitting atop of fat 401(k) accounts. Money alone will not lure them. An adjustment in corporate attitudes may be necessary. (Brock, 1999)

In addition, rigid government and organizational policies do not offer enough flexibility for innovative employment plans for older workers. Recently, Social Security liberalized restrictions to allow older workers to keep more of their income without docking their benefits. However, the IRS prohibits pension distributions to individuals who continue to work but have not reached traditional normal retirement ages (Watson Wyatt, 1999). So, a 55 year-old worker cannot retire gradually by reducing work hours and supplementing his/her income with pension benefits from the same employer, even if he or she has worked sufficient years to be eligible for the pension. For example, a recent early retirement plan offered to Massachusetts public school teachers with 30 or more years of service does not allow them to take substitute teaching assignments within the state public school system. So, the most qualified people in the state cannot work as substitute teachers. In addition, many organizations have retirement plans that calculate retirement benefits based on an employee's *last* 3 years of employment. So, employees who reduce their work hours also can lose pension benefits.

The few organizations that do have successful programs designed to capitalize on the strengths and advantages of older workers seem to share some common characteristics:

- Top management support
- Identification of their own organizational barriers
- Willingness to eliminate these barriers
- Flexibility
- Appreciation of the contributions of older workers

The Aerospace Corporation and Vita Needle are examples of two very different types of organizations that have successfully utilized the talents of older workers. The former is a $186 million a year corporation that employs over 3,000 employees, mostly highly educated scientists and engineers, to conduct government research. The latter is a small privately held manufacturer with 35 employees, located in a second-floor former theater. The Aerospace Corporation has a well-developed phased retirement program that allows the organization to retain the skills of a technical workforce. The Vita Needle Company simply values the contributions of older workers and has structured its operations around the needs of its older workforce.

THE AEROSPACE CORPORATION

Although individuals have always had the option of finding part-time or contract work to "bridge the gap" between full-time employment and retirement, few companies have instituted and maintained formalized phased retirement programs for their own employees. A notable exception is The Aerospace Corporation, El Segundo, CA, an independent nonprofit organization that receives yearly contracts that exceed $400 million in federally funded research.

The Aerospace Corporation was founded in 1960 at the request of the then Secretary of the Air Force. The organizational mission is to provide engineering services "objective technical analyses and assessments for space programs . . . [by operating] a federally funded research and development center (FFRDC) sponsored by the Department of Defense" (*1999 Annual Report*). The Department of Defense has identified five core competencies for The Aerospace Corporation: space launch certification; system-of-systems engineering, systems development and acquisition, process implementation, and technology application. Organized in a matrix structure, the heart of the $186 million corporation is the technical knowledge and expertise of its highly educated and skilled 3,000+ workforce. Consequently, it is to The Aerospace Corporation's advantage to retain this institutional memory on long-term projects.

This corporation has a "Retirement Transition Program" that offers its highly skilled technical employees four options: preretirement leaves of absence, part-time status in preparation for retirement, postretirement employment on a consulting basis, and postretirement employment on a "casual basis." The latter category is the most popular program. As a casual employee, the corporation's retirees can work in this phased retirement program up to 999 hours per year and still maintain their full pension benefits. Over 300 employees, 80 percent of them employed as engineers or scientists, take advantage of this program each year. In an interview on *Good Morning America*, Shirley McCarty, a participant in the plan, described it as a way to keep your "identity and self-esteem" (*Good Morning America*, February 8, 2000).

VITA NEEDLE

Innovative programs that utilize the talents and skills of older workers need not be limited to large organizations. Vita Needle, Needham, MA, is a manufacturer of stainless steel tubing and needles that has a reputation for quality and service and a policy of hiring primarily older workers. The average age of Vita Needle's 35 employees is 73 years. The oldest employee is 89 years old. The president, Fred Hartman, in an interview with Tom Brokaw for *NBC Nightly News*, said that he actively recruits older workers to assemble small metal components by hand because they are "extremely conscientious employees: loyal, dedicated, aware of quality requirements, and very reliable."

Founded in 1932 by the current president's great-grandfather, Oscar E. Nutter, a 68 year-old retiree from the textile industry, the company originally manufactured reusable medical needles, but these product lines now account for less than 20 percent of the business. Responding to the changing needs of a marketplace for disposable needles, Vita Needle expanded its product lines. The company now has more than 1,000 customers who use its products in medicine, sports equipment, and even the body-piercing business. The company produces some of the smallest needles in the world for eye surgery, most of the inflating needles for U.S. basketball manufacturers, and supplies 90 percent of the golf pro shops with needles used to inject solvent under golf club grips for repair and replacement. Stainless steel tube and wire products now make up 60–70 percent of the current sales. With yearly sales of $4 million, annual growth has averaged 20 percent over the past 5 years.

The Vita Needle Company's management practices illustrate how even a small business can simultaneously meet the employees' needs and its production and profit goals by utilizing flexible schedules and policies. Hartman allows his employees to work the ultimate in flextime. Each employee has a key to the factory and can start and finish work at any hour. It is common for workers to be on the job before 5 A.M. The first one in turns up the heat, and the last person who leaves is expected to put out the lights. Most workers put in 15 to 40 hours per week.

Rather than take advantage of such freedom, the production workers are so reliable and focused on quality that the company features them as a competitive advantage in its brochure. They are described as a "mature team of New England craftspeople (2/3 over age 70) with extraordinary attention to detail." Personnel costs are lower because the workers already have medical benefits through Medicare, do not need to take time off for child care needs, and have low turnover rates.

Employees join the company after retirement from careers such as nursing, engineering, and baking—one was even a circus performer. Some are there because they find Social Security and pension benefits inadequate and others because they find retirement boring and lonely. Hartman says it best, "There is a huge benefit to be gained from the experience, the values, [the] loyalty, and the dedication to quality that senior citizens bring to the workplace. We profit from it and so do our customers" (*Thomas's Register Trendletter*, 1999).

These two organizations illustrate that win-win solutions can be developed when there is an appreciation for the contributions of older workers. As the baby boomers moved through the stages of their lifetimes, their sheer numbers changed so many aspects of American society. As they move to retirement age, perhaps they will be the driving force that improves job opportunities for older workers.

Discussion Questions

1. List some of the stereotypes that often prevent older workers from having more employment opportunities. What are some of the things that managers could do to overcome these stereotypes? What are some of the things that older workers could do?

2. Make a list of the types of organizational barriers that could prevent organizations from developing programs like those at The Aerospace Corporation and Vita Needle.

3. Will the development of new uses for technology, like telecommuting, provide additional work opportunities for older workers? Why or why not?

References

Ackerman, Jerry. "Seniors Choosing Work over Retirement." *The Boston Globe*, October 15, 2000, pp. H1 and H6.

Anonymous. (1999). "Employees Inject Vitality into Needle Production." *Thomas's Register Trendletter,* #108, pp. 1–2.

American Association of Retired Persons. (1998). "Boomers Approaching Midlife." Available at research.aarp.org

American Association of Retired Persons (AARP) (2000). "Companies Do Not Use Strategies That Would Better Utilize Older Workers." Available at www. aarp.org/press/2000.

Brock, Fred. "Labor Shortage: Color It Gray." *New York Times*, February 5, 1999, p. 7.

Committee for Economic Development. (1999). "New Opportunities for Older Workers." p. 2. Available at www.ced.org

Flaherty, Julie. "A Company Where Retirement is a Dirty Word." *The New York Times*, December 28, 1997, Section 3, pp. 1 and 11.

Good Morning America. Interview with Diane Sawyer, February 8, 2000.

Mason, Jon. "Time Stands Still Here." *The Boston Globe*, December 31, 1997, p. 1.

National Center for Health Statistics. (1992). Vol. 11, section 6 life tables. Available at www.lifeexpectancy.com/usle.html

Public Health Service and National Center for Health Statistics. (1996). Available at www.lifeexpectancy.com/usle.html

The Aerospace Corporation. *1999 Annual Report*, p. 4.

Watson, Wyatt. (1999). "Phased Retirement: Reshaping the End of Work." Available at www.watsonwyatt.com

Pamela D. Sherer, Ph.D., is on the faculty of the Management Department at Providence College, where she teaches courses in managing workplace diversity, organizational change and development, and international human resource management. She was also the founding director of Providence College's Center for Teaching Excellence and Chair of its Faculty Development Committee. Her research interests include diversity issues, faculty development practices, collaborative learning, and pedagogy and its technology.

SECTION THREE

Perspectives on Some Dimensions of Diversity

The Power of Talk:
Who Gets Heard and Why

Deborah Tannen

The head of a large division of a multinational corporation was running a meeting devoted to performance assessment. Each senior manager stood up, reviewed the individuals in his group, and evaluated them for promotion. Although there were women in every group, not one of them made the cut. One after another, each manager declared, in effect, that every woman in his group did not have the self-confidence needed to be promoted. The division head began to doubt his ears. How could it be that all the talented women in the division suffered from a lack of self-confidence?

In all likelihood, they didn't. Consider the many women who have left large corporations to start their own businesses, obviously exhibiting enough confidence to succeed on their own. Judgments about confidence can be inferred only from the way people present themselves, and much of that presentation is in the form of talk.

The CEO of a major corporation told me that he often has to make decisions in 5 minutes about matters on which others may have worked 5 months. He said he uses this rule: If the person making the proposal seems confident, the CEO approves it. If not, he says no. This might seem like a reasonable approach, but my field of research, sociolinguistics, suggests otherwise. The CEO obviously thinks he knows what a confident person sounds like. But his judgment, which may be dead right for some people, may be dead wrong for others.

Communication isn't as simple as saying what you mean. How you say what you mean is crucial, and differs from one person to the next, because using language is learned social behavior: How we talk and listen are deeply influenced by cultural experience. Although we might think that our ways of saying what we mean are natural, we can run into trouble if we interpret and evaluate others as if they necessarily felt the same way we'd feel if we spoke the way they did.

Since 1974, I have been researching the influence of linguistic style on conversations and human relationships. In the past 4 years, I have extended that research to the workplace, where I have observed how ways of speaking learned in childhood affect judgments of competence and confidence, as well as who gets heard, who gets credit, and what gets done.

The division head who was dumbfounded to hear that all the talented women in his organization lacked confidence was probably right to be skeptical. The senior managers were judging the women in their groups by their own linguistic norms, but women—like people who have grown up in a different culture—have often learned different styles of speaking than men, which can make them seem less competent and self-assured than they are.

WHAT'S LINGUISTIC STYLE?

Everything that is said must be said in a certain way—in a certain tone of voice, at a certain rate of speed, and with a certain degree of loudness. Whereas often we consciously consider what to say before speaking, we rarely think about how to say it, unless the situation is obviously loaded—for example, a job interview or a tricky performance review. Linguistic style refers to a person's characteristic speaking pattern. It includes such features as directness or indirectness, pacing and pausing, word choice, and the use of such elements as jokes, figures of speech, stories, questions, and apologies. In other words, linguistic style is a set of culturally learned signals by which we not only communicate what we mean but also interpret others' meaning and evaluate one another as people.

Consider turn taking, one element of linguistic style. Conversation is an enterprise in which people take turns: One person speaks, then the other responds. However, this apparently simple exchange requires a subtle negotiation of signals so that you know when the other person is finished and it's your turn to begin. Cultural factors such as country or region of origin and ethnic background influence how long a pause seems natural. When Bob, who is from Detroit, has a conversation with his colleague Joe, from New York City, it's hard for him to get a word in edgewise because he expects a slightly longer pause between turns than Joe does. A pause of that length never comes because, before it has a chance to, Joe senses an uncomfortable silence, which he fills with more talk of his own.

Both men fail to realize that differences in conversational style are getting in their way. Bob thinks that Joe is pushy and uninterested in what he has to say, and Joe thinks that Bob doesn't have much to contribute. Similarly, when Sally relocated from Texas to Washington, DC, she kept searching for the right time to break in during staff meetings—and never found it. Although in Texas she was considered outgoing and confident, in Washington she was perceived as shy and retiring. Her boss even suggested she take an assertiveness training course. Thus, slight differences in conversational style—in these cases, a few seconds of pause—can have a surprising impact on who gets heard and on the judgments, including psychological ones, that are made about people and their abilities.

Every utterance functions on two levels. We're all familiar with the first one: Language communicates ideas. The second level is mostly invisible to us, but it plays a powerful role in communication. As a form of social behavior, language also negotiates relationships. Through ways of speaking, we signal—and create—the relative status of speakers and their level of rapport. If you say, "Sit down!" you are signaling that you have higher status than the person you are addressing, that you are so close to each other that you can drop all pleasantries, or that you are angry. If you say, "I would be honored if you would sit down," you are signaling great respect—or great sarcasm, depending on your tone of voice, the situation, and what you both know about how close you really are. If you say, "You must be so tired—why don't you sit down," you are communicating either closeness and concerns or condescension. Each of these ways of saying the same thing—telling someone to sit down—can have a vastly different meaning.

In every community known to linguists, the patterns that constitute linguistic style are relatively different for men and women. What's "natural" for most men speaking a given language is, in some cases, different from what's "natural" for most women. That is because we learn ways of speaking as children growing up, especially from peers, and children tend to play with other children of the same sex. The research of sociologists, anthropologists, and psychologists observing American children at play has shown that, although both girls and boys find ways of creating rapport and negotiating status, girls tend to learn conversational rituals that focus on the rapport dimension of relationships whereas boys tend to learn rituals that focus on the status dimension.

Girls tend to play with a single best friend or in small groups, and they spend a lot of time talking. They use language to negotiate how close they are; for example, the girl you tell your secrets to becomes your best friend. Girls learn to downplay ways in which one is better than the others and to emphasize ways in which they are all the same. From childhood, most girls learn that sounding too sure of themselves will make them unpopular with their peers—although nobody really takes such modesty literally. A group of girls will ostracize a girl who calls attention to her own superiority and criticize her by saying, "She thinks she's something"; and a girl who tells others what to do is called "bossy." Thus, girls learn to talk in ways that balance their own needs with those of others—to save face for one another in the broadest sense of the term.

Boys tend to play very differently. They usually play in larger groups in which more boys can be included, but not everyone is treated as an equal. Boys with high status in their group are expected to emphasize rather than downplay their status, and usually one or several boys will be seen as the leader or leaders. Boys generally don't accuse one another of being bossy, because the leader is expected to tell lower-status boys what to do. Boys learn to use language to negotiate their status in the group by displaying their abilities and knowledge, and by challenging others and resisting challenges. Giving orders is one way of getting and keeping the high-status role. Another is taking center stage by telling stories or jokes.

This is not to say that all boys and girls grow up this way or feel comfortable in these groups or are equally successful at negotiating within these norms. But, for the most part, these childhood play groups are where boys and girls learn their conversational styles. In this sense, they grow up in different worlds. The result is that women and men tend to have different habitual ways of saying what they mean, and conversations between them can be like cross-cultural communication: You can't assume that the other person means what you would mean if you said the same thing in the same way.

My research in companies across the United States shows that the lessons learned in childhood carry over into the workplace. Consider the following example: A focus group was organized at a major multinational company to evaluate a recently implemented flextime policy. The participants sat in a circle and discussed the new system. The group concluded that it was excellent, but they also agreed on ways to improve it. The meeting went well and was deemed a success by all, according to my own observations and everyone's comments to me. But the next day, I was in for a surprise.

I had left the meeting with the impression that Phil had been responsible for most of the suggestions adopted by the group. But as I typed up my notes, I noticed that Cheryl had made almost all those suggestions. I had thought that the key ideas came from Phil because he had picked up Cheryl's points and supported them, speaking at greater length in doing so than she had in raising them.

It would be easy to regard Phil as having stolen Cheryl's ideas and her thunder. But that would be inaccurate. Phil never claimed Cheryl's ideas as his own. Cheryl herself told me later that she left the meeting confident that she had contributed significantly and that she appreciated Phil's support. She volunteered, with a laugh, "It was not one of those times when a woman says something and it's ignored, then a man says it and it's picked up." In other words, Cheryl and Phil worked well as a team, the group fulfilled its charge, and the company got what it needed. So what was the problem?

I went back and asked all the participants who they thought had been the most influential group member, the one most responsible for the ideas that had been adopted. The pattern of answers was revealing. The two other women in the group named Cheryl. Two of the three men named Phil. Of the men, only Phil named Cheryl. In other words, in this instance, the women evaluated the contribution of another woman more accurately than the men did.

Meetings like this take place daily in companies around the country. Unless managers are unusually good at listening closely to how people say what they mean, the talents of someone like Cheryl may well be undervalued and underutilized.

One Up, One Down

Individual speakers vary in how sensitive they are to the social dynamics of language—in other words, to the subtle nuances of what others say to them. Men tend to be sensitive to the power dynamics of interaction, speaking in ways that position themselves as one up and resisting being put in a one down position by others. Women tend to react more strongly to the rapport dynamic, speaking in ways that save face for others and buffering statements that could be seen as putting others in a one-down position: These linguistic patterns are pervasive; you can hear them in hundreds of exchanges in the workplace every day. And, as in the case of Cheryl and Phil, they affect who gets heard and who gets credit.

Getting Credit   Even so small a linguistic strategy as the choice of pronoun can affect who gets credit. In my research in the workplace, I heard men say "I" in situations where I heard women say "we." For example, one publishing company executive said, "I'm hiring a new manager. I'm going to put him in charge of my marketing division, as if he owned the corporation." In stark contrast, I recorded women saying "we" when referring to work they alone had done. One woman explained that it would sound too self-promoting to claim credit in an obvious way by saying, "I did this." Yet she expected—sometimes vainly—that others would know it was her work and would give her the credit she did not claim for herself.

Managers might leap to the conclusion that women who do not take credit for what they've done should be taught to do so. But that solution is problematic because we associate ways of speaking with moral qualities: The way we speak is who we are and who we want to be.

Veronica, a senior researcher in a high-tech company, had an observant boss. He noticed that many of the ideas coming out of the group were hers but that often someone else trumpeted them around the office and got credit for them. He advised her to "own" her ideas and make sure she got the credit. But Veronica found she simply didn't enjoy her work if she had to approach it as what seemed to her an unattractive and unappealing "grabbing game." It was her dislike of such behavior that had led her to avoid it in the first place. Whatever the motivation, women are less likely than men to have learned to blow their own horn. And they are more likely than men to believe that if they do so, they won't be liked.

Many have argued that the growing trend of assigning work to teams may be especially congenial to women, but it may also create complications for performance evaluation. When ideas are generated and work is accomplished in the privacy of the team, the outcome of the team's effort may become associated with the person most vocal about reporting results. There are many women and men—but probably relatively more women—who are reluctant to put themselves forward in this way and who consequently risk not getting credit for their contributions.

Confidence and Boasting   The CEO who based his decisions on the confidence level of speakers was articulating a value that is widely shared in U.S. businesses: One way to judge confidence is by an individual's behavior, especially verbal behavior. Here again, many women are at a disadvantage.

Studies show that women are more likely to downplay their certainty, and men are more likely to minimize their doubts. Psychologist Laurie Heatherington and her colleagues devised an ingenious experiment, which they reported in the journal *Sex Roles* (Volume 29, 1993). They asked hundreds of incoming college students to predict what grades they would get in their first year. Some subjects were asked to make their predictions privately by writing them down and placing them in an envelope; others were asked to make their predictions publicly, in the presence of a researcher. The results showed that more women than men predicted lower grades for themselves if they made their predictions publicly. If they made their predictions privately, the predictions were the same as those of the men—and the same as their actual grades. This study provides evidence that what comes across as lack of confidence—predicting lower grades for oneself—may reflect not one's actual level of confidence but the desire not to seem boastful.

These habits with regard to appearing humble or confident result from the socialization of boys and girls by their peers in childhood play. As adults, both women and men find these behaviors reinforced by the positive responses they get from friends and relatives who share the same norms. But the norms of behavior in the U.S. business world are based on the style of interaction that is more common among men—at least, among American men.

Asking Questions   Although asking the right questions is one of the hallmarks of a good manager, how and when questions are asked can send unintended signals about competence and power. In a group, if only one person asks questions, he or she risks being seen as the only ignorant one. Furthermore, we judge others not only by how they speak but also by how they are spoken to. The person who asks questions may end up being lectured to and looking like a novice under a schoolmaster's tutelage. The way boys are socialized makes them more likely to be aware of the underlying power dynamic by which a question asker can be seen in a one-down position.

One practicing physician learned the hard way that any exchange of information can become the basis for judgments—or misjudgments—about competence. During her training, she received a negative evaluation that she thought was unfair, so she asked her supervising physician for an explanation. He said that she knew less than her peers. Amazed at his answer, she asked how he had reached that conclusion. He said, "You ask more questions."

Along with cultural influences and individual personality, gender seems to play a role in whether and when people ask questions. For example, of all the observations I've made in lectures and books, the one that sparks the most enthusiastic flash of recognition is that men are less likely than women to stop and ask for directions when they are lost. I explain that men often resist asking for directions because they are aware that it puts them in a one-down position and because they value the independence that comes with finding their way by themselves. Asking for directions while driving is only one instance—along with many others that researchers have examined—in which men seem less likely than women to ask questions. I believe this is because they are more attuned than women to the potential face-losing aspect of asking questions. And men who believe that asking questions might reflect negatively on them may, in turn, be likely to form a negative opinion of others who ask questions in situations where they would not.

Conversational Rituals

Conversation is fundamentally ritual in the sense that we speak in ways our culture has conventionalized and expect certain types of responses. Take greetings, for example. I have heard visitors to the United States complain that Americans are hypocritical because they ask how you are but aren't interested in the answer. To Americans, "How are you?" is obviously a ritualized way to start a conversation rather than a literal request for information. In other parts of the world, including the Philippines, people ask each other "Where are you going?" when they meet. The question seems intrusive to Americans, who do not realize that it, too, is a ritual query to which the only expected reply is a vague "Over there."

It's easy and entertaining to observe different rituals in foreign countries. But we don't expect differences, and are far less likely to recognize the ritualized nature of our conversations, when we are with our compatriots at work. Our differing rituals can be even more problematic when we think we're all speaking the same language.

Apologies   Consider the simple phrase *I'm sorry.*

> CATHERINE: How did that big presentation go?
>> BOB: Oh, not very well. I got a lot of flak from the VP for finance, and I didn't have the numbers at my fingertips.
> CATHERINE: Oh, I'm sorry. I know how hard you worked on that.

In this case, *I'm sorry* probably means "I'm sorry that happened," not "I apologize," unless it was Catherine's responsibility to supply Bob with the numbers for the presentation. Women tend to say *I'm sorry* more frequently than men, and often they intend it in this way—as a ritualized means of expressing concern. It's one of many learned elements of conversational style that girls often use to establish rapport. Ritual apologies—like other conversational rituals—work well when both parties share the same assumptions about their use. But people who utter frequent ritual apologies may end up appearing weaker, less confident, and literally more blameworthy than people who don't.

Apologies tend to be regarded differently by men, who are more likely to focus on the status implications of exchanges. Many men avoid apologies because they see them as putting the speaker in a one-down position. I observed with some amazement an encounter among several lawyers engaged in a negotiation on a speakerphone. At one point, the lawyer in whose office I was sitting accidentally elbowed the telephone and cut off the call. When his secretary got the parties back on again, I expected him to say what I would have said: "Sorry about that. I knocked the phone with my elbow." Instead, he said, "Hey, what happened? One minute you were there; the next minute you were gone." This lawyer seemed to have an automatic impulse not to admit fault if he didn't have to. For me, it was one of those pivotal moments when you realize that the world you live in is not the one everyone lives in and that the way you assume is the way to talk is really only one of many.

Those who caution managers not to undermine their authority by apologizing are approaching interaction from the perspective of the power dynamic. In many cases, this strategy is effective. On the other hand, when I asked people what frustrated them in their jobs, one frequently voiced complaint was working with or for someone who refuses to apologize or admit fault. In other words, accepting responsibility for errors and admitting mistakes may be an equally effective or superior strategy in some settings.

Feedback   Styles of giving feedback contain a ritual element that often is the cause for misunderstanding. Consider the following exchange: A manager had to tell her marketing director to rewrite a report. She began this potentially awkward task by citing the report's strengths and weaknesses and then moved to the main point: the weaknesses that needed to be remedied. The marketing director seemed to understand and accept his supervisor's comments, but his revision contained only minor changes and failed to address the major weaknesses. When the manager told him of her dissatisfaction, he accused her of misleading him: "You told me it was fine."

The impasse resulted from different linguistic styles. To the manager, it was natural to buffer the criticism by beginning with praise. Telling her subordinate that his report is inadequate and has to be rewritten puts him in a one-down position. Praising him for the parts that are good is a ritualized way of saving face for him. But the marketing director did not share his supervisor's assumption about how feedback should be given. Instead, he assumed that what she mentioned first was the main point and that what she brought up later was an afterthought.

Those who expect feedback to come in the way the manager presented it would appreciate her tact and would regard a more blunt approach as unnecessarily callous. But those who share the marketing director's assumptions would regard the blunt approach as honest and no-nonsense, and the manager's as obfuscating. Because each one's assumptions seemed self-evident, each blamed the other: The manager thought the marketing director was not listening, and he thought she had not communicated clearly or had changed her mind. This is significant because it illustrates that incidents labeled vaguely as "poor communication" may be the result of different linguistic styles.

Compliments   Exchanging compliments is a common ritual, especially among women. A mismatch in expectations about this ritual left Susan, a manager in the human resources field, in a one-down position. She and her colleague Bill had both given presentations at a national conference. On the airplane home, Susan told Bill, "That was a great talk!" "Thank you," he said. Then she asked, "What did you think of mine?" He responded with a lengthy and detailed critique as she listened uncomfortably. An unpleasant feeling of having been put down came over her. Somehow she had been positioned as the novice in need of his expert advice. Even worse, she had only herself to blame, since she had, after all, asked Bill what he thought of her talk.

But had Susan asked for the response she received? When she asked Bill what he thought about her talk, she expected to hear not a critique but a compliment. In fact, her question had been an attempt to repair a ritual gone awry. Susan's initial compliment to Bill was the kind of automatic recognition she felt was more or less required after a colleague gives a presentation, and she expected Bill to respond with a matching compliment. She was just talking automatically, but he either sincerely misunderstood the ritual or simply took the opportunity to bask in the one-up position of critic. Whatever his motivation, it was Susan's attempt to spark an exchange of compliments that gave him the opening.

Although this exchange could have occurred between two men, it does not seem coincidental that it happened between a man and a woman. Linguist Janet Holmes discovered that women pay more compliments than men (*Anthropological Linguistics*, Volume 28, 1986). And, as I have observed, fewer men are likely to ask, "What did you think of my talk?" precisely because the question might invite an unwanted critique.

In the social structure of the peer groups in which they grow up, boys are indeed looking for opportunities to put others down and take the one-up position for themselves. In contrast, one of the rituals girls learn is taking the one-down position but assuming that the other person will recognize the ritual nature of self-denigration and pull them back up.

The exchange between Susan and Bill also suggests how women's and men's characteristic styles may put women at a disadvantage in the workplace. If one person is trying to minimize status differences, maintain an appearance that everyone is equal, and save face for the others while another person is trying to maintain the one-up position and avoid being positioned as one down, the person seeking the one-up position is likely to get it. At the same time, the person who has not been expending any effort to avoid the one-down position is likely to end up in it. Because women are more likely to take (or accept) the role of advice seeker, men are more inclined to interpret a ritual question from a woman as a request for advice.

Ritual Opposition   Apologizing, mitigating criticism with praise, and exchanging compliments are rituals common among women that men often take literally. A ritual common among men that women often take literally is ritual opposition.

A woman in communications told me she watched with distaste and distress as her office mate argued heatedly with another colleague about whose division should suffer budget cuts. She was even more surprised, however, that a short time later they were as friendly as ever. "How can you pretend that fight never happened?" she asked. "Who's pretending it never happened?" he responded, as puzzled by her question as she had been by his behavior. "It happened," he said, "and it's over." What she took as literal fighting to him was a routine part of daily negotiation: a ritual fight.

Many Americans expect the discussion of ideas to be a ritual fight—that is, an exploration through verbal opposition. They present their own ideas in the most certain and absolute form they can and wait to see if they are challenged. Being forced to defend an idea provides an opportunity to test it. In the same spirit, they may play devil's advocate in challenging their colleagues' ideas—trying to poke holes and find weaknesses—as a way of helping them explore and test their ideas.

This style can work well if everyone shares it, but those unaccustomed to it are likely to miss its ritual nature. They may give up an idea that is challenged, taking the objections as an indication that the idea was a poor one. Worse, they may take the opposition as a personal attack and may find it impossible to do their best in a contentious environment. People unaccustomed to this style may hedge when stating their ideas in order to fend off potential attacks. Ironically, this posture makes their arguments appear weak and is more likely to invite attack from pugnacious colleagues than to fend it off.

Ritual opposition can even play a role in who gets hired. Some consulting firms that recruit graduates from the top business schools use a confrontational interviewing technique. They challenge the candidate to "crack a case" in real time. A partner at one firm told me, "Women tend to do less well in this kind of interaction, and it certainly affects who gets hired. But, in fact, many women who don't 'test well' turn out to be good consultants. They're often smarter than some of the men who looked like analytic powerhouses under pressure."

The level of verbal opposition varies from one company's culture to the next, but I saw instances of it in all the organizations I studied. Anyone who is uncomfortable with this linguistic style—and that includes some men as well as many women—risks appearing insecure about his or her ideas.

Negotiating Authority

In organizations, formal authority comes from the position one holds, but actual authority has to be negotiated day to day. The effectiveness of individual managers depends in part on their skill in negotiating authority and on whether others reinforce or undercut their efforts. The way linguistic style reflects status plays a subtle role in placing individuals within a hierarchy.

Managing Up and Down   In all the companies I researched, I heard from women who knew they were doing a superior job and knew that their coworkers (and sometimes their immediate bosses) knew it as well, but believed that the higher-ups did not. They frequently told me that something outside themselves was holding them back and found it frustrating because they thought that all that should be necessary for success was to do a great job, that superior performance should be recognized and rewarded. In contrast, men often told me that if women weren't promoted it was because they simply weren't up to snuff. Looking around, however, I saw evidence that men more often than women behaved in ways likely to get them recognized by those with the power to determine their advancement.

In all the companies I visited, I observed what happened at lunchtime. I saw young men who regularly ate lunch with their boss, and senior men who ate with the big boss. I noticed far fewer women who sought out the highest-level person they could eat with. But one is more likely to get recognition for work done if one talks about it to those higher up, and it is easier to do so if the lines of communication are already open. Furthermore, given the opportunity for a conversation with superiors, men and women are likely to have different ways of talking about their accomplishments because of the different ways in which they were socialized as children. Boys are rewarded by their peers if they talk up their achievements, whereas girls are rewarded if they play theirs down. Linguistic styles common among men may tend to give them some advantages when it comes to managing up.

All speakers are aware of the status of the person they are talking to and adjust accordingly. Everyone speaks differently when talking to a boss than when talking to a subordinate. But, surprisingly, the ways in which they adjust their talk may be different and thus may project different images of themselves.

Communications researchers Karen Tracy and Eric Eisenberg studied how relative status affects the way people give criticism. They devised a business letter that contained some errors and asked 13 male and 11 female college students to role-play delivering criticism under two scenarios. In the first, the speaker was a boss talking to a subordinate; in the second, the speaker was a subordinate talking to his or her boss. The researchers measured how hard the speakers tried to avoid hurting the feelings of the person they were criticizing.

One might expect people to be more careful about how they deliver criticism when they are in a subordinate position. Tracy and Eisenberg found that hypothesis to be true for the men in their study but not for the women. As they reported in *Research on Language and Social Interaction* (Volume 2.4, 1990/1991), the women showed more concern about the other person's feelings when they were playing the role of superior. In other words, the women were more careful to save face for the other person when they were managing down than when they were managing up. This pattern recalls the way girls are socialized: Those who are in some way superior are expected to downplay rather than flaunt their superiority.

In my own recordings of workplace communication, I observed women talking in similar ways. For example, when a manager had to correct a mistake made by her secretary, she did so by acknowledging that there were mitigating circumstances. She said laughing, "You know, it's hard to do things around here, isn't it, with all these people coming in!" The manager was saving face for her subordinate, just like the female students role-playing in the Tracy and Eisenberg study.

Is this an effective way to communicate? One must ask, effective for what? The manager in question established a positive environment in her group, and the work was done effectively. On the other hand, numerous women in many different fields told me that their bosses say they don't project the proper authority.

Indirectness   Another linguistic signal that varies with power and status is indirectness—the tendency to say what we mean without spelling it out in so many words. Despite the widespread belief in the United States that it's always best to say exactly what we mean, indirectness is a fundamental and pervasive element in human communication. It also is one of the elements that vary most from one culture to another, and it can cause enormous misunderstanding when speakers have different habits and expectations about how it is used. It's often said that American women are more indirect than American men, but in fact everyone tends to be indirect in some situations and in different ways. Allowing for cultural, ethnic, regional, and individual differences, women are especially likely to be indirect when it comes to telling others what to do, which is not surprising, considering girls' readiness to brand other girls as bossy. On the other hand, men are especially likely to be indirect when it comes to admitting fault or weakness, which also is not surprising, considering boys' readiness to push around boys who assume the one-down position.

At first glance, it would seem that only the powerful can get away with bald commands such as "Have that report on my desk by noon." But power in an organization also can lead to requests so indirect that they don't sound like requests at all. A boss who says, "Do we have the sales data by product line for each region?" would be surprised and frustrated if a subordinate responded, "We probably do" rather than "I'll get it for you." Examples such as these notwithstanding, many researchers have claimed that those in subordinate positions are more likely to speak indirectly, and that is surely accurate in some situations. For example, linguist Charlotte Linde, in a study published in *Language in Society* (Volume 17, 1988), examined the black-box conversations that took place between pilots and copilots before airplane crashes. In one particularly tragic instance, an Air Florida plane crashed into the Potomac River immediately after attempting take-off from National Airport in Washington, DC, killing all but 5 of the 74 people on board. The pilot, it turned out, had little experience flying in icy weather. The copilot had a bit more, and it became heartbreakingly clear on analysis that he had tried to warn the pilot but had done so indirectly. Alerted by Linde's observation, I examined the transcript of the conversations and found evidence of her hypothesis. The copilot repeatedly called attention to the bad weather and to ice buildup on other planes:

> **Copilot:** Look how the ice is just hanging on his, ah, back there, see that? See all those icicles on the back there and everything?
>   **Pilot:** Yeah.
> [The copilot also expressed concern about the long waiting time since deicing.]
> **Copilot:** Boy, this is a, this is a losing battle here on trying to decide those things; it [gives] you a false feeling of security, that's all that does.
> [Just before they took off, the copilot expressed another concern—about abnormal instrument readings—but again he didn't press the matter when it wasn't picked up by the pilot.]
> **Copilot:** That don't seem right, does it? [3-second pause]. Ah, that's not right. Well—
>   **Pilot:** Yes it is, there's 80.
> **Copilot:** Naw, I don't think that's right. [7-second pause] Ah, maybe it is.

Shortly thereafter, the plane took off, with tragic results. In other instances as well as this one, Linde observed that copilots, who are second in command, are more likely to express themselves indirectly or otherwise mitigate, or soften, their communication when they are suggesting courses of action to the pilot. In an effort to avert similar disasters, some airlines now offer training for copilots to express themselves in more assertive ways.

This solution seems self-evidently appropriate to most Americans. But when I assigned Linde's article in a graduate seminar I taught, a Japanese student pointed out that it would be just as effective to train pilots to pick up on hints. This approach reflects assumptions about communication that typify Japanese culture, which places great value on the ability of people to understand one another without putting everything into words. Either directness or indirectness can be a successful means of communication as long as the linguistic style is understood by the participants.

In the world of work, however, there is more at stake than whether the communication is understood. People in powerful positions are likely to reward styles similar to their own, because we all tend to take as self-evident the logic of our own styles. Accordingly, there is evidence that in the U.S. workplace, where instructions from a superior are expected to be voiced in a relatively direct manner, those who tend to be indirect when telling subordinates what to do may be perceived as lacking in confidence.

Consider the case of the manager at a national magazine who was responsible for giving assignments to reporters. She tended to phrase her assignments as questions. For example, she asked, "How would you like to do the X project with Y?" or said, "I was thinking of putting you on the X project. Is that okay?" This worked extremely well with her staff; they liked working for her, and the work got done in an efficient and orderly manner. But when she had her midyear evaluation with her own boss, he criticized her for not assuming the proper demeanor with her staff.

In any work environment, the higher ranking person has the power to enforce his or her view of appropriate demeanor, created in part by linguistic style. In most U.S. contexts, that view is likely to assume that the person in authority has the right to be relatively direct rather than to mitigate orders. There also are cases, however, in which the higher ranking person assumes a more indirect style. The owner of a retail operation told her subordinate, a store manager, to do something. He said he would do it, but a week later he still hadn't. They were able to trace the difficulty to the following conversation: She had said, "The bookkeeper needs help with the billing. How would you feel about helping her out?" He had said, "Fine." This conversation had seemed to be clear and flawless at the time, but it turned out that they had interpreted this simple exchange in very different ways. She thought he meant, "Fine, I'll help the bookkeeper out." He thought he meant, "Fine, I'll think about how I would feel about helping the bookkeeper out." He did think about it and came to the conclusion that he had more important things to do and couldn't spare the time.

To the owner, "How would you feel about helping the bookkeeper out?" was an obviously appropriate way to give the order "Help the bookkeeper out with the billing." Those who expect orders to be given as bold imperatives may find such locutions annoying or even misleading. But those for whom this style is natural do not think they are being indirect. They believe they are being clear in a polite or respectful way.

What is atypical in this example is that the person with the more indirect style was the boss, so the store manager was motivated to adapt to her style. She still gives orders the same way, but the store manager now understands how she means what she says. It's more common in U.S. business contexts for the highest-ranking people to take a more direct style, with the result that many women in authority risk being judged by their superiors as lacking the appropriate demeanor—and, consequently, lacking confidence.

WHAT TO DO?

I am often asked, what is the best way to give criticism or what is the best way to give orders? In other words, what is the best way to communicate? The answer is that there is no one best way. The results of a given way of speaking will vary depending on the situation, the culture of the company, the relative rank of speakers, their linguistic styles, and how those styles interact with one another. Because of all those influences, any way of speaking could be perfect for communicating with one person in one situation and disastrous with someone else in another. The critical skill for managers is to become aware of the workings and power of linguistic style, to make sure that people with something valuable to contribute get heard.

It may seem, for example, that running a meeting in an unstructured way gives equal opportunity to all. But awareness of the differences in conversational style makes it easy to see the potential for unequal access. Those who are comfortable speaking up in groups, who need little or no silence before raising their hands, or who speak out easily without waiting to be recognized are far more likely to get heard at meetings. Those who refrain from talking until it's clear that the previous speaker is finished, who wait to be recognized, and who are inclined to link their comments to those of others will do fine at a meeting where everyone else is following the same rules but will have a hard time getting heard in a meeting with people whose styles are more like the first pattern. Given the socialization typical of boys and girls, men are more likely to have learned the first style and women the second, making meetings more congenial for men than for women. It's common to observe women who participate actively in one-on-one discussions or in all-female groups but who are seldom heard in meetings with a large proportion of men. On the other hand, there are women who share the style more common among men, and they run a different risk—of being seen as too aggressive.

A manager aware of those dynamics might devise any number of ways of ensuring that everyone's ideas are heard and credited. Although no single solution will fit all contexts, managers who understand the dynamics of linguistic style can develop more adaptive and flexible approaches to running or participating in meetings, mentoring or advancing the careers of others, evaluating performance, and so on. Talk is the lifeblood of managerial work, and understanding that different people have different ways of saying what they mean will make it possible to take advantage of the talents of people with a broad range of linguistic styles. As the workplace becomes more culturally diverse and business becomes more global, managers will need to become even better at reading interactions and more flexible in adjusting their own styles to the people with whom they interact.

Discussion Questions

1. What evidence have you seen to support or refute Tannen's article in either students' behaviors in this class or at work?
2. What is the relationship between American corporate culture and the idea that women's learned conversation styles work against them in the workplace while men's conversation styles are an advantage?
3. Why does merely adding women to a team not necessarily result in women's points of views being equally represented in a discussion?
4. What is the relationship between conversational styles and sexual harassment in the workplace?

Deborah Tannen is university professor and a professor of linguistics at Georgetown University in Washington, DC. She is the author of 15 books, including *You Just Don't Understand: Women and Men in Conversation* (William Morrow, 1990), which introduced to the general public the idea of female and male styles of communication. The material in this article is drawn from *Talking from 9 to 5* (Avon Books, 1995).

The Male Role Stereotype
Doug Cooper Thompson

When you first consider that many men now feel that they are victims of sex role stereotyping, your natural response might be: "Are you kidding? Why should men feel discriminated against? Men have the best jobs; they are the corporation presidents and the political leaders. Everyone says, 'It's a man's world.' What do men have to be concerned about? What are their problems?"

It is obvious that men hold most of the influential and important positions in society, and it does seem that many men "have it made." The problem is that men pay a high cost for the ways they have been stereotyped and for the roles that they play.

To understand why many men and women are concerned, we need to take a look at the male role stereotype. Here is what men who conform to the stereotype must do.

CODE OF CONDUCT:
THE MALE ROLE STEREOTYPE

1. **Act "Tough."** Acting tough is a key element of the male role stereotype. Many boys and men feel that they have to show that they are strong and tough, and they can "take it" and "dish it out" as well. You've probably run into some boys and men who like to push people around, use their strength, and act tough. In a conflict, these males would never consider giving in, even when surrender or compromise would be the smartest or most compassionate course of action.
2. **Hide Emotions.** This aspect of the male role stereotype teaches males to suppress their emotions and to hide feelings of fear or sorrow or tenderness. Even as small children, they are warned not to be "crybabies." As grown men, they show that they have learned this lesson well, and they become very efficient at holding back tears and keeping a "stiff upper lip."
3. **Earn "Big Bucks."** Men are trained to be the primary source of income for the family. So men try to choose occupations that pay well, and then they stick with those jobs, even when they might prefer to try something else. Boys and men are taught that earning a good living is important. In fact, men are often evaluated not on how kind or compassionate or thoughtful they are, but rather on how much money they make.
4. **Get the "Right" Kind of Job.** If a boy decides to become a pilot, he will receive society's stamp of approval, for that is the right kind of a job for a man. But if a boy decides to become an airline steward, many people would think that quite strange. Boys can decide to be doctors, mechanics, or business executives, but if a boy wants to become a nurse, secretary, librarian, ballet dancer, or kindergarten teacher, he will have a tough time. His friends and relatives will probably try to talk him out of his decision, because it's just not part of the male role stereotype.

Reprinted with permission from *As Boys Become Men: Learning New Male Roles* by Doug Cooper Thompson. Copyright 1985. New York: Irvington Publishers, Inc.

5. **Compete—Intensely.** Another aspect of the male role stereotype is to be super-competitive. This competitive drive is seen not only on athletic fields, but in school and later at work. This commitment to competition leads to still another part of the male stereotype: getting ahead of other people to become a winner.

6. **Win—At Almost Any Cost.** From the Little League baseball field to getting jobs that pay the most money, boys and men are taught to win at whatever they may try to do. They must work and strive and compete so that they can get ahead of other people, no matter how many personal, and even moral, sacrifices are made along the way to the winner's circle.

Those are some of the major features of the male stereotype. Certainly, some of them may not appear to be harmful. Yet when we look more closely, we find that many males who do "buy" the message of the male role stereotype end up paying a very high price for their conformity.

THE COST OF THE CODE: WHAT MEN GIVE UP

1. Men who become highly involved in competition and winning can lose their perspective and good judgment. Competition by itself is not necessarily bad, and we have all enjoyed some competitive activities. But when a man tries to fulfill the male stereotype, and compete and win at any cost, he runs into problems. You have probably seen sore losers (and even sore winners)—sure signs of overcommitment to competition. Real competitors have trouble making friends because they are always trying to go "one-up" on their friends. When cooperation is needed, true-blue competitors have a difficult time cooperating.

2. Hiding emotions can hurt. For one thing, hiding emotions confuses people as to what someone's real feelings are. Men who hide their emotions can be misunderstood by others who might see them as uncaring and insensitive. Men who are always suppressing their feelings may put themselves under heavy psychological stress. This pressure can be physically unhealthy as well.

3. The heavy emphasis that the male stereotype puts on earning big money also creates problems. Some men choose careers they really do not like, just because the job pays well. Others choose a job they like at first, only later to find out that they would rather do something else. But they stay with their jobs anyway, because they cannot afford to earn less money.

In trying to earn as much as possible, many men work long hours and weekends. Some even take second jobs. When men do this, they begin to lead one-track lives—the track that leads to the office or business door. They drop outside interests and hobbies. They have less and less time to spend with their families. That is one reason why some fathers never really get to know their own children, even though they may love them very much.

4. Many men who are absorbed by competition, winning, and earning big bucks pay a terrible price in terms of their physical health. With the continual pressure to compete, be tough, earn money, with little time left for recreation and other interests, men find themselves much more likely than women to fall victim to serious disease. In fact, on the average, men die eight years sooner than women. Loss of life is a high cost to pay for following the code of the male role stereotype.

5. Those boys and men who do not follow the male code of conduct may also find their lives more difficult because of this stereotype. For example, some boys choose to become nurses rather than doctors, kindergarten teachers rather than lawyers, artists rather than electricians. Social pressure can make it terribly difficult for males who enter these nonstereotyped careers. Other boys and men feel very uncomfortable with the continual pressure to compete and win.

And some boys do not want to hide their feelings in order to project an image of being strong and tough. These males may be gentle, compassionate, sensitive human beings who are puzzled with and troubled by the male role stereotype. When society stereotypes any group—by race, religion, or sex—it becomes difficult for individuals to break out of the stereotype and be themselves.

Discussion Questions

1. How are the six characteristics of the male role stereotype connected?
2. What characteristics does Thompson omit, and how do they relate to his six?
3. Explain the costs to men of conforming to this stereotype.
4. What other costs might Thompson have included?

White Privilege and Male Privilege: A Personal Account of Coming to See Correspondences Through Work in Women's Studies

Peggy McIntosh
Wellesley College

Through work to bring materials and perspectives from Women's Studies into the rest of the curriculum, I have often noticed men's unwillingness to grant that they are over privileged in the curriculum, even though they may grant that women are disadvantaged. Denials which amount to taboos surround the subject of advantages which men gain from women's disadvantages. These denials protect male privilege from being fully recognized, acknowledged, lessened, or ended.

Thinking through unacknowledged male privilege as a phenomenon with a life of its own, I realized that since hierarchies in our society are interlocking, there was most likely a phenomenon of white privilege which was similarly denied and protected, but alive and real in its effects. As a white person, I realized I had been taught about racism as something which puts others at a disadvantage, but had been taught not to see one of its corollary aspects, white privilege, which puts me at an advantage.

I think whites are carefully taught not to recognize white privilege, as males are taught not to recognize male privilege. So I have begun in an untutored way to ask what it is like to have white privilege. This paper is a partial record of my personal observations, and not a scholarly analysis. It is based on my daily experiences within my particular circumstances.

I have come to see white privilege as an invisible package of unearned assets which I can count on cashing in each day, but about which I was "meant" to remain oblivious. White privilege is like an invisible weightless knapsack of special provisions, assurances, tools, maps, guides, codebooks, passports, visas, clothes, compass, emergency gear, and blank checks.

Since I have had trouble facing white privilege, and describing its results in my life, I saw parallels here with men's reluctance to acknowledge male privilege. Only rarely will a man go beyond acknowledging that women are advantaged to acknowledging that men have unearned advantage, or that unearned privilege has not been good for men's development as human beings, or for society's development, or that privilege systems might ever be challenged and *changed.*

I will review here several types or layers of denial which I see at work protecting, and preventing awareness about, entrenched male privilege. Then I will draw parallels, from my own experience, with the denials which veil the facts of white privilege. Finally, I will list 46 ordinary and daily ways in which I experience having white privilege, within my life situation and its particular social and political frameworks.

Writing this paper has been difficult, despite warm receptions for the talks on which it is based.[1] For describing white privilege makes one newly accountable. As we in Women's Studies work reveal male privilege and ask men to give up some of their power, so one who writes about having white privilege must ask, "Having described it, what will I do to lessen or end it?"

The denial of men's overprivileged state takes many forms in discussions of curriculum-change work. Some claim that men must be central in the curriculum because they have done most of what is important or distinctive in life or in civilization. Some recognize sexism in the curriculum but deny that it makes male students seem unduly important in life. Others agree that certain *individual* thinkers are blindly male-oriented but deny that there is any systemic tendency in disciplinary frameworks or epistemology to overempower men as a group. Those men who do grant that male privilege takes institutionalized and embedded forms are still likely to deny that male hegemony has opened doors for them personally. Virtually all men deny that male overreward alone can explain men's centrality in all the inner sanctums of our most powerful institutions. Moreover, those few who will acknowledge that male privilege systems have overempowered them usually end up doubting that we could dismantle these privilege systems. They may say they will work to improve women's status, in the society or in the university, but they can't or won't support the idea of lessening men's. In curricular terms, this is the point at which they say that they regret they cannot use any of the interesting new scholarship on women because the syllabus is full. When the talk turns to giving men less cultural room, even the most fair-minded of the men I know well tend to reflect, or fall back on, conservative assumptions about the inevitability of present gender relations and distributions of power, calling on precedent or sociobiology and psychobiology to demonstrate that male domination is natural and follows inevitably from evolutionary pressures. Others resort to arguments from "experience" or religion or social responsiblity or wishing and dreaming.

After I realized, through faculty development work in Women's Studies, the extent to which men work from a base of unacknowledged privilege, I understood that much of their oppressiveness was unconscious. Then I remembered the frequent charges from women of color that white women whom they encounter are oppressive. I began to understand why we are justly seen as oppressive, even when we don't see ourselves that way. At the very least, obliviousness of one's privileged state can make a person or group irritating to be with. I began to count the ways in which I enjoy unearned skin privilege and have been conditioned into oblivion about its existence, unable to see that it put me "ahead" in any way, or put my people ahead, overrewarding us and yet also paradoxically damaging us, or that it could or should be changed.

My schooling gave me no training in seeing myself as an oppressor, as an unfairly advantaged person, or as a participant in a damaged culture. I was taught to see myself as an individual whose moral state depended on her individual moral will. At school, we were not taught about slavery in any depth; we were not taught to see slaveholders as damaged people. Slaves were seen as the only group at risk of being dehumanized. My schooling followed the pattern which Elizabeth Minnich has pointed out: Whites are taught to think of their lives as morally neutral, normative, and average, and also ideal, so that when we work to benefit others, this is seen as work which will allow "them" to be more like "us." I think many of us know how obnoxious this attitude can be in men.

After frustration with men who would not recognize male privilege, I decided to try to work on myself at least by identifying some of the daily effects of white privilege in my life. It is crude work, at this stage, but I will give here a list of special circumstances and conditions I experience which I did not earn but which I have been made to feel are mine by birth, by citizenship, and by virtue of being a conscientious law-abiding "normal" person of good will. I have chosen those conditions which I think in my case *attach somewhat more to skin-color privilege* than to class, religion, ethnic status, or geographical location, though of course all these other factors are intricately intertwined. As far as I can see, my Afro-American co-workers, friends, and acquaintances with whom I come into daily or frequent contact in this particular time, place, and line of work cannot count on most of these conditions.

1. I can if I wish arrange to be in the company of people of my race most of the time.
2. I can avoid spending time with people whom I was trained to mistrust and who have learned to mistrust my kind or me.
3. If I should need to move, I can be pretty sure of renting or purchasing housing in an area which I can afford and in which I would want to live.
4. I can be pretty sure that my neighbors in such a location will be neutral or pleasant to me.
5. I can go shopping alone most of the time, pretty well assured that I will not be followed or harassed.
6. I can turn on the television or open to the front page of the paper and see people of my race widely represented.
7. When I am told about our national heritage or about "civilization," I am shown that people of my color made it what it is.
8. I can be sure that my children will be given curricular materials that testify to the existence of their race.
9. If I want to, I can be pretty sure of finding a publisher for this piece on white privilege.
10. I can be pretty sure of having my voice heard in a group in which I am the only member of my race.
11. I can be casual about whether or not to listen to another woman's voice in a group in which she is the only member of her race.

12. I can go into a music shop and count on finding the music of my race represented, into a supermarket and find the staple foods which fit with my cultural traditions, into a hairdresser's shop and find someone who can cut my hair.

13. Whether I use checks, credit cards, or cash, I can count on my skin color not to work against the appearance of financial reliability.

14. I can arrange to protect my children most of the time from people who might not like them.

15. I do not have to educate my children to be aware of systemic racism for their own daily physical protection.

16. I can be pretty sure that my children's teacher and employers will tolerate them if they fit school and workplace norms; my chief worries about them do not concern others' attitudes toward their race.

17. I can talk with my mouth full and not have people put this down to my color.

18. I can swear, or dress in second-hand clothes, or not answer letters, without having people attribute these choices to the bad morals, the poverty, or the illiteracy of my race.

19. I can speak in public to a powerful male group without putting my race on trial.

20. I can do well in a challenging situation without being called a credit to my race.

21. I am never asked to speak for all the people of my racial group.

22. I can remain oblivious of the language and customs of persons of color who constitute the world's majority without feeling in my culture any penalty for such oblivion.

23. I can criticize our government and talk about how much I fear its policies and behavior without being seen as a cultural outsider.

24. I can be pretty sure that if I ask to talk to "the person in charge," I will be facing a person of my race.

25. If a traffic cop pulls me over or if the IRS audits my tax return, I can be sure I haven't been singled out because of my race.

26. I can easily buy posters, postcards, picture books, greeting cards, dolls, toys, and children's magazines featuring people of my race.

27. I can go home from most meetings of organizations I belong to feeling somewhat tied in, rather than isolated, out-of-place, outnumbered, unheard, held at a distance, or feared.

28. I can be pretty sure that an argument with a colleague of another race is more likely to jeopardize her chances for advancement than to jeopardize mine.

29. I can be pretty sure that if I argue for the promotion of a person of another race, or a program centering on race, this is not likely to cost me heavily within my present setting, even if my colleagues disagree with me.

30. If I declare there is a racial issue at hand, or there isn't a racial issue at hand, my race will lend me more credibility for either position than a person of color will have.

31. I can choose to ignore developments in minority writing and minority activist programs, or disparage them, or learn from them, but in any case, I can find ways to be more or less protected from negative consequences of any of these choices.

32. My culture gives me little fear about ignoring the perspectives and powers of people of other races.

33. I am not made acutely aware that my shape, bearing, or body odor will be taken as a reflection of my race.
34. I can worry about racism without being seen as self-interested or self-seeking.
35. I can take a job with an affirmative action employer without having my co-workers on the job suspect that I got it because of my race.
36. If my day, week, or year is going badly, I need not ask of each negative episode or situation whether it has racial overtones.
37. I can be pretty sure of finding people who would be willing to talk with me and advise me about my next steps, professionally.
38. I can think over many options, social, political, imaginative, or professional, without asking whether a person of my race would be accepted or allowed to do what I want to do.
39. I can be late to a meeting without having the lateness reflect on my race.
40. I can choose public accommodation without fearing that people of my race cannot get in or will be mistreated in the places I have chosen.
41. I can be sure that if I need legal or medical help, my race will not work against me.
42. I can arrange my activities so that I will never have to experience feelings of rejection owing to my race.
43. If I have low credibility as a leader I can be sure that my race is not the problem.
44. I can easily find academic courses and institutions which give attention only to people of my race.
45. I can expect figurative language and imagery in all of the arts to testify to experiences of my race.
46. I can choose blemish cover or bandages in "flesh" color and have them more or less match my skin.

I repeatedly forgot each of the realizations on this list until I wrote it down. For me, white privilege has turned out to be an elusive and fugitive subject. The pressure to avoid it is great, for in facing it I must give up the myth of meritocracy. If these things are true, this is not such a free country; one's life is not what one makes it; many doors open for certain people through no virtues of their own. These perceptions mean also that my moral condition is not what I had been led to believe. The appearance of being a good citizen rather than a troublemaker comes in large part from having all sorts of doors open automatically because of my color.

A further paralysis of nerve comes from literary silence protecting privilege. My clearest memories of finding such analysis are in Lillian Smith's unparalleled *Killers of the Dream* and Margaret Andersen's review of Karen and Mamie Fields' *Lemon Swamp*. Smith, for example, wrote about walking toward black children on the street and knowing they would step into the gutter; Andersen contrasted the pleasure which she, as a white child, took on summer driving trips to the south with Karen Fields' memories of driving in a closed car stocked with all necessities lest, in stopping, her black family should suffer "insult, or worse." Adreinne Rich also recognizes and writes about daily experiences of privilege, but in my observation, white women's writing in this area is far more often on systemic racism than on our daily lives as light-skinned women.[2]

In unpacking this invisible knapsack of white privilege, I have listed conditions of daily experience which I once took for granted, as neutral, normal, and universally available to everybody, just as I once thought of a male-focused curriculum as the neutral or accurate account which can speak for all. Nor did I think any of these perquisites as bad for the holder. I now think that we need a more finely differentiated taxonomy of privilege, for some of these varieties are only what one would want for everyone in a just society, and others give license to be ignorant, oblivious, arrogant, and destructive. Before proposing some more finely-tuned categorization, I will make some observations about the general effects of these conditions on my life and expectations.

In this potpourri of examples, some privileges make me feel at home in the world. Others allow me to escape penalties or dangers which others suffer. Through some, I escape fear, anxiety, or a sense of not being welcome or not being real. Some keep me from having to hide, to be in disguise, to feel sick or crazy, to negotiate each transaction from the position of being an outsider or, within my group, a person who is suspected of having too close links with a dominant culture. Most keep me from having to be angry.

I see a pattern running through the matrix of white privilege, a pattern of assumptions which were passed on to me as a white person. There was one main piece of cultural turf; it was my own turf, and I was among those who could control the turf. I could measure up to the cultural standards and take advantage of the many options I saw around me to make what the culture would call a success of my life. *My skin color was an asset for any move I was educated to want to make.* I could think of myself as "belonging" in major ways, and of making social systems work for me. I could freely disparage, fear, neglect, or be oblivious to anything outside of the dominant cultural forms. Being of the main culture, I could also criticize it fairly freely. My life was reflected back to me frequently enough so that I felt, with regard to my race, if not to my sex, like one of the real people.

Whether through the curriculum or in the newspaper, the television, the economic system, or the general look of people in the streets, we received daily signals and indications that my people counted, and that others *either didn't exist or must be trying not very successfully, to be like people of my race.* We were given cultural permission not to hear voices of people of other races, or a tepid cultural tolerance for hearing or acting on such voices. I was also raised not to suffer seriously from anything which darker-skinned people might say about my group, "protected," though perhaps I should more accurately say *prohibited,* through the habits of my economic class and social group, from living in racially mixed groups or being reflective about interactions between people of differing races.

In proportion as my racial group was being made confident, comfortable, and oblivious, other groups were likely being made inconfident, uncomfortable, and alienated. Whiteness protected me from many kinds of hostility, distress, and violence, which I was being subtly trained to visit in turn upon people of color.

For this reason, the word "privilege" now seems to me misleading. Its connotations are too positive to fit the conditions and behaviors which "privilege systems" produce. We usually think of privilege as being a favored state, whether earned, or conferred by birth or luck. School graduates are reminded they are privileged and urged to use their (enviable) assets well. The word "privilege" carries the connotation of being something everyone must want. Yet some of the conditions I have described here work to systemically overempower certain groups. Such privilege simply *confers dominance,* gives permission to control, because of one's race or sex. The kind of privilege which gives license to some people to be, at best, thoughtless and, and at worst, murderous should not continue to be referred to as a desirable attribute. Such "privilege" may be widely desired without being in any way beneficial to the whole society.

Moreover, though "privilege" may confer power, it does not confer moral strength. Those who do not depend on conferred dominance have traits and qualities which may never develop in those who do. Just as Women's Studies courses indicate that women survive their political circumstances to lead lives which hold the human race together, so "underprivileged" people of color who are the world's majority have survived their oppression and lived survivor's lives from which the white global minority can and must learn. In some groups, those dominated have actually become strong through *not* having all of these unearned advantages, and this gives them a great deal to teach the others. Members of the so-called privileged groups can seem foolish, ridiculous, infantile, or dangerous by contrast.

I want, then, to distinguish between earned strength and unearned power conferred systemically. Power from unearned privilege can look like strength when it is in fact permission to escape or to dominate. But not all of the privileges on my list are inevitably damaging. Some, like the expectation that neighbors will be decent to you, or that your race will not count against you in court, should be the norm in a just society and should be considered as the entitlement of everyone. Others, like the privilege not to listen to less powerful people, distort the humanity of the holders as well as the ignored groups. Still others, like finding one's staple foods everywhere, may be a function of being a member of a numerical majority in the population. Others have to do with not having to labor under pervasive negative sterotyping and mythology.

We might at least start by distinguishing between positive advantages which we can work to spread, to the point where they are not advantages at all but simply part of the normal civic and social fabric, and negative types of advantage which unless rejected will always reinforce our present hierarchies. For example, the positive "privilege" of belonging, the feeling that one belongs within the human circle, as Native Americans say, fosters development and should not be seen as privilege for a few. It is, let us say, an entitlement which none of us should have to earn; ideally it is an *unearned entitlement.* At present, since only a few have it, it is an *unearned advantage* for them. The negative "privilege" which gave me cultural permission not to take darker-skinned Others seriously can be seen as arbitrarily conferred dominance and should not be desirable for anyone. This paper results from a process of coming to see that some of the power which I originally saw as attendant on being a human being in the United States consisted in *unearned advantage* and *conferred dominance,* as well as other kinds of special circumstance not universally taken for granted.

In writing this paper I have also realized that white identity and status (as well as class identity and status) give me considerable power to choose whether to broach this subject and its trouble. I can pretty well decide whether to disappear and avoid and not listen and escape the dislike I may engender in other people through this essay, or interrupt, take over, dominate, preach, direct, criticize, or control to some extent what goes on in reaction to it. Being white, I am given considerable power to escape many kinds of danger or penalty as well as to choose which risks I want to take.

There is an analogy here, once again, with Women's Studies. Our male colleagues do not have a great deal to lose in supporting Women's Studies, but they do not have a great deal to lose if they oppose it either. They simply have the power to decide whether to commit themselves to more equitable distributions of power. They will probably feel few penalties whatever choice they make; they do not seem, in any obvious short-term sense, the ones at risk, though they and we are all at risk because of the behaviors which have been rewarded in them.

Through Women's Studies work I have met very few men who are truly distressed about systemic, unearned male advantage and conferred dominance. And so one question for me and others like me is whether we will be like them, or whether we will get truly distressed, even outraged, about unearned race advantage and conferred dominance and if so, what we will do to lessen them. In any case, we need to do more work in identifying how they actually affect our daily lives. We need more down-to-earth writing by people about these taboo subjects. We need more understanding of the ways in which white "privilege" damages white people, for these are not the same ways in which it damages the victimized. Skewed white psyches are an inseparable part of the picture, though I do not want to confuse the kinds of damage done to the holders of special assets and to those who suffer the deficits. Many, perhaps most, of our white students in the United States think that racism doesn't affect them because they are not people of color; they do not see "whiteness" as a racial identity. Many men likewise think that Women's Studies does not bear on their own existences because they are not female; they do not see themselves as having gendered identities. Insisting on the universal *effects* of "privilege" systems, then, becomes one of our chief tasks, and being more explicit about the *particular* effects in particular contexts is another. Men need to join us in this work.

In addition, since race and sex are not the only advantaging systems at work, we need to similarly examine the daily experience of having age advantage, or ethnic advantage, or physical ability, or advantage related to nationality, religion, or sexual orientation. Professor Marnie Evans suggested to me that in many ways the list I made also applies directly to heterosexual privilege. This is a still more taboo subject than race privilege: the daily ways in which heterosexual privilege makes married persons comfortable or powerful, providing supports, assets, approvals, and rewards to those who live or expect to live in heterosexual pairs. Unpacking that content is still more difficult, owing to the deeper imbeddedness of heterosexual advantage and dominance, and stricter taboos surrounding these.

But to start such an analysis I would put this observation from my own experience: The fact that I live under the same roof with a man triggers all kinds of societal assumptions about my worth, politics, life, and values, and triggers a host of unearned advantages and powers. After recasting many elements from the original list I would add further observations like these:

1. My children do not have to answer questions about why I live with my partner (my husband).
2. I have no difficulty finding neighborhoods where people approve of our household.

3. My children are given texts and classes which implicitly support our kind of family unit, and do not turn them against my choice of domestic partnership.
4. I can travel alone or with my husband without expecting embarrassment or hostility in those who deal with us.
5. Most people I meet will see my marital arrangements as an asset to my life or as a favorable comment on my likability, my competence, or my mental health.
6. I can talk about the social events of a weekend without fearing most listener's reactions.
7. I will feel welcomed and "normal" in the usual walks of public life, institutional, and social.
8. In many contexts, I am seen as "all right" in daily work on women because I do not live chiefly with women.

Difficulties and dangers surrounding the task of finding parallels are many. Since racism, sexism, and heterosexism are not the same, the advantaging associated with them should not be seen as the same. In addition, it is hard to disentangle aspects of unearned advantage which rests more on social class, economic class, race, religion, sex, and ethnic identity than on other factors. Still, all of the oppressions are interlocking, as the Combahee River Collective statement of 1977 continues to remind us eloquently.[3]

One factor seems clear about all of the interlocking oppressions. They take both active forms which we can see and embedded forms which as a member of the dominant group one is taught not to see. In my class and place, I did not see myself as racist because I was taught to recognize racism only in individual acts of meanness by members of my group, never in invisible systems conferring unsought racial dominance on my group from birth. Likewise, we are taught to think that sexism or heterosexism is carried on only through individual acts of discrimination, meanness, or cruelty toward women, gays, and lesbians, rather than in invisible systems conferring unsought dominance on certain groups. Disapproving of the systems won't be enough to change them. I was taught to think that racism could end if white individuals changed their attitudes; many men think sexism can be ended by individual changes in daily behavior toward women. But a man's sex provides advantage for him whether or not he approves of the way in which dominance has been conferred on his group. A "white" skin in the United States opens many doors for whites whether or not we approve of the way dominance had been conferred on us. Individual acts can palliate, but cannot end, these problems. To redesign social systems we need first to acknowledge their colossal unseen dimensions. The silences and denials surrounding privilege are the key political tools here. They keep thinking abut equality or equity incomplete, protecting unearned advantage and conferred dominance by making these taboo subjects. Most talk by whites about equal opportunity seems to me now to be about equal opportunity to try to get in to a position of dominance while denying that *systems* of dominance exist.

It seems to me that obliviousness about white advantage, like obliviousness about male advantage, is kept strongly inculturated in the United States so as to maintain the myth of meritocracy, the myth that democratic choice is equally available to all. Keeping most people unaware that freedom of confident action is there for just a small number of people props up those in power, and serves to keep power in the hands of the same groups that have most of it already. Though systemic change takes many decades, there are pressing questions for me and I imagine for some others like me if we raise our daily consciousness on the perquisites of being light-skinned. What will we do with such knowledge? As we know from watching men, it is an open question whether we will choose to use unearned advantage to weaken hidden systems of advantage, and whether we will use any of our arbitrarily-awarded power to try to reconstruct power systems on a broader base.

Discussion Questions

1. What does the author mean by the concept of "white privilege?"
2. Reread the author's list of 46 examples of white privilege. Select the five examples that seem the most significant in helping you to understand that white people are privileged. Explain your selections.
3. In addition to white privilege, the author also cites examples of heterosexual privilege. Develop a list of privileges that the able bodied enjoy that the physically challenged do not experience.
4. Most of us have experienced privilege in some form. Describe an example from your experience.
5. How does this article help you to understand the oppression that members of other groups may experience?

Notes

1. This paper was presented at the Virginia Women's Studies Association conference in Richmond in April 1986 and the American Educational Research Association conference in Boston in October 1986 and discussed with two groups of participants in the Dodge Seminars for Secondary School Teachers in New York and Boston in the spring of 1987.
2. Andersen, Margaret. "Race and the Social Science Curriculum: a Teaching and Learn-ing Discussion." *Radical Teacher,* November 1984, pp. 17–20; Smith, Lillian. 1949. *Killers of the Dream.* New York: WW Norton.
3. "A Black Feminist Statement." The Combahee River Collective. In Hull, Scott, and Smith. (eds.,). *All the Women Are White, all the Blacks Are Men. But Some of Us Are Brave: Black Women's Studies.* The Feminist Press, 1982, pp. 13–22.

The Continuing Challenge of Sexual Diversity at Work

Gerald Callan Hunt
Ryerson Polytechnic University

The tragic murder in 1998 of Matthew Shepard, an openly gay, 21-year-old, first-year political science student at the University of Wyoming, once again focused attention on the high cost one can pay for being "different." Matthew was lured from a campus bar shortly after midnight on October 7th, driven to a remote area near Laramie, tied to a split-rail fence, tortured, beaten, and pistol whipped while he begged for his life. He was left for dead in near freezing temperatures but was found alive by strangers who took him to a hospital. Matthew never regained consciousness and died on October 12th. Many people believe that Matthew was killed to make the point that homosexuals deserve to die.

Matthew's murder stood in stark contrast to the view that gays and lesbians have achieved full citizenship in American society. In some ways, gays and lesbians have moved toward greater acceptance. There have been important and supportive shifts in the legal situation, public opinion, and some workplace cultures. Gay characters have become an accepted part of situational comedy television (*Ellen* and *Will and Grace*). Influential organizations such as General Motors now offer same-sex partner benefits, and Disney World holds an annual "gay day" in Orlando. At the same time, anti-gay bias in law, housing, the workplace, the media, and some churches can still be a harsh fact of life if you are gay or lesbian, and even more stark if you are transgendered (dress and behave opposite to one's biological sex). In 18 of the United States, sexual activity between adults of the same sex in private is still on the books as a criminal offense; 39 states refuse to ban job discrimination on the basis of sexual orientation; and the American military continues to proclaim that no openly gay man or lesbian should ever be allowed to serve in the defense of their country. For the casual observer, it is a bit confusing. Have gays and lesbians come a long way, just a little way, or no way at all? Is sexual diversity a workplace issue or not?

Increasingly positive public attitudes, significant changes in the legal environment, expanding marketplace activity, union support, and "activist" employees provide indisputable evidence that sexual orientation is part of the diversity mosaic that organizations can no longer ignore. At the same time, organizational response to this form of diversity challenge has been very mixed and uneven. Some organizations fully embrace issues related to sexual orientation and have removed as many discriminatory policies and procedures as legally possible. Others have resisted any change at all, some going so far as to fight for the right to fire and openly discriminate against this group.

GAYS AND LESBIANS AT WORK

In the late 1940s, in his pioneering work on human sexuality, Kinsey (1948) found upwards of 10 percent of the American population to be engaged in homosexual activity. Recent American and Canadian studies place the figure somewhat lower, finding 5–6 percent of the population to be predominately homosexual, identifying exclusively as gay or lesbian. However, that percentage rises to as high as 13–15 percent when bisexuals and transsexuals are included (Bagley and Trembley, 1998). These figures mean that the gay and lesbian population is slightly higher than the number of Jewish people living in the United States (estimated at 3 percent). Unlike most other minority groups, however, homosexuals are not readily visible, and many have chosen to remain invisible, especially at work, because they fear the negative consequences that might result from revealing their sexual orientation. This is with good reason: In Nazi Germany, homosexuals were rounded up and forced into concentration camps where many died in the gas chambers (Plant, 1986). As the murder of Matthew Shepard illustrated, being openly and visibly gay can still cost your life.

The true case of Mark Sension illustrates the kind of dilemmas gays and lesbians can still confront within the labor market. Mark was hired by the University of Denver to be the associate director of operations of the Ricks Center for Gifted Children. About a month after he was hired, his supervisor learned that he was gay. Soon after, Mark was fired without warning and escorted from the building by university security personnel. He was told his firing was an "issue of trust" because he did not make his sexual orientation clear during the hiring interview. At the same time, if Mark had revealed his sexual orientation he would not have been offered the job. What happened to Mark in Colorado was completely legal; if it had happened in New York or California, it would have been illegal.

In spite of the very real risks, in recent years, more and more gays and lesbians have decided it is time to come out of the "closet" and fight for equal rights. Because of the centrality of work in most people's sense of well-being, many gays and lesbians have found living in the closet to be too demeaning a price to pay for "protection" from discrimination. The workplace is not only a place where people spend much of their time and make a living; it is also where they develop a sense of self-worth and status. Employment-related issues such as firing, hiring, harassment, violence, promotions, benefits, perks, leaves of absence, pension provisions, housing allowances, and retirement plans all have the potential to discriminate against gays and lesbians in ways that can be economically and psychologically harmful. Workplace benefits, for example, can account for up to 40 percent of overall compensation. As a result, including sexual orientation in nondiscrimination policies, and gaining access to benefits and perks for same-sex partners, has become an important rallying point for people concerned about equity and fairness at work.

Spokespersons for sexual minorities offer a clear message: Gays and lesbians believe they are discriminated against and treated inequitably at work. They seek change in institutional policies and practices to do with recruiting, hiring, promotion, discipline, and employee benefits (specifically to include same-sex partners), and they look to organizational leaders to foster and promote an environment that is positive and supportive of human difference and diversity.

The demands made by sexual minorities closely parallel the demands that have been made by women and minorities. In many ways, the gay rights movement is only now catching up with other human rights movements. Although there are differences within and between the experience of women, racial minorities, and the disabled, all minorities come together in sharing a history of various forms of prejudice and workplace disadvantage.

The overwhelming difference between sexual orientation and other diversity issues is that for some people it is more controversial. Homosexuality continues to be a fact of life that makes some people feel extremely uncomfortable and angry. Some very conservative thinkers portray gays and lesbians as immoral and degenerate people who voluntarily choose a deviant lifestyle, opting to ignore evidence to the contrary suggesting homosexuality is relatively fixed and does not involve free choice. Some people who are guided by biblical teachings, for example, quote from the Bible to defend their views (Leviticus 18:22 states that homosexuality is an abomination). These people fail to note that Leviticus 10:10 also indicates that eating shellfish is an abomination and that Exodus 35:2 clearly states that a neighbor who insists on working on the Sabbath should be put to death. Ultimately, however, in countries based on a notion of secular government, and on the idea that various religious and spiritual traditions should coexist (many of which are mute on the subject of homosexuality), the idea that the religious or moral philosophy of one group should override all others, and directly influence the state and workplace, becomes intolerable.

Although some organizations have gone to extensive efforts to ensure policies and benefits are equal for everyone and to value their gay and lesbian employees equally with other workers, in other settings, little has been done. So, before considering what organizations have done, might do, and should do, it is important to understand the rapidly changing social, legal, and economic landscape that has brought this issue to the foreground.

SOCIAL, LEGAL, AND ECONOMIC DEVELOPMENTS

A changing social, legal, and economic environment, combined with increasing pressure from unions and gay/lesbian activist employee groups, exerts considerable pressure on organizational leaders to rethink policies and practices to do with their gay and lesbian workers.

Social Forces

With each passing year, gays and lesbians acquire a higher and more positive public profile. Yeager (1999) estimates there are 124 openly gay and lesbian elected officials serving at the federal, state, and municipal levels. These people range from member of Congress Barney Frank to Margo Frasier, an elected sheriff in Austin, Texas. More and more high-profile people have publicly declared their sexuality.

Over the past couple of decades, public opinion polls have shown a steadily increasing tolerance toward homosexuals in general, and gay rights at work in particular. A comprehensive review of public opinion polling in several countries including the United States, for example, found that by 1988 most people supported gay equality rights, leading the authors to conclude that, "over the course of a generation, a major shift towards a more liberal position on the principle of equality rights for lesbians and gay men has been evident" (Rayside and Bowler, 1988:649). Since 1988, polling results indicate that public support for homosexual rights has been increasing. Research conducted in 1998 (Yang, 1999) found that a majority of Americans supported the idea of gays and lesbians having equality in employment (84 percent); housing (81 percent); inheritance rights (62 percent); social security benefits (57 percent); gays in the military (66 percent). The same study found that disapproval of same-sex relationships dropped from a peak of 75 percent in 1987 to 56 percent in 1996. Wilcox and Wolpert (2000:28), summarizing polling data from throughout the 1990s, found that attitudes have moved in a positive direction since 1992, even though they indicate that there remains a minority "voicing strongly negative reactions, often rooted in basic emotional reactions." In other words, although there may not be widespread public involvement in fighting for homosexual rights, some people continue to be vocal in their opposition. There is little basis for believing that the citizens of the United States support either overt or covert discrimination in the workplace on the basis of sexual orientation.

Legal Change

The increased visibility of gays and lesbians, combined with more assertive demands for equal rights, has generated considerable legal action. For the past decade, federal, state, and municipal legislators have been debating changes in legislation that would affect gays and lesbians in almost every aspect of their lives including violence and harassment, employment and housing discrimination, adoption and child care, domestic partner benefits and the freedom to marry. In some jurisdictions, the legal changes have been widespread; in others, there has been little or no change.

At one time, all states had laws regulating and criminalizing consensual homosexual activity between adults. When the new millennium unfolded, such laws had been repealed, or struck down, in 32 states but remained on the statutes in 18 states plus Puerto Rico. In Oklahoma, for instance, a law remains on the books that makes a "crime against nature" (unspecified act) punishable by up to 10 years. This law originally applied to both same- and opposite-sex couples, but the state high court did narrow the law to apply only to same-sex couples. Such laws have been used to justify job dismissal, apartment rental refusals, and taking away children from lesbian and gay parents. Most of these laws are under challenge by groups such as the American Civil Liberties Union.

At the same time, increasing numbers of governments have passed bills to include sexual orientation as a protected grounds, particularly in employment and housing (Mills and Herrschaft, 1999). By the year 2000, over 240 state, local, and federal governments had nondiscrimination policies that included sexual orientation. In 1999, Nevada became the eleventh state to ban job workplace discrimination on the basis of sexual orientation, following on the heels of California, Connecticut, Hawaii, Massachusetts, Minnesota, New Hampshire, New Jersey, Rhode Island,

Vermont, and Wisconsin. Seven others states have executive orders barring discrimination in public employment, and two states (Illinois and Michigan) have state civil service rules prohibiting discrimination based on sexual orientation. Nearly 90 state and local governments offer inclusive domestic partner benefits.

One of the most spectacular developments has been in Vermont. In December 1999, the state made history by becoming the first American jurisdiction to equalize benefits for all people. Under this arrangement, lesbians and gays who enter civil unions will be eligible to receive the same protections and benefits that Vermont currently provides to married couples. Vermont was a logical place for this to happen because it was the first state to offer domestic partner benefits to state workers, one of the first to approve same-sex adoptions, and one of the first states to prohibit discrimination on the basis of sexual orientation. So far, however, there has not been a line-up to mirror Vermont's progressive initiatives.

A very dramatic development has also occurred in the city of San Francisco. In 1997, the city passed an equal benefits ordinance law requiring any company doing business with the city or county of San Francisco to offer the same benefits to the domestic partners of its employees as it offered to the legal spouses of employees. It was soon after the passage of San Francisco's law that many organizations, such as Shell and United Airlines, implemented domestic partner benefits. Since then, Seattle has initiated a similar law.

Labor Union Activity

Although initially unsupportive, labor organizations now support gay rights in a number of ways (Bain, 1999; Frank, 1999). This support varies among unions, sectors, and regions of the country and ranges from formal nondiscrimination clauses that include sexual orientation to the formation of subcommittees and caucuses focusing on issues of concern to gay and lesbian workers. In 1997, the American Federation of Labor-CIO approved "Pride at Work" as a funded constituency group, and many state and local labor councils have adopted similar measures. A few unions, such as the American Federation of State, County, and Municipal Employees (AFSCME), Service Employees International Union (SEIU), and Union of Needletrades, Industrial, and Textile Employees (UNITE), have negotiated inclusive domestic partner benefits in areas such as health care insurance, bereavement leave, and pension coverage in their collective agreements.

One of the most dramatic examples of union activity has been with the United Auto Workers (UAW). For a number of years, the issue of lesbian and gay rights had been subject to some of the most divisive debate in the union's history. A 1997 *New Yorker* article, for example, profiled the story of Ron Woods, a UAW worker at Chrysler's Trenton, Michigan, plant (Stewart, 1997). In the early 1990s, Ron helped to organize a caucus with the goal of pressuring the union to take on gay issues. Initially, the union's response was unsupportive, but gradually the tide turned. By 1998, the UAW had pressured General Motors and Ford to adopt a nondiscrimination policy that included sexual orientation, but Chrysler continued to refuse to take this step. By August 2000, the "Big Three" had all agreed not only to an inclusive nondiscrimination policy, but to medical, dental, and prescription coverage for same-sex partners, covering over 466,000 workers throughout the United States, as well.

Economic Forces

Gay and lesbian activists now target the marketplace as a focal point for exerting pressure on corporations to change. This group represents both an important market segment and a group with considerable clout if it decides to boycott a product, service, or organization believed to be homophobic. Badgett (2000) argues that gays and lesbians are not as affluent as many believe, and on average earn no more than heterosexuals, but do spend money just like everyone else, although with more political sensitivity. As well, this group (especially gay men) is less likely to have children, probably making discretionary income levels higher than average. Buford (2000) points out that advertising for "gay dollars" in the media generally and in the gay media in particular, especially in categories such as Web sites, travel, events, cars, music, and clothing, has become big business. He suggests that what matters about this group from a marketing point of view is not affluence but discretionary income and more free time.

Activists have waged proxy contests against homophobic companies, urged public institutions to buy the shares of companies that prohibit anti-gay discrimination and to sell the shares of companies that do not, and lobbied for legislation to prohibit states and municipalities from purchasing products and services from companies that discriminate against homosexuals.

Surveys are now routinely done to uncover gay-friendly companies. Baker (Baker, Strub, Henning, 1995) examined over 200 large corporations to determine their treatment of employees and how company attitudes were reflected in donations and response to the AIDS epidemic. The bimonthly magazine, *The Advocate,* also publishes an annual listing of the top 10 corporations for gay and lesbian workers. These lists include high-profile firms such as Lotus, Levi Strauss, Ikea, Ben and Jerry's, and Microsoft. Given the financial and organizing strength of the gay community, being on these lists, and equally importantly, not being on lists of the "worst" companies, could well have a direct impact on the corporate bottomline.

ORGANIZATIONAL RESPONSE

Corporate Sector

More and more organizations are responding positively to the concerns about discrimination that have been raised by lesbians and gays. Increasing numbers of organizations have adopted antidiscrimination policies and instituted domestic partner benefit packages inclusive of same-sex partners. According to a recent survey, less than 24 employers offered domestic partner benefits at the beginning of the 1990s, but this number had risen to nearly 3,500 by the end of the decade (Mills and Herrschaft, 1999).

During the 1990s, the information technology sector tended to lead the way in implementing inclusive benefits, although by the end of the decade oil companies, major banks, hospitality, airlines, and accounting firms were leading the pack. As summarized in Table 3-1, many of the private-sector employers that have instituted gay-friendly policies are among the most prestigious, prosperous, and best known organizations in the United States. Included in the 95 *Fortune* 500 companies that offer domestic partner health benefits are brand names such as Ford, IBM, AT&T,

Boeing, Chase Manhattan Bank, Walt Disney, American Airlines, Xerox, Eastman Kodak, Gap Inc., Nike, America Online, and New York Times Co.

Public Sector

Many public-sector organizations have also been responding positively (see Table 3-1). Nearly 300 American colleges and universities have implemented nondiscrimination polices, and well over 100 of them have inclusive benefit packages. Among the post-secondary institutions that have nondiscrimination policies are 44 of the top 50 national universities.

FEDERAL GOVERNMENT

In 1998, President Clinton introduced an executive order banning discrimination based on sexual orientation throughout the federal civil service. Even though the federal government does not yet offer same-sex benefits, all cabinet-level departments and 24 independent agencies have adopted nondiscrimination policies (*New York Times*, 2000).

Growing numbers of American organizations now have groups or caucuses dealing with sexual orientation issues. Initially, many of these groups were created as a way of pressuring organizations to adopt gay-friendly policies and procedures. Most groups have seen a measure of success but continue as social groups and/or as activist groups pushing for full equality in the workplace. Among the organizations with lesbian, gay, bisexual, and transgender employee groups are 3M, American Express, Bell Atlantic, Coca-Cola, federal government, Ford, Levi Strauss, Maryland Gay Law Enforcement Association, Kaiser Permanente, McKinsey and

---

TABLE 3-1   Employers with Gay-Friendly Policies (as of June 2000)

A) Employers with nondiscrimination policies that include sexual orientation (total number: 1,623)
- *Fortune* 500 companies (total number: 256)
- Other private companies, nonprofits, and unions (total number: 834)
- Colleges and universities (total number: 291)
- State and local governments (total number: 291)
- Federal government (total number: 36)

B) Employers that offer domestic partner benefits that include same-sex partners (total number 3,424)
- *Fortune* 500 companies (total number: 97)
- Other private companies, nonprofits, and unions (total number: 513)
- Colleges and universities (total number: 110)
- State and local governments (total number: 88)
- Additional employers (from the San Francisco Human Rights Commission) (total number: 2,616)

C) Organizations with formal gay, lesbian, bisexual, and transgender employee groups (total number: 127)

Source: Mills and Herrschaft, 1999, with a June 2000 update published at www.hrc.org

Co., Microsoft, NBC, and Warner-Lambert. The employee group at IBM, called EAGLE, is large enough to have subgroups in Texas, California, and New York.

Some organizations, however, steadfastly refuse to alter their polices and practices. Some companies offer no protection to gay and lesbian employees against wrongful dismissal, let alone offering things such as partner benefits. Others have rescinded such protections and benefits after mergers and changes in ownership. In 1998, for example, Perot Systems Corporation became the first major American company to end its policy of offering domestic partner benefits to its gay and lesbian employees once Ross Perot returned to the CEO position after his absence to seek the presidency. Another high-profile case involves the merger of Mobile Oil and Exxon. Prior to the merger, Mobile had a nondiscrimination policy and offered domestic partner benefits, whereas Exxon did not. After the merger, a policy was put into place to allow same-sex partners of former Mobile employees to continue receiving benefits, but excluding former employees of Exxon or new employees of ExxonMobile from gaining access to these perks. The decision stood in stark contrast to the other major oil companies—Amoco, Chevron, and Shell—which offer benefits without prejudice.

DEVELOPMENTS IN CANADA

The situation for gays and lesbians has undergone spectacular change in many other parts of the world. This is particularly the case in Canada. By most standards, Canada now ranks among the most favorable in the world for sexual minorities (along with countries such as Denmark, the Netherlands, and Sweden). Although the Charter of Rights and Freedoms (roughly equivalent to the U.S. Constitution) did not specifically include sexual orientation when it was enacted in 1982, by the early 1990s the Supreme Court had determined that sexual orientation should be "read into" the charter. Now, the federal and all provincial human rights codes include sexual orientation as a protected grounds in housing and employment. Same-sex couples cannot marry, but on almost every other front there is now extensive legal equality. The three largest provinces, Ontario, Quebec, and British Columbia, now recognize same-sex relationships in family law, including the right to adopt children.

These legislative changes in some ways followed initiatives already underway in many Canadian organizations. As early as the mid-1980s, some unions such as the Canadian Auto Workers and the Canadian Union of Public Employees were fighting for nondiscrimination policies and negotiating same-sex benefit packages in collective agreements (Hunt, 1999). By the time they were legislatively mandated to do so, most universities, colleges, and public-sector organizations, and many in the private sector, had already moved toward inclusive policies and practices. One measure of the speed and depth of change is the Canadian military. Until the early 1990s, the armed forces could dismiss members found to be gay or lesbian. However, a 1992 court challenge under the Charter of Rights and Freedoms forced the military to drop the ban on homosexuals. By 1998, the armed forces were advertising in their recruiting that they provided the same benefits, opportunities, and protections to all members and their families, regardless of sexual orientation (albeit only for those sufficiently brave to be open and disclosing in what many believe is still an unwelcoming organizational culture in relation to sexual diversity).

In spite of the legal changes, though, there continue to be confusing and sometimes contradictory laws governing family and inheritance laws, with significant differences in what is legal, available, and tolerated among provinces and regions of the country. The changes have meant that most organizations no longer have the legal option of denying protection and benefits to sexual minorities (with the exception of a few specific religious institutions). Some Canadian institutions change their policies in relation to same-sex relationship-based benefit and pension packages only when confronted with litigation (which they invariably lose). One example is Dave Mitges' battle with Imperial Oil Ltd. For 8 years, Dave presented his case for same-sex partner benefits at the annual meeting of the shareholders. Each time he asked, the answer was no. Only on the eve of a new Ontario law requiring it, did Imperial finally relent and agree to offer these benefits.

The Canadian situation highlights the fact that access to a legal system does not necessarily change a culture of exclusion and exclusivity. If organizational leaders, and the culture they produce, remain opposed to equity for gays and lesbians, then bias and subtle discrimination are likely to remain in force. As a result, people committed to diversity initiatives within Canada tend to focus their efforts on education in an effort to address the values and attitudes that underlay prejudice.

CONCLUSIONS

I began this paper by suggesting it can be a bit confusing to know if sexual orientation continues to be a workplace diversity challenge. On the one hand, there have been significant changes in the social and legal situation regarding this minority, and many organizations have taken steps to curb heterosexual bias. On the other hand, some jurisdictions have refused to change the legal situation for gays and lesbians, and in a few cases even overturned pro-gay laws and existing ordinances. In far too many situations, it is still possible to fire someone merely for being gay or lesbian. The legal situation in Canada is more uniformly supportive than in the United States, but here as well some organizations resist any kind of proactive approach and will not implement new policies until an employee is brave enough to ask.

Overall, the challenge of sexual diversity in the workplace continues, but differs in form from the 1990s. Sexual orientation and the set of concerns it generates are firmly situated on the organizational diversity agenda—no one could deny that—but the responses generated are unpredictable and variable, ranging from rage to embarrassment to positive embracement. Progressive organizations have taken up the challenge sexuality issues present by finding ways to acknowledge and value this form of difference in terms of policy and education initiatives. Some jurisdictions such as the city of Seattle even require that companies doing business with them conform to the same equity policies. Benchmark organizations make every effort to ensure that all the benefits, rights, and obligations of heterosexual and homosexual employees are the same. In particular, they ensure that relationship-based benefits are inclusive, and that same- and opposite-sex partnerships have equity in such things as pension plans, access to recreational facilities, and discounted loans if these sorts of perks are available.

Ultimately, a progressive organization must make clear through its disciplinary policies that anti-gay behavior would no more be tolerated than would sexist or racist behaviors.

Discussion Questions

1. What factors or forces continue to discourage organizations from tackling the issue of gay and lesbian rights in the workplace? How might these factors or forces be overcome?
2. A coworker has just told you that she thinks another coworker may be a lesbian, and that she is totally grossed out. How will you respond?
3. You are working in the human resources department of a large manufacturing organization and you are deeply concerned about the lack of policy around sexual orientation. Several "out" gays and lesbians have spoken to you about the verbal harassment they experience working on the assembly floor; one woman even claims she was beaten up in the parking lot amid taunts of "fat dyke" (she has indicated she is too afraid to press charges). You live in a state where you are not required to do anything around sexual orientation issues, but you would like to be proactive. You approached your boss and she said she would support you, but that you will have to sell the idea to the vice president of administration, who comes across as very macho and has a reputation for being a bit sexist. How will you approach this situation?

References

Badgett, M. (2000). "The Myth of Gay and Lesbian Affluence." *The Gay and Lesbian Review*, Vol. VII(2), Spring, pp. 22–25.

Bagley, C., and P. Tremblay. (1998). "On the Prevalence of Homosexuality and Bisexuality, in a Random Community Survey of 750 Men Aged 18–27." *Journal of Homosexuality*, Vol. 36(2).

Bain, C. (1999). "A Short History of Lesbian and Gay Labor Activism in the United States." In Hunt, G. *Laboring for Rights: Unions and Sexual Diversity Across Nations.* Philadelphia: Temple University Press.

Baker, D., S. Strub, and B. Henning. (1995). *Cracking the Corporate Closet: The 200 Best (and Worst) Companies to Work, Buy From, and Invest In if You're Gay or Lesbian—and Even if You Aren't.* New York: Harper-Business.

Buford, H. (2000). "Understanding Gay Consumers." *The Gay and Lesbian Review*, Vol. VII(2), Spring, pp. 26–27.

Frank, M. (1999). "Lesbian and Gay Caucuses in the U.S. Labor Movement." In Hunt, G. *Laboring for Rights: Unions and Sexual Diversity Across Nations,* Philadelphia: Temple University Press.

Hunt, G. (1999). "No Longer Outsiders: Labor's Response to Sexual Diversity in Canada." In Hunt, G. *Laboring for Rights: Unions and Sexual Diversity Across Nations.* Philadelphia: Temple University Press.

Kinsey, A., et al. (1948). *Sexual Behaviour in the Human Male.* New York: Saunders.

Mills, K., and D. Herrschaft. (1999). *The State of the Workplace for Lesbian, Gay, Bisexual and Transgendered Americans.* Washington, DC: Human Rights Campaign.

Mitchell, J. (1999). "The Pink Ceiling." *The Globe and Mail Report on Business Magazine,* June, pp. 78–84.

"Gays Under Fire." *Newsweek,* September 14, 1992, pp. 35–40.

"More Companies Offering Same-Sex Benefits." *New York Times,* September 26, 2000.

Plant, R. (1986). *The Pink Triangle: The Nazi War Against Homosexuals.* New York: Henry Holt.

Rayside, D. and S. Bowler. (1988). "Public Opinion and Gay Rights." *Canadian Review of Sociology and Anthropology,* 25(4), pp. 649–660.

Stewart, J. (1997) "Coming Out at Chrysler." *The New Yorker,* pp. 38–49.

Wilcox, C. and R. Wolpert. (2000). "Gay Rights in the Public Sphere: Public Opinion on Gay and Lesbian Equality." In Rimmerman, C., K. Wald and C. Wilcox. *The Politics of Gay Rights.* Chicago: The University of Chicago Press.

Yang, A. (1999). *From Wrongs to Rights, 1973–1999: Public Opinion on Gay and Lesbian Americans Moves Toward Equality.* Washington, DC: Policy Institute of the National Gay and Lesbian Task Force.

Yeager, K. (1999). *Trailblazers: Profiles of America's Gay and Lesbian Elected Officials.* New York: The Hawthorn Press.

Gerald Hunt is an associate professor of organizational behavior and industrial relations at Ryerson Polytechnic University in Toronto. He has published several articles as well as a book dealing with the response of labor organizations to sexual diversity issues. He is currently studying the response of international labor organizations to sexual diversity issues.

Social Class in the Workplace

Adalberto Aguirre, Jr.
University of California–Riverside

Alexis de Tocqueville collected the observations he made during his 9-month visit to the new republic in his book, *Democracy in America*. In the introduction to the book, Tocqueville writes, "Amongst the novel objects that attracted my attention during my stay in the United States, nothing struck me more forcibly than the general equality of condition among the people" (1956:26). Tocqueville's visit to the new republic convinced him that despite vestiges of inequality rooted in wealth and poverty, the new republic was an open territory filled with opportunity for the taking. Individuals such as Cornelius Vanderbilt, J. P. Morgan, and Andrew Carnegie are portrayed as successful venture capitalists that took advantage of opportunity (Domhoff, 1967). It is not surprising then to find that poverty is less appealing than success because it textures the perception that poor people have chosen to be poor; they have chosen not to make use of opportunities before them. Regarding the perceptions in popular thinking Parenti (1997:319) notes, "The entertainment media present working people not only as unlettered and uncouth but also as less desirable and less moral than other people. Conversely, virtue is more likely to be ascribed to those whose speech and appearance are soundly middle or upper-middle class."

THE IDEA OF INEQUALITY

Casual observations of everyday life suggest that people are the same in some ways but different in others. The car a person drives, the logos on his/her clothing, and other noticeable aspects of behavior serve as a basis for making social evaluations of the people around us. Usually, one's social evaluations are graded into high, for those we find appealing, and low, those we find unappealing. The result is a continuum, running from high to low, that serves as a guide for assigning social status to people.

For example, the homeless person asking for food or money on the street corner has lower status than the person driving an expensive car and talking on the car phone. Keep in mind, we are only talking about noticeable behavior. Ironically, the homeless person may be a ruse by a wealthy person to measure public sentiment toward the homeless, whereas the person in the expensive car may have just robbed a bank and is talking on the car phone with his accomplices. The important point is that the assignment of social status to persons around us implies that people are not viewed as being equal to each other.

THE IDEA OF SOCIAL CLASS

The dynamic quality of inequality is rooted in the hierarchical organization of people based on status characteristics (for example, sex, age, income, occupation, or education). Society evaluates a college degree higher than a high school degree, a white-collar occupation as better than a blue-collar job, and wealth as more rewarding than poverty. Those who share status characteristics can be said to belong to the same social group. Social evaluations of status characteristics for social groups in society allow us to see the hierarchical arrangement of social relations between people. It helps one observe the degree of similarity in status characteristics within social groups. It also helps one observe the degree of difference between social groups based on their status characteristics. A comparative examination of in-group versus out-group status characteristics illuminates the criteria used by society to structure hierarchical relations among social classes. This hierarchical arrangement of social relations provides a behavioral description of social class: "Classes may be thought of as groupings in which people share not only similar occupations, incomes, and levels of education but also similar lifestyles" (Marger, 1999:24).

In contrast to a behavioral description of social class is a description based on economic dimensions. Taken together, income, occupation, and education provide a description of the economic structuring of classes in society.

Exceptions can often be observed in society that can raise questions about the interdependency among the three variables. The 19-year-old computer nerd who dropped out of high school and started a multimillion-dollar dot-com company makes people question the association between income and education. The salaries for college professors with Ph.D. degrees that are often lower than the salaries for bus drivers or factory workers makes people question the association between income, education, and occupation. In a sense, the exceptions reinforce the value of inequality in society because they make people believe that opportunities are there for the taking. That is, the exceptions convince people that everybody benefits from a system based on unequal social relations between persons.

CLASS IN THE WORKPLACE

If one accepts the proposition that social relations are determined by economic factors, then individuals do not enter the workplace on an equal footing; they enter the workplace as members of a class. According to Clegg and Dunkerley (1980:431), "Not only do we not enter organizations randomly, we are also treated differently as a result of being at different levels and in possession of different skills." Position in the class structure provides social capital (for example, life chances) that determines one's entry point and placement level in the workplace. Ironically, placement in the workplace mirrors placement in society's class structure.

Collins (1988) and Nichols and Wanamaker (1995) suggest that the middle-class members in society occupy work positions that can be viewed as order givers and that working-class members occupy work positions that can be viewed as order takers. For the sake of discussion, let us assume that:

1) Entry into middle-class work positions is dependent on educational credentials and social networking skills; and (a) educational credentials are an outcome of social capital, but (b) social networking skills are an effect of social capital.

2) Entry into working-class work positions is dependent on proficiency with work-related skills that are (a) not an outcome of educational credentials, but (b) may be affected by marginal social networking skills.

It is possible, but not highly probable, for someone to occupy a middle-class work position without possessing educational credentials similar to those of others in those positions. In most cases, one can explain these instances by looking at the person's social background: class ("the boss' daughter is doing a school internship") or social networks ("it's a favor for a family friend"). It is also possible, but not very probable, for someone to occupy a workplace position without the required job skills. A father may convince his supervisor to hire his son on a part-time basis in order to "keep him out of trouble," or a supervisor may hire a family friend as "a return favor." In order for these types of instances to occur, a person must be sponsored by somebody within the organization. That is, someone in the economic organization must be willing to legitimate the presence of a person in a workplace position for which they lack the educational credentials or job skills shared by the persons around them.

For the purpose of discussion, the term *social capital* refers to the quality of life indicators derived from one's class position in society. Examples of quality of life indicators are social networks (family and friendships), level of education, and cultural knowledge (classical music, art, and so forth). People with high social capital participate in influential social networks that facilitate placement in economic organizations; they have extensive, and often prestigious, educational training and proficiency with cultural knowledge. In comparison, people with low social capital do not participate in influential social networks; they have limited educational training and limited proficiency with cultural knowledge. Thus quality of life indicators increase in status and prestige as one moves up the class structure in society. For example, one would expect to find people in the upper-class with quality of life indicators more socially desirable and visible than those in either the middle class or working class. In this sense, there is a correspondence between the quality of life indicators found in the workplace and those associated with class position.

Some interesting questions can be asked at this point in our discussion. How does the workplace mediate class among workers? What are the economic organization's costs in mediating class differences between workers? These questions open a window to questions of class diversity in organizations.

Class Diversity and Workplace

If social class shapes social capital in society, then one would expect to find class differences in peoples' perceptions of the workplace. The intersection between social class and the workplace also extends into home life. For example, Ritchie (1997) argues that parents who work in jobs that stress conformity to hierarchical authority promote conformity and deference in socializing their children. By comparison, parents who work in jobs that stress individual initiative and autonomy promote autonomy and self-direction in socializing their children.

Carter (1994) has noted that office automation procedures in the workplace affect the class identity workers bring with them. In studying class identification among female office workers, Carter observed that office automation procedures in small workplace settings reduce the visibility of class differences between workers and managers because the procedures appear to place all workers on the same level. On the other hand, office automation procedures in large workplace settings enhance class differences between workers and managers because the procedures signal the hierarchical structure of the workplace. For example, in the former, workers and managers may perceive themselves to be on the same level because they share use of the automation procedures, whereas in the latter, workers may spend more time than managers with office automation procedures in the workplace.

Few studies in the literature examine social class in the workplace. However, Gerteis and Savage examined data from the *Comparative Project on Class Structure and Class Consciousness* that focus on class and political identification among workers. There were clear differences in opinions about the workplace based on a worker's placement in the workplace. For example, working-class workers are more likely to agree than middle-class workers that corporations benefit owners at the expense of workers and consumers. Working-class workers may perceive themselves as absorbing greater costs than middle-class workers from profit making among owners. During times of economic uncertainty, such as an economic recession, owners may strive to maintain profit levels for themselves, as well as their demanding stockholders, by reorganizing the workplace (for an example, see Brueggemann and Boswell, 1998). Working-class workers may perceive themselves as more likely targets of reorganization efforts than middle-class workers. The organization's logic may argue that working-class workers are more of a safety valve (for example they can be laid off and rehired) than are middle-class workers, who if they are laid off can seek employment with a competing economic organization.

Working-class workers are also more likely than middle-class workers to support the opinion that management should be prohibited from hiring workers to replace striking workers. Working-class workers may be well aware of the power differential between themselves and management—management can enforce actions that reinforce the workers' powerlessness: Workers can be easily replaced. As a result, working-class workers may have an understanding of the structured ordering of power in the economic organization. In contrast, middle-class workers may not perceive themselves to be separated structurally from management. They may have an unfocused view of how power is structured between themselves and management.

In addition, the sense of powerlessness working-class workers may have about themselves finds expression in their agreement that nonmanagement employees could run things without bosses, and that workers are justified in preventing strikebreakers from entering the place of work. These opinions may express the belief that management is not as important in the workplace as they (workers) are, and that one way of reducing their own powerlessness is by preventing strikebreakers from taking their place. In short, working-class workers appear to have a clear sense of their unequal social relations in the workplace.

By comparison, middle-class workers may not perceive themselves to be in danger of being replaced by temporary workers because they are not likely to go on strike. The fact they are more likely to be salaried employees, while working-class workers are more likely to be hourly wage earners, suggests that middle-class workers may perceive their roles to be continuous with the economic organization's activity. That is, their link (for example, salary) with the organization's reward structure may result in the perception that they have stable and continuous work roles in the organization. If this is the case, then it helps us understand why these workers are not likely to agree that nonmanagement employees could run things without bosses and that workers are justified in preventing strikebreakers from entering the workplace.

Now What?

If opinions about the workplace are shaped by class background, then how does the economic organization maintain continuity in social relations among workers? Why are social relations among workers not likely to disrupt work routines?

Organizational processes mask class differences between workers. For example, the most direct intervention for blurring class differences in the workplace is the economic organization's promotion of workplace democracy. Workplace democracy describes workplaces in which workers are given opportunities to make decisions about the governance and structure of the workplace (Bachrach and Botwinick, 1992; Schurman and Eaton, 1996). Workers are empowered to believe that they are collectively responsible for creating effective working relationships that promote organizational goals. According to Gamble and Gregg (1998:431), "Thousands of managers and workers attend conferences and workshops to hear other managers and workers describe how 'empowered' workers have created 'lean' and effective work sites and new working relationships."

Workplace democracy promotes beliefs among workers that they are making workplace decisions that affect the integrity of the economic organization. At the individual level, workers are identified as associates or representatives. One can buy a cup of coffee at Starbucks from a sales representative, a pair of shoes at Macy's where one is attended by a sales associate, or fly on Southwest Airlines where employees see themselves as working together to give each passenger a rewarding experience. As a result, class differences between workers are masked by organizational processes. More importantly, these processes constrain workers from identifying along class lines in the workplace. That is, polarization between workers on the basis of class is reduced (for example, see Smith, 1998). In the end, the economic organization is guaranteed of stable and continuous social relations between workers in the workplace.

CONCLUDING REMARKS

The discussion has been mostly exploratory because class has not been regarded as a diversifying factor in the workplace. However, we may need to pay closer attention to social class. First, if social class is a dynamic dimension in the workplace, then we need to see if economic organizations differ from each other based on their workers' class backgrounds. For example, do U.S. postal workers have class backgrounds that set them apart from workers at Microsoft? Do U.S. postal workers act differently than workers at Microsoft given their class background? Does organizational structure prevent U.S. postal workers from pursuing jobs at Microsoft and vice versa? If it does, does it show that economic organizations are crucial to supporting the class structure in society?

Second, much attention is being given to changing demographics in U.S. society and their impact on social institutions, especially the workplace. In particular, women and minorities are perceived as the new wave of entrants into the workplace (Aguirre, 2000; Allison, 1999; Bond and Pyle, 1998). Not only are women and minorities likely to change the gender and racial/ethnic composition of the workplace, but they may also challenge the class structure of the workplace. Women and minorities are nontraditional entrants in the workplace because they come from diverse social backgrounds that do not fit the traditional white middle class–male-dominated image of most economic organizations. If their class background typifies the diversity of women and minorities in the workplace, then we need to see how the economic organization will respond to their class backgrounds. Will the economic organization mask their class differences by focusing on gender and racial/ethnic dimensions? Will gender and racial/ethnic dimensions be masked by organizational processes, such as workplace democracy, that blur class identification in the workplace? The diversification of the workplace by women and minorities in the twenty-first century will provide an opportunity for observing how economic organizations will address workplace dimensions affected by gender, race/ethnicity, and social class.

Discussion Questions

1. If *inequality* is a feature of social relations between people in society, how does inequality affect social relations in the workplace?
2. How does the economic or work organization mediate the effects of social class in the workplace?
3. How does the structure of the workplace reflect workers' social class position?
4. How does workplace democracy affect worker social class identification in the work organization?

References

Aguirre, Jr., Adalberto. (2000). *Women and Minority Faculty in the Academic Workplace: Recruitment, Retention, and Academic Culture.* San Francisco: Jossey-Bass.

Aguirre, Jr., Adalberto, and David Baker. (2000). *Structured Inequality in the United States: Discussions on the Continuing Significance of Race, Ethnicity, and Gender.* Upper Saddle River, N.J.: Prentice Hall.

Aguirre, Jr., Adalberto, Anthony Hernandez, and Ruben Martinez. (1994). "Perceptions of the Workplace: Focus on Minority Women Faculty." *Initiatives,* 56, pp. 41–50.

Aguirre, Jr., Adalberto, Ruben Martinez, and Anthony Hernandez. (1993). "Majority and Minority Faculty Perceptions in Academe." *Research in Higher Education,* 34, pp. 371–385.

Allison, Maria. (1999). "Organizational Barriers to Diversity in the Workplace." *Journal of Leisure Research,* 31, pp. 78–91.

Aschaffenburg, Karen, and Ineke Mass. (1997). "Cultural and Educational Careers: The Dynamics of Social Reproduction." *American Sociological Review,* 62, pp. 573–587.

Bachrach, Peter, and Aryeh Botwinick. (1992). *Power and Empowerment: A Radical Theory of Participatory Democracy.* Philadelphia: Temple University Press.

Bond, Meg. (1999). "Gender, Race, and Class in Organizational Contexts."

American Journal of Community Psychology, 27, pp. 327–355.

Bond, Meg, and Jean Pyle. (1998). "The Ecology of Diversity in Organizational Settings: Lessons from a Case Study." *Human Relations,* 51, pp. 589–623.

Bourdieu, Pierre. (1977). "Cultural Reproduction and Social Reproductions," In *Power and Ideology in Education,* J. Karabel and A. H. Halsey, (eds). New York: Oxford University Press, pp. 487–511.

Bourdieu, Pierre, and Jean-Claude Passeron. (1990). *Reproduction in Education, Society, and Culture* (2d ed.). London: Sage.

Brueggemann, John, and Terry Boswell. (1998). "Realizing Solidarity: Social Interracial Unionism During the Great Depression." *Work and Occupations,* 25, pp. 436–482.

Carter, Valerie. (1994). "The Family, the Workplace, and Work Technology: An Integrated Model of Class Identification Among Women Office Workers." *Work and Occupations,* 21, pp. 308–334.

Clegg, Stewart. (1975). *Power, Rule and Domination: A Critical and Empirical Understanding of Power in Sociological Theory and Organizational Life.* London: Routledge and Kegan Paul.

Clegg, Stewart, and David Dunkerley. (1980). *Organization, Class, and Control.* London: Routledge and Kegan Paul.

Collins, R. (1988). "Women and Men in the Class Structure." *Journal of Family Issues,* 9, pp. 27–50.

Domhoff, G. William. (1967). *Who Rules America?* Upper Saddle River, N.J.: Prentice Hall.

Edwards, Richard. (1979). *Contested Terrain: The Transformation of the Workplace in the Twentieth Century.* New York: Basic Books.

Feagin, Joe. (1975). *Subordinating the Poor.* Upper Saddle River, N.J.: Prentice Hall.

Fink, Ross, Robert Robinson, and David Wyld. (1996). "English-Only Work Rules: Balancing Fair Employment Considerations in a Multicultural and Multilingual Healthcare Workplace." *Hospital and Health Services Administration,* 41, pp. 473–483.

Gamble, Doug, and Nina Gregg. (1998). "Rethinking the Twenty-First Century Workplace: Unions and Workplace Democracy." *Journal of Labor and Employment Law,* 1, pp. 429–456.

Gerteis, Joseph, and Mike Savage. (1998). "The Salience of Class in Britain and America: A Comparative Analysis." *British Journal of Sociology,* 49, pp. 252–274.

Gerth, Hans, and C. Wright Mills. (1946). From *Max Weber: Essays in Sociology.* New York: Oxford University Press.

Gilbert, Dennis. (1998). *The American Class Structure: In an Age of Growing Inequality.* (5th ed.). Belmont, Calif.: Wadsworth.

Granovetter, Mark. (1995). *Getting a Job: A Study of Contacts and Careers.* (2d ed.). Chicago: University of Chicago Press.

Heilbroner, Robert. (1992). *The Worldly Philosophers.* (6th ed.). New York: Touchstone.

Hurst, Charles. (1998). *Social Inequality: Forms, Causes, and Consequences.* (3d ed.). Boston: Allyn and Bacon.

Kerbo, Harold. (2000). *Social Stratification and Inequality: Class Conflict in Historical, Comparative, and Global Perspective.* (4th ed.). New York: McGraw-Hill.

Marger, Martin. (1999). *Social Inequality: Patterns and Processes.* Mountain View, Calif.: Mayfield.

Marx, Karl. (1967). *Capital: A Critical Analysis of Capitalist Production.* (Vol. 1). New York: International.

Marx, Karl. (1964). *The Economic and Political Manuscripts.* New York: International.

Marx, Karl, and Friedrich Engels. (1955, original publication 1848). *The Communist Manifesto.* New York: Appleton-Century-Crofts.

Mills, Albert, and Tony Simmons. (1999). *Reading Organization Theory: A Critical Approach to the Study of Organizational Behavior and Structure.* Toronto: Garamond Press.

Nichols, Laurie, and Nancy Wanamaker. (1995). "Needs and Priorities in Balancing Paid and Family Work: A Gender and Social Class Analysis." *Family and Consumer Sciences Research Journal,* 24, pp. 71–86.

Parenti, Michael. (1997). "Class and Virtue." In *Signs of Life in the USA: Readings on Popular Culture for Writers.* Sonia Maasik and Jack Solomon, Boston: Bedford Books, pp. 318–321.

Podolny, Joel, and James Baron. (1997). "Resources and Relationships: Social Networks and Mobility in the Workplace." *American Sociological Review,* 62, pp. 673–693.

Ritchie, David. (1997). "Parents' Workplace Experiences and Family Communication Patterns." *Communication Research,* 24, pp. 175–187.

Romanelli, Elaine. (1991). "The Evolution of New Organizational Forms." *Annual Review of Sociology,* 17, pp. 79–103.

Schurman, Susan, and Adrienne Eaton. (1996). "Labor and Workplace Democracy: Past, Present and Future." *Labor Studies Journal,* 21, pp. 3–26.

Smith, Vicki. (1998). "The Fractured World of the Temporary Worker: Power, Participation, and Fragmentation in the Contemporary Workplace." *Social Problems,* 45, pp. 411–430.

Steers, Richard, and J. Stewart Black. (1994). *Organizational Behavior.* New York: HarperCollins.

Tocqueville, Alexis de, 1805–1859. (1999). *Democracy in America.* (English trans.) New York: Westvaco. (5th ed.).

Weber, Max. (1968). *Economy and Society.* New York: Bedminster.

Weber, Max. (1958). *The Protestant Ethic and the Spirit of Capitalism.* New York: Scribner's.

Weber, Max. (1947). *The Theory of Social and Economic Organization.* Glencoe, Ill.: Free Press.

Adalberto Aguirre, Jr., is professor of sociology at the University of California at Riverside. He received his B.A. in sociology from the University of California at Santa Cruz and his Ph.D. in sociology and linguistics from Stanford University. His research interests are in equity issues for women and minority faculty in higher education, social class as a diversifying feature in the workplace, immigrant populations in California, and the sociolinguistic features of the Chicano speech community. His articles have appeared in such journals as *Sociological Perspectives, The Social Science Journal, Social Problems, International Journal of Comparative Sociology,* and *Research in Higher Education.* His most recent publications are *American Ethnicity: The Dynamics and Consequences of Discrimination* (3rd ed.) (McGraw-Hill, 2001), *Structured Inequality in the United States* (Prentice Hall, 2000), and *Women and Minority Faculty in the Academic Workplace* (Jossey-Bass, 2000).

Religion, Culture, and Management in the New Millennium

Asha Rao
Rutgers University

Spirituality could be the ultimate competitive advantage.
—Ian Mitroff, A Spiritual Audit of Corporate America

Across the country, major-league executives are meeting for prayer breakfasts and spiritual conferences. In Minneapolis, 150 business chiefs lunch monthly at a private ivy-draped club to hear chief executives such as Medtronic Inc's William George and Carlson Co's Marilyn Carlson Nelson draw business solutions from the Bible. In Silicon Valley, a group of high-powered, high-tech Hindus—including Suhas Patil, founder of Cirrus Logic, Desh Despande, founder of Cascade Communications, and Krishna Kalra, founder of BioGenex—are part of a movement to connect technology to spirituality.
—*Business Week,* Nov. 1999

As we end a millennium and move into the twenty-first century, the world of business and management is turbulent and evolving faster than it has in the past. We live and work in "Internet time" where firms form, go public, and disband before decision trees and 5-year plans can be developed (Conlin, 1999). In this time of rapid change, there seems to be a renewed interest in old traditions: spirituality and religion in business. American CEOs and executives are drawing on the Bible, Bhagvad Gita, Talmud, and other scriptures for inspiration (Brahm, 1999; Conlin, 1999; Leigh, 1997).

The trend is not limited to the United States; Asian leaders have espoused the role of "Asian values" derived from Confucianism in the rapid economic development of the ASEAN region (*The Economist,* 1992; Hofstede and Bond, 1988). In countries ranging from India to Burma to France, religion has played a part in management processes and economic development (or the lack thereof). At an individual level, we now truly live in a global village where more people than ever are internationally mobile or work in cross-cultural environments in global teams, which are often temporary or even virtual teams (Adler, 1997; Conlin, 1999).

Consequently, people are directly affected by the cultural beliefs, religious norms, and practices of others.

This article examines the role of religion or faith in culturally derived values, beliefs, and management practices across the globe and discusses the implications for international managers. It focuses on work issues raised by major religions or faiths such as Christianity, Confucianism, Hinduism, Islam, and Judaism to examine their impact on management today, and potentially for the future. Although some of these religions directly affect the behavior of people at work, others have a more subtle effect through ethnic culture.

CONCEPTUAL FRAMEWORK

The statistics indicate that 95 percent of Americans say that they believe in God or a religious faith, and 48 percent bring religion into the workplace (Conlin, 1999). Our future global leaders, the presidential candidates in the current U.S. elections, report turning to the Bible for advice on a range of their decisions (*New York Times,* 2000). United States's attendance rates at religious services are among the highest in the world (Gannon, 1994). Recent reports suggest that top executives from a range of firms believe that faith has an impact on the bottom line (Conlin, 1999). Indeed, Ian Mitroff states that in the new millennium, spirituality could be the ultimate competitive advantage by raising productivity in the workplace (Mitroff, 1999).

The impact of religion is not always blatant or intentional. It can have an indirect, more subtle impact through national or ethnic culture. For instance, the concept of the 5-day workweek in the West is firmly rooted in Christianity, but most Christians or even Americans see this as an accepted business practice rather than a religious one. To understand the subtle impact of religion on business today, one needs to understand national or ethnic cultures.

CULTURE

Three critical mechanisms explain the origins of different cultures. They are religion, language, and geographical proximity (Ronen and Shenkar, 1985). Because religion is only one of three determinants of culture, it is clear that cultures sharing religious roots can differ because of variations in the latter two mechanisms. This explains the differences in cultures between the Latin American cluster and the Anglo cluster. The power of religion is evident in the similarities of culture in the Islamic nations and in the overseas Chinese. Cultural bonds, or the collective programming, is usually difficult to break even later in adulthood. We maintain culturally derived values, beliefs, and behavior in the workplace and even when traveling across cultures as demonstrated by much research in the field of cross-cultural management (Adler, 1997).

Cultures have several layers, as depicted in Figure 3-1.

Elements in layer one change with time. These include language, clothing, or appearance and behavior. These elements are based on the deeper levels of culture. At the next level lie attitudes and rituals—key among them being the attitude toward women in the workplace. These too can change with time, but they adapt at a much slower pace. At the core of the culture, in the third layer, lie values and be-

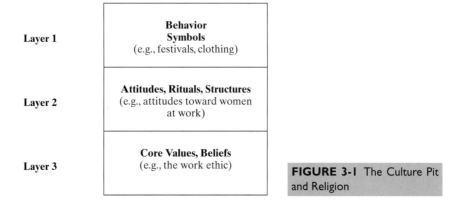

Layer 1	**Behavior** **Symbols** (e.g., festivals, clothing)
Layer 2	**Attitudes, Rituals, Structures** (e.g., attitudes toward women at work)
Layer 3	**Core Values, Beliefs** (e.g., the work ethic)

FIGURE 3-1 The Culture Pit and Religion

liefs that are stable, often across generations, and relatively impermeable to the passage of time. Religious beliefs and practices can be linked to each layer of culture. The following discussion begins with the bottom layer and draws upon it in examining the upper layers of culture.

RELIGION AND CULTURAL VALUES

The impact of religion at the level of core values and beliefs is strong. Take for instance the meaning of work in different cultures, cultural assumptions, and ethics. Religions differ in their emphasis on the role of work in life. Much has been written about the Protestant Work Ethic, which helps explain the criticality of work in the United States. Succinctly, the ethic holds that a good Protestant will work hard on earth and be successful in order to reap rewards later in heaven. A person's work, or their calling, comes from God. In working hard, people make evident their worth to both God and themselves. In the United States, the Protestant ethic was joined by Social Darwinism, as so well expressed by Russell Conwell, a Methodist minister and the first president of Temple University (Burr, 1917). He extolled his followers, "I say you ought to be rich; you have no right to be poor . . . I must say that you ought to spend some time getting rich." He went on to conclude that it was absurd to believe that people should not want wealth, because wealth enables people to truly accomplish something of value on earth (Gannon, 1991). In this fashion, the work value is united with both drive and a high need for achievement in the United States.

Other religions also speak of the value of work. The book of Islam, the Quran, indicates that work is an obligation. Indeed, the prophet Muhammad was a trader by profession. But Islam also breeds an element of fatalism in the workplace, letting employees off the hook, because destiny is in the hand of God, who is the ultimate creator of wealth (Rice, 1999). Hindu philosophy offers *dharma* (duty) as one of the four means to salvation. This aspect of Hindu religion espoused in the *Bhagvad Gita* as *karma,* which represents work or duty without an attachment towards immediate rewards. Kalra, founder and CEO of BioGenex laboratories says, "The

Bhagvad Gita teaches that I have rights on action, but no rights on the fruits of action, nor should I be attached to inaction as a result. So I have the right to be the best CEO but no right to how much money I can earn . . . As a result of this, I have no fear of failure, and I can take risks," (Brahm, 1999).

Work helps the Hindu earn a living, satisfy worldly interests, gain power and status, and take care of the family (Gannon, 1994). But, Hinduism dictates that the role of work changes during different stages in life. The role of work is strongest in the second stage of life, where the *grahasta* is obliged to work and fulfil his duty to society. At later stages, the Hindu needs to withdraw from worldly accomplishments such as work to focus on the search for the truth.

Differences in power relations can also be traced back to religions. For instance, Confucius declared that the stability of society is based on unequal relationships and listed five basic and unequal relationships as follows: father–son, husband–wife, ruler–subject, older brother–younger brother, older friend–younger friend. This philosophy helps explain the power differentials between men and women, bosses and subordinates, and the relevance of seniority in cultures such as China, Japan, and Korea. Also, these relationships are held together by mutual and complementary obligations, which helps explain the power of *guanxi* in Chinese business (Leong and Tung, 1998).

Religion and culture have been linked to economic development. In one analysis, cultures where long-term values of persistence, ordered relationships, thrift, and a sense of shame were dominant tended to experience rapid economic growth. Cultures that clung to short-term Confucian values of personal steadiness, face, tradition, and reciprocity of favors tended to be slow developers (Hofstede and Bond, 1988). Taking this a level higher, the rulers of South Korea and Singapore have long used Confucian principles as a means of societal change and control.

Religion and Ethics

Religious values and management interface in discussions of ethics and social responsibility but surface in different forms in different cultures (Laczniak, 1999; Rice, 1999; Vogel, 1992). U.S. firms today are formulating codes of ethical conduct for their employees worldwide. In trying to explain why the level of public interest in business ethics in the United States exceeds that in the rest of the world, Vogel (1992) draws upon America's Protestant heritage, which makes the creation of wealth "God's work"; it raises people's expectations of the moral behavior of businesspeople. Most Americans also believe that these ethics are or should be universal, compared to Eastern cultures that allow for situational or contextual variations (Trompenaars, 1993).

In discussing Islamic ethics, Rice (1999) states that Islam requires the free-market system to be complemented by a moral filter so that scarce resources are equitably distributed in society. The religion stresses brotherhood, equality, and socioeconomic justice for all. In the Gulf countries, oil has brought amazing wealth to a few, but interestingly that wealth has also trickled down to the masses through social welfare programs. *Zakat,* or alms tax, is one of the five pillars of Islam. [1] According to Rice, the Quranic injunction "there is no compulsion in religion" leads people to follow a strong moral code.

Jewish business ethics also acknowledge the centrality of the community (Pava, 1998) as reflected in three talmudic principles. First is the recognition of different levels of responsibility for charity; second, the *Kofin* principles "formalize a minimum standard. If B's situation can improve at no cost to A, A should willingly waive legal rights." Third, *lifnim mishurat hadin* calls for ethical conduct beyond meeting legal norms. The emphasis on community over wealth is apparent in Brahm's (1999) account of Arron Feuerstein's (President/CEO, Malden Mills Industries) decision to keep his mill open and his employees on the payroll even after the mill burned down. Feuerstein drew on the teachings of the Talmud, which stress that money is not as crucial as taking care of others and acquiring a good name, which is "the greatest treasure a man can acquire." Feuerstein paid his employees for the next few months and was rewarded with his employees' motivation and loyalty.

These contrasting approaches show that global religions focus on different aspects of ethics. It is interesting to note that in the United States the focus is on creating ethical codes of conduct to control managerial behavior such as bribery and the misuse of resources, whereas Islamic societies focuses on the welfare of all, that is, socioeconomic issues.

ATTITUDES, SOCIAL STRUCTURES AND THE CONCEPT OF TIME

The concepts discussed in this section are based on the values and core assumptions described in the previous one, but these include rituals or artifacts that are observable as well as discernable attitudes that are based on core values. Some of the key concepts include attitudes such as those towards women and work, and structures such as the Hindu caste system, Islamic banking, and ethical codes such as Catholic Social Teaching (Lacznaik, 1999).

Women in Management

Sadly, most religions can be held accountable for the lower status of women in the workforce. Christianity, Islam, Hinduism, Judaism, and Confucianism all assign women to nurturing, family primary roles, allowing for power differentials between men and women. In the United States, the Southern Baptist Convention recently declared that wives should be submissive to their husbands (*New York Times,* 2000). Fundamentalist leaders in different cultures have used religion to drastically limit the ability of women to acquire an education and to participate in the workforce (for example, the Taliban in Afghanistan).

The beliefs on the appropriate role of women in society affect state policy. For instance, until 1977 the Federal Republic of Germany had laws that gave husbands the right to prevent their wives from working outside the home. In South Africa, a husband could control his wife's right to negotiate and undertake contracts until 1984 (Adler and Israeli,1988). In a more indirect fashion, the family primary role advocated for women legitimizes the social limits to their career choices along with business practices such as unequal pay for equal work prevalent in most cultures (Adler and Israeli, 1988).

Social Hierarchies and Business Codes

Although educated Indians deem caste a medieval degeneration, it has been a basic feature of Hindu society. The caste system mandated a religious division of labor into four castes of priests (*brahamans*), warriors (*kshatryias*), businessfolk (*vaishyas*) and workers (*sudras*). The discriminatory negative consequences of this inherited division of labor are well known. Yet, much of Indian enterprise, in India and overseas, can be traced to the business families belonging to the *viashya* clans (Saha, 1993). The knowledge that it was their mandated role in society and centuries of specialization helped the *vaishya* business houses develop their skills.

In Islamic countries such as Saudi Arabia, business law is derived from the Quran and the Hadith. The fact that the prophet Mohammad prohibited *riba,* or unearned profit, has lead to the development of systems of Islamic banking where banks invest in business or enter into partnership so that the lender and borrower share the same risk and reward rather than profit from another's work.

SURFACE CULTURE

Values, core assumptions, attitudes, and rituals are manifested in the surface culture. This layer is paradoxically the most evident, yet the most mutable layer of culture. Some evident manifestations of the cultural layers include schedules and calendars, festivals, and the concept of the workweek.

Calendars, Schedules, and the Workweek

Although the 5-day workweek is common in many countries, it is most accepted in Christian ones. In 1992 when merchants in Montreal sought to overturn legislation that kept stores closed on Sunday, people raised the issue that even God rested on Sunday after creating the world and so should Quebec residents. The president of YKK (North America) found this to be a point of conflict between American and Japanese employees. The former hated working over weekends, which was a common practice for Japanese expatriates. He traced the difference to differences in faith or religion because the Japanese picked up the workweek concept from the Americans after World War II, and didn't take it too seriously (Ishino, 1994). Sunday has no religious significance for much of the world. In the Islamic world, the weekend begins on Thursday. In predominantly Hindu India, the workweek is 5-1/2 days.

Devout Christians go to church on Sunday, a holiday in the Western world, but Jews and Muslims have to make adjustments to manage the clash between their religious rituals and work. Given that Orthodox Jews cannot operate machines (such as cars) from Friday sundown to Saturday sundown, it poses a challenge for people who are asked to work late on Fridays. Prayer is one of the five pillars of Islam, and a devout Muslim must pray five times a day. A colleague in Princeton keeps a prayer mat rolled up in his drawer at work and schedules his prayer times between meetings.

Religious days for many groups including the Hindus and Muslims are determined by the lunar calendar and change from year to year. This is important for the modern business traveler because, across the globe, most mandated holidays are religious ones. Mapping them has become a business necessity and enterprise. Work slows down in the Muslim world during the month of Ramadan (the ninth month in the Islamic calendar) when people generally fast from sunrise to sunset and focus on prayer. A similar phenomenon occurs around Christmas in the United States and Diwali in India. In an interesting development in international negotiations, South Americans realized that U.S. businesspeople were tempted to make concessions and close deals so that they could return home for Christmas. They then scheduled negotiations around the holidays to gain an advantage (Adler, 1997).

Finally, religious norms often dictate dress in the workplace. In Islamic cultures where modesty is a virtue, women wear loose-fitting clothing in public. Women often wear the veil, which represents honor, dignity, chastity, purity, and integrity, to work. Devout Muslim men often have beards and wear skull caps. Jewish men, too, may wear skullcaps to work. In both religions, the cap is viewed as a symbol of subservience to their God.

Causes

The popular press suggests many motives for the current interest in religion and spirituality in the workplace. For one, the changing nature of business, especially in the high-technology area, leads managers into uncharted territory. Although the formal attendance rates at churches in the United States is high, the number usually increases during periods of crisis (Gannon, 1994). A potential explanation for the interest in religion is that the pace of change in the business environment, and the stress of working in this environment, creates an internal crisis that draws people to their religion.

Consequences

In sum, the impact of religion on management is widespread through its impact on culture. However, what we see happening today is a more direct application of religion and spirituality in the workforce by executives, rather than the incidental application through culture. The current belief is that this is conducive to the workplace because it spurs the development of employee programs such as on-site day care and flextime, enhances motivation, and increases productivity (Mitroff, 1999). But what of its consequence in a global economy? To some extent, it is positive because managers can theoretically schedule work to take advantage of religious differences—such as having non-Christians work over Christmas, and non-Muslims over Ramadan. But, on another level, it is bound to create conflict when different religious practices and beliefs collide. Conflicts that emerge from differences in beliefs and values are usually difficult to resolve because people become committed to positions based on principles and will not compromise (Lewicki, Litterer, and Saunders, 1988). Managers need to consider the implications of these trends and consider ways to deal with the negative consequences. Because religion and culture have many layers, some are more critical to people than others. Mapping the similarities and differences of dominant religions will help managers reduce conflict and build on universal norms. Unlike other management trends, religion is a personal issue at the core of most people's values. The inappropriate application of religious principles can have potentially dangerous consequences.

Discussion Questions

1. Identify a belief, value, or attitude of yours that you can attribute to your religion.
2. Examine its impact on your work and career.
3. How could your religion affect your role and performance in a multicultural workplace?
4. In small group discussions, map some of the similarities and differences in religious beliefs, attitudes, and behavior of people following different world religions and faiths. Present your findings to the class.

References

Adler, N. J. (1997). *International Dimensions of Organizational Behavior,* Ohio: SouthWestern.

Adler, N. J., and D. N. Israeli. (1988). *Woman in Management Worldwide,* Sharpe: Armonk, N.Y.

Alexandrin, G. (1993). "Elements of Buddhist Economies." *International Journal of Social Economics,* 20(2), pp. 3–11.

Ananth, S. (1998). *Vaastu: The Classical Indian Science of Architecture and Design,* Penguin: India.

Brahm, J. (1999). "The Spiritual Side." *Industry Week,* 248(3), pp. 48–56.

Burr, Agnes Rush. (1917). *Russell H. Conwell and His Work, One Man's Interpretation of Life.* Philadelphia: John C. Winston Company.

"Motorola's Cultural Sensitivity Pays Off from Hong Kong to Texas." *Business Week,* 1991.

Conlin, M. (1999). "Religion in the Workplace: The Growing Presence of Spirituality in Corporate America." *Business Week,* Nov. 1, pp. 151–159.

Copeland, L., and L. Griggs. (1985). *Going International.* N.Y.: Random House.

Digh, P. "Religion in the Workplace: Make a Good-Faith Effort to Accommodate." *HR Magazine,* 43(13), pp. 84–91.

Ferraro, G. P. (1994). *The Cultural Dimensions of International Business,* Prentice Hall: Upper Saddle River, N.J.

Flynn, G. (1988). "Accomodating Religion on the Job: Few Rules, Lots of Common Sense." *Workforce,* 77(9), pp. 94–97.

Gannon, M. (1994). *Understanding Global Cultures: Metaphorical Journeys Through 17 Countries.* Sage: Thousand Oaks, Calif.

Hofstede G. (1980). *Cultures Consequences: International Differences in Work Related Values.* Sage: Beverly Hills.

Hofstede, Geert, and Michael Harris Bond. "The Confucius Connection: From Cultural Roots to Economic Growth." *Organizational Dynamics,* Spring 1988, 16(4), pp. 4–22.

Ishino, Y. "Religion in Management," presented at McGill University, 1994.

Laczniak, G. R. (1999). "Distributive Justice, Catholic Social Teaching, and the Moral Responsibility of Marketeers." 18(1), pp. 125–129.

Leigh, P. (1997). "The New Spirit at Work." *Training and Development,* 51(3), pp. 26–33.

Lloyd, Bruce, and Trompenaars, Fons. (1993). "Culture and Change: Conflict or Consensus?" *Leadership and Organizational Journal,* 14(6), p. 17.

Mitroff, I. (1999). *A Spiritual Audit of Corporate America.* Jossey Bass: N.Y.

Pava, M. I. (1998). "The Substance of Jewish Business Ethics" *Journal of Business Ethics,* 17(6), pp. 603–617.

Rice, G. (1999). "Islamic Ethics and the Implications for Business." *Journal of Business Ethics,* 18(4), pp. 345–358.

Ronen, S., and O. Shenkar. (1985). "Clustering Countries on Attitudinal Dimensions: A Review and Synthesis." *Academy of Management Review,* 19(3), pp. 435–54.

Saha, A. (1993). "The Caste System in India and Its Consequences." *International Journal of Sociology and Social Policy,* 13(3), pp. 1–76.

"Teaching New Values." *The Economist,* Nov. 28, 1992, 325(7787), p. 31.

"The 2000 Campaign: Al Gore's Journey." *The New York Times,* October 22, 2000, p. 20.

Vogel, D. (1992). "The Globalization of Business Ethics: Why America Remains Distinctive." *California Management Review,* 35(1).

Yeung, I., and R. Tung. (1996). "Achieving Business Success in Confucian Societies: The Importance of Guanxi." *Organizational Dynamics,* 25(2), pp. 54–65.

Endnotes

1. The other four pillars are the belief in one God, *salat* or prayer, the observance of *ramadan,* and pilgrimage to Mecca in one's lifetime.

Internet Assignments

1. Examine the holidays and observances listed in the society and culture section of Yahoo! Compare the holidays for Buddhists, Christians, Hindus, Muslims, and Jews.

2. Examine the Web sites of some *Fortune* 500 firms to learn about their policy on religion in the workplace.

3. Universities often describe their policies on religious accommodation on their Web sites. (for example, www.uwo.ca/univsec/handbook/general/religiou.html) What is your university's policy on religious accommodation?

Asha Rao is an assistant professor of management at Rutgers University. Her research focusing on issues of cross-cultural conflict and its resolution in joint venture negotiations, multinational management, and domestic diversity situations has been published in academic journals such as *Journal of International Business Studies, Human Relations, Leadership Quarterly,* and *Advances in International and Comparative Management.* She teaches business courses on the dynamics of managing conflict and negotiations, cross-cultural management, and managerial effectiveness at Rutgers.

SECTION FOUR

Perspectives on Diversity: Cases

Nightmare on Wall Street

Melinda Ligos

In this unprecedented bull market, selling in the financial industry is more lucrative than ever. It's also hell for many women, who are blatantly harassed and discriminated against by their managers. When saleswomen head to Wall Street, they dream of big money, million-dollar deals, chauffeured limos, and a house in the Hamptons.

What many find instead is the stuff of nightmares—demeaning managers, crude jokes, physical assaults, and a glass ceiling so impenetrable it might as well he made of titanium steel. "The [financial industry] is the last bastion of testosterone gone wild," says Marybeth Cremin, the original plaintiff in one of two major class-action sexual discrimination/harassment lawsuits recently settled against two of the nation's largest securities firms. "This industry has been discriminating against women for years."

At the time this article went to press, both Merrill Lynch and Company and Salomon Smith Barney were reaching financial agreements with thousands of women who had filed discrimination suits against them. In the Smith Barney case, more than 22,500 former and current sales assistants and brokers throughout the country alleged widespread sexual harassment and discrimination. At Merrill Lynch, more than 900 current and former female brokers contend that the firm had discriminated against women in wages, promotions, account distributions, maternity leaves, and other areas. And as the result of the filing of a discrimination claim, the Equal Employment Opportunity Commission (EEOC) is currently investigating allegations of discriminatory practices alleged by a high-earning female broker at a third firm, Morgan Stanley Dean Witter [now Morgan Stanley].

While the very existence of these suits might seem disturbing, they seem to expose a much larger problem. Many financial industry insiders say sexual harassment and discrimination in the industry are not unique to the companies mentioned in these lawsuits. For many women who sell on Wall Street—especially in securities and investment banking businesses—harassment simply comes with the job. What's worse, sales managers not only tolerate this hostile environment, but actively promote it.

"Stereotypes about women's abilities run rampant in the financial industry," says Sheila McFinney, an organizational psychologist familiar with Wall Street. "A lot of men in management feel that women don't have the stomach for selling on Wall Street. They think they can't handle the adverse climate."

In addition, McFinney says, veteran Wall Street managers may not feel that women deserve to be in positions where they could potentially earn a lot of cash. "There's a lot of money coming into some of these firms," she says, "and there's this machismo culture that doesn't feel women should get a piece of the pie."

Reprinted with permission from *Sales and Marketing Management*, February 2000, Vol. 152, Issue 2, pp. 66–72.

These stereotypes drive all kinds of business decisions, McFinney says, from who gets which accounts to who gets promoted to who gets which perks. And the problems are created by a group of predominately male managers who foster a culture in which women are, at best, made to feel uncomfortable and, at worst, driven to the point of personal and financial ruin. Of course, the financial industry isn't the only one in which sexual harassment and discrimination occur, but it does offer a particularly disturbing example of how things can go terribly wrong if managers allow these practices to fester.

A REAL TYRANT

Why do managers discriminate against women in the financial industry? Because they can. For years, most firms in the industry have required employees to sign mandatory arbitration agreements, which limit their ability to file claims in federal or state court. Instead, employees must submit complaints of discrimination to an arbitrator, who acts as judge and jury in determining the validity of an employee's claims. (Class-action suits—suits with multiple plaintiffs—traditionally have been exempt from mandatory arbitration.)

Industry insiders say the process is flawed, because the arbitrators tend to be older white males who often discount discrimination claims. "Managers have no fear of accountability," says Linda Friedman, a partner at Stowell and Friedman, the law firm representing the plaintiffs in both the Merrill Lynch and Smith Barney class-action suits. "There's no fear of repercussions, no fear of embarrassment or public scorn. Most managers believe they can get off scot-free." That's what one branch manager at Salomon Smith Barney may have believed—and apparently bragged about as he allegedly harassed and discriminated against female brokers and sales assistants in the company's Garden City, New York, branch for years.

When Roberta Thomann first came in contact with branch manager Nicholas Cuneo, she says, she tried to avoid him. Thomann, a successful sales assistant for the top broker at the branch in the early 1990s, says Cuneo was "a real tyrant. He treated women like garbage." Thomann says she tried to ignore it when Cuneo and other male brokers openly used crude language when referring to women in the office. According to court records, Cuneo once paraded a female sales assistant around the office who had worn culottes to work and told her to spread her legs at each male broker's desk so the broker could vote on whether the culottes violated Cuneo's dress code. (Note: Cuneo did not return repeated phone calls to discuss these allegations. In addition, Joan Walsh, director of employee relations at Smith Barney, said she could not comment on the specifics of the lawsuit.)

Thomann says she kept quiet at the beginning. "I would just think to myself, 'What an ass—,' and get back to work," Thomann says. Then, in 1994, Thomann, who was at that time a senior sales assistant, became pregnant and could no longer ignore Cuneo. She went on maternity leave for 8 weeks and was scheduled to return to work in mid-June. At four o'clock on the Friday before she was to come back, Thomann says she got a call from Cuneo. "He said that my position had been replaced, and I was going to be demoted," she says.

Thomann says she was offered a lowly sales assistant position in the bullpen, a notoriously rowdy area reserved for 11 broker trainees. "I was treated as if I had a disease," she says about her return to work. At one point, Thomann claims, the top broker she used to work for sent her and other sales assistants a memo promising that any charges of sexual harassment would be deliberated in the "Boom Boom Room," a room Cuneo had allegedly created in the basement of the office building, which was decorated in fraternity-house style, with a toilet bowl hanging from the ceiling.

Thomann says she wrote a letter to the branch's human resources department complaining of discriminatory treatment. "I thought, 'Now, they're really going to be in trouble,'" she says. But shortly after she filed the complaint, Thomann says, Cuneo began walking by her desk every 15 minutes, allegedly singing, "You're dead, you're dead, you're dead." Throughout the whole ordeal, according to court documents, Cuneo often openly displayed his lack of concern that Smith Barney would discipline him for violating its written antidiscrimination policies.

"I thought, 'Oh my God, nothing's going to happen,'" Thomann says. Two weeks later, her fears were confirmed when she got a letter from the human resources department stating that an investigation had revealed no discrimination. That was the last straw for Thomann. She quit her job in 1994 and gave up her Wall Street aspirations for good. She later became one of the original plaintiffs in the Smith Barney suit. "He thought he was invincible," Thomann says of her former boss.

As invincible as Cuneo may have felt, he allegedly tried to further safeguard himself from discrimination complaints by attempting to intimidate broker Pamela Martens and other female workers at the branch. Court records state that when Martens filed a discrimination complaint against Cuneo, he told at least one coworker that if he got into trouble because of the complaint, he would "f—[Martens] where she bleeds" and "snap [Martens'] neck." Martens was terminated by Smith Barney in October 1995, two days after Cuneo's retirement.

Wall Street insiders say Cuneo's reported air of invincibility is typical of managers in the financial industry. One successful female broker who works at a major Wall Street firm says her former manager used to call her and the only other female broker in the office "C—t One" and "C—t Two." "These guys are making big bucks, and they're real cocky," she says. "Their attitude is like, 'I'm not going to let some dumb bitch get in my way.'"

ANSWER YOUR OWN DAMN PHONE

Sexual harassment is only part of the story in the financial industry. Many female brokers who aren't harassed still face discrimination—sometimes in not-so-subtle ways. In both the Smith Barney and Merrill Lynch lawsuits, dozens of managers are accused of refusing to hire female brokers and managers, and of denying women the same pay and opportunities as their male counterparts, among other discriminatory acts.

When the Smith Barney case was filed, the plaintiffs claimed that less than 5 percent of Smith Barney's 11,000 brokers were female, and, although the company had 460 branch offices, fewer than 10 branch managers were women. "Indeed, the substantial majority of Smith Barney's employees are white males," the court filing alleged. The Merrill Lynch lawsuit tells a similar story. When that suit was filed, its plaintiffs complained that out of 76 sales managers, only seven were female, and only about 14 of its 125 brokers were women.

Why were the numbers so low? The plaintiffs in both cases allege that their managers purposely made it difficult for them to succeed. While Thomann and her female coworkers were struggling in Smith Barney's Garden City office, trouble was brewing in the Kansas City branch for broker Beverly Trice, who later became another of the lawsuit's original plaintiffs. Trice worked for Smith Barney from 1990 until 1996, and claims she was denied the same privileges enjoyed by the office's male brokers. For instance, when her sales assistant left the company, her sales manager allegedly refused to fill the position for 7 months, telling Trice that she could "answer her own damn phone." "I would be talking to a very important client, and I'd have to say, 'Hold on a minute,' and answer my other line, or I'd miss calls," Trice says. "It got so bad that after I interrupted a long-term client several times in one call, he told me that he couldn't handle it anymore."

In addition to being denied privileges of employment, Trice says her sales efforts were undermined by her male peers and supervisors. For example, on one occasion, she says her manager prevented her from mailing out her quarterly statement to clients in a timely fashion by falsely telling her that she couldn't send certain articles typically sent by brokers to their clients. Another time, a male broker in the office reportedly stole Trice's quarterly monitors from her desk and hid them for his own use.

After she filed several complaints with human resources, Trice claims that her boss fired her. His reason? "He said my desk was too messy," Trice says. "Then he started laughing raucously, and told me if I sued, I would never get a job in the business again." Sure enough, her manager was right. Trice says she had five major job offers withdrawn—some with salaries of more than a million dollars—after her former boss told the prospective employers that she was suing the firm. "This is a very small community," says Trice, who is still unemployed and spends her time working on a book about her experiences.

Managers at Smith Barney and Merrill Lynch might not be the only ones who allegedly have used such tactics to keep women in the industry's lower ranks. At least one woman, Allison Schieffelin, at a third brokerage firm, has filed a complaint with the EEOC against her current employer. For more than a dozen years, Schieffelin was on Wall Street's fast track, eventually taking home more than $1 million per year as a senior salesperson in the convertible bond department at Morgan Stanley Dean Witter.

But her progress began to stall a few years ago, when, she claims, she was denied many of the privileges that males in her position received. According to her lawyer, Wayne Outten, Schieffelin was excluded from male-only events, including trips to Manhattan strip clubs, and her division's annual 5-day golf outing to the Doral Resort and Spa in Florida. "The [golf trips] were very important opportunities to mingle with senior executives and clients, and Allison lost out," Outten says.

In 1996, although she was one of the company's superstars, her lawyer says, Schieffelin claims she was passed over when she became eligible to become a managing director. She was bypassed again the next 2 years. In the spring of 1998, her lawyer says, she was told that she would never become a managing director, even though men who seemed less qualified had received the title. "The only rationale

[Morgan Stanley] has provided is extremely vague," Outten says. Outten alleges that Morgan Stanley has only one female managing director out of 40 in its North American division. Morgan Stanley refused to comment on the case, which is still in progress, and would not provide information about the number of females in top management.

Outten says super-successful saleswomen like Schieffelin—who is still working at the company—are often even more likely to experience some of these discriminatory actions than women who are less successful. "A lot of these guys have a sort of western gunslinger mentality," he says. "They don't care if women get jobs as clerks or secretaries. But when they think they could take away another guy's paycheck, they're going to fight nasty."

THE ANTI-MOMMY SENTIMENT

At one Wall Street firm, there's a cruel joke that goes like this: "There's only one thing worse than a female broker—a pregnant broker." "As soon as you're pregnant, they find some way to drum you out the door," says a male broker who works for the firm, which is among the most respected in the industry. Such appeared to be the case with Marybeth Cremin. For 13 years, Cremin, a broker at Merrill Lynch's branch office in Northbrook, Illinois, was managing more than $60 million in assets. A mother of three with an MBA, Cremin said she ignored remarks by her branch manager about how women couldn't balance work and family. She also claims that the manager refused to send her to financial planning seminars and other training opportunities "because he said I was too busy raising my children." "He pushed pregnant women out the door all the time," she says, "while telling male [brokers] that they should have more kids and a big mortgage so that they would be motivated to sell more. It was a big double standard."

When Cremin announced that she was pregnant with her fourth child, she says, the manager began pressuring her to transfer her book of customer accounts to other male brokers at Merrill Lynch. "He threatened to break up my partnership with a male colleague and reduce my support staff if I didn't give up my clients," she says. "But I told him I had worked very hard to get where I was, and I wanted to provide for my children."

Later in her pregnancy, Cremin had to go on total bed rest, and the manager turned up the heat, Cremin says. In June 1995, shortly after she gave birth, he reportedly told Cremin that he would give her a financial incentive—and a permanent part-time position as a financial planner—if she gave up her accounts. She took the offer. In August 1995, the week before Cremin was to start her new position, she says the manager's secretary called her to let her know the company was putting through her termination papers.

"I was dumbfounded," she says. "I said that there must be some kind of screw up." It turns out there was no mistake. The same secretary the following week confirmed the termination, Cremin says, and the manager "even had the nerve to call me on the phone and tell me why." Merrill Lynch maintains that Cremin resigned from her position. In addition, the company "is committed more than ever to improving the diversity of its workforce, particularly among [brokers]," says Joe Haldin, a Merrill Lynch spokesperson.

CHANGING THEIR WAYS?

To some victims of harassment and discrimination, Haldin's assertion may sound like corporate-speak aimed at deflecting criticism. But the fact is, executives at Wall Street firms are at least making efforts to address these problems. A recent study of Wall Street from the United States Commission on Civil Rights states that the industry deserves credit for having at least started to embrace diversity (though Mary Frances Berry, the Commission's chairwoman, laments a "dismal lack of progress").

As part of their respective settlement agreements, Merrill Lynch and Smith Barney have pledged to make sweeping changes in the way they treat women. Merrill Lynch is boosting its recruitment efforts, and between 1997 and 1998, Haldin says, the number of female brokers hired by the firm increased by about 7 percent. Merrill Lynch also has ended the practice of mandatory arbitration (a second Wall Street firm, Paine Webber, followed suit); and according to Haldin, the company is implementing a new policy this year governing the distribution of accounts, which ensures that female brokers "receive their fair share." In addition, the company is in the process of working out financial settlements with each plaintiff

As part of its class-action settlement, Salomon Smith Barney has committed $15 million to diversity initiatives and last year hired a substantial number of female brokers. "Between 32 percent and 35 percent of all new brokers hired are females," says Walsh, Smith Barney's director of employee relations. In addition, she says, the company has conducted sexual harassment prevention training programs every year since 1995, and more than 8,000 managers have completed the workshop. Women are also encouraged to explore promotional opportunities with the company, she says.

These efforts may help some women—but they won't help many of the plaintiffs involved in the two class-action lawsuits. Some of those women left the financial industry after their experiences. Others remain with the companies they sued, or have gotten jobs at other firms. "Many of their lives are destroyed," says Friedman, the attorney representing both groups, "and their spirits are destroyed as well. Unlike women who are 20 years older than they are, most of these women grew up being told every day that there were no limits; that they could be anything they wanted to be. When they found out that wasn't true, it was a harsh reality that many won't recover from."

Managers who harass or discriminate also face harsh realities. Not only do they leave themselves open to lawsuits, but they also seriously jeopardize their companies' bottom lines. "Women are beginning to control a lot of money in this country," Cremin says. "As they become more sophisticated investors, they're going to want to buy from other women. And they're sure as hell not going to entrust their money to a firm that has a reputation for not being women-friendly."

MANAGING IN A MALE-DOMINATED INDUSTRY

Sexual harassment and discrimination happen in virtually every industry—but it's especially prevalent in industries that traditionally employ males. Here are some tips from Greg Rasin, a partner at Jackson Lewis, a New York–based law firm that specializes in labor and employment law, on what managers in male-dominated fields can do to make sure their sales force is female-friendly.

Create a Zero-Tolerance Policy

"Managers need to convince their male employees that discrimination and harassment won't be tolerated," Rasin says. Managers should create a policy prohibiting such behavior and distribute it to all employees.

Keep It Clean

"Seemingly innocuous jokes and sexual comments should be considered off limits," Rasin says. Employees who make lewd remarks should be disciplined immediately.

Rethink Social Outings

Taking clients to strip bars and similar outings isn't acceptable, Rasin says. "Women who work in an environment where this happens are put in an awful situation," he says. "They're either forced to go and potentially be embarrassed, or they're excluded. It's just wrong in today's world to entertain a client in this way—and it's discriminatory.

Distribute Accounts Fairly

That means, in part, working out a plan so that women who take maternity leave aren't unfairly penalized as a result. "Treat all medical leaves the same," he says. If a male salesperson is out for 3 months following a heart attack, you'd better treat him the same as you would a woman who's out on maternity leave."

AN OASIS FOR WOMEN

While most Wall Street firms are ruled by male managers, here's a big exception: Fiduciary Trust Company International, a global asset management firm, not only has a female CEO and president, it employs dozens of female vice presidents. In fact, 40 percent of the firm's professional staffers are women, and 26 percent of the senior staff is female. Many credit the large number of high-level females to the hiring practices of CEO Anne Tatlock, who says she strongly believes that "sex does not define your capability." But, she says, the company got its female-friendly reputation years before she came to Fiduciary in 1984. "Part of the reason was that the firm was founded to manage private wealth," she says, "and our clients wanted family-type relationships with our employees. Women are exceptional in this environment," Tatlock says.

A money manager for more than 37 years, Tatlock herself has had some struggles moving up the ranks. In the 1960s, she says, she was the first woman hired at Smith Barney "who was not a secretary." As she climbed the ladder in the financial world, Tatlock remembers "having to be smuggled in through the back door" of all-male clubs in order to give presentations to clients. She also remembers cases where she "did all the work" on an account, only to have a male colleague present her work to superiors as his own. Interestingly, though, Tatlock says she probably experienced less discrimination than women who entered the industry in the 1970s and later. "At first, I didn't have very high expectations for my career, so I probably didn't present myself as much of a threat," she says. Now, this high-ranking Wall Streeter is an inspiration to other women at the firm. Marilyn Fee White, Fiduciary's vice president of institutional new business, says Tatlock's presence at the helm sold her on the job. "It's wonderful to work in an organization that is attuned to the different strengths that both men and women bring to the business," she says.

Discussion Questions

1. From this article, what are the similarities and differences between the ways that women were treated at Fiduciary Trust Corporation International and how they were treated at Merrill Lynch & Co., Inc., Salomon Smith Barney, and Morgan Stanley Dean Whitter?
2. What potential advantages could women bring to this industry?
3. If you were a diversity consultant for Salomon Smith Barney, Merrill Lynch, or Morgan Stanley Dean Whitter, what policy changes would you recommend? Why?

First Union Case: Lessons in the Politics of Space

Susan Stites-Doe
Melissa Waite
SUNY College at Brockport

Rajnandini Pillai
California State University–
San Marcos

THE CASE: AN OFFICE WITHOUT WALLS

Meet Meg Rabb

Meg Rabb was a self-made woman. Having started her full-time career at 18, she was at the pinnacle of her career as vice president of training for First Union Federal, a large (fictitious name) savings and loan located in the eastern United States. Meg's division was responsible for both employee training and management development, and the services that her staff provided were very visible in the organization. Her unit was known as a "staff" one in the organization; that is, the training and development division served the needs of other units that were directly tied to serving consumers. These later "line" divisions were closer to final customers and, therefore, enjoyed high status in the organization.

Having recently survived several years of financial crisis and regulatory scrutiny, First Union was embarking on a new customer focus that it took very seriously. Significant amounts of financial resources were directed to employee training. All branch delivery mechanisms and systems were aimed at the achievement of a single service target: meeting consumers' changing financial needs. New approaches to service focused on customers' convenience needs and on the delivery of consistently high-quality personal service. At the same time, attention to cost containment was necessary to avoid further financial crisis and please the board of directors; the organization spent resources available for internal programs very carefully. In sum, then, the fact that the training and development division was getting a big slice of the available resources gave them some stature in the organization, and the clout that went with it, even though they were still a staff function and not involved in direct customer interactions and/or service delivery.

Meg's achievements were financially rewarding and personally satisfying. She was very good at both the design and implementation phases of the training process, and the 12 trainers and management development specialists under her charge were

169

highly qualified, and respectful of her developmental and caring leadership style. Vice president titles at First Union Federal were hard to get, and Meg had only recently been promoted to the position of vice president. Five years ago, when she had been hired at the level of assistant vice president, not a single woman enjoyed the V.P. rank and title, and only a handful of men were V.P.s, out of a total work force of 1,700 employees. After 5 years of hard work and measurable success in her job, Meg was promoted to the level of vice president. One week after the announcement of her promotion, her boss, Dan Cummings told her that she would receive a new office and that new furniture would be available to her, should she be interested in replacing her existing desk and other fixtures, lamps, and equipment.

The Office As an Incentive

Being a V.P. at First Union brought certain perquisites, or nonfinancial rewards. An office, a travel allowance, a larger share of human and other departmental financial resources, and a parking space in the corporate lot—all of these traditionally accompanied an assistant vice president in the trip up the corporate ladder to vice president.

Meg looked forward to the privacy that her new office would afford. That, above all other nonfinancial perquisites, was to be cherished in her very busy office. The office was characteristically noisy, with lots of people shuffling in and out of the office area all day long to attend training sessions or to schedule programs.

The physical office layout in her department was uncomplicated. Each employee, in a total staff of 12, had his or her own "section"—a partitioned area walled with movable screens. Employees had variable quality office furniture within their areas, depending on their level in the organizational hierarchy. All areas had desks; however, the lowest level employees received cheaper quality furniture of a hand-me-down quality, a desk chair, and possibly a guest chair. Lower level employees typically had just enough room to move around in their spaces and often had to share space within screened-off areas with other employees. Meg herself had been seated within a screened-off area located in the corner of the work area; this space had two floor-to-ceiling glass walls that overlooked the expansive city, 10 stories below. Her plan was to make this same space her office.

The Walls Came Down

The construction of the office was completed quickly, within 3 weeks of her promotion. The office was simply decorated, with grey carpet and sparse decorations—including some tasteful (but inexpensive) modern prints, a desk lamp of modern design (selected from an office supply catalog), and utilitarian desk accessories of simple design. Meg planned on using her existing office furniture in order to economize: The old furniture suited the decor of the new office, and she felt good about saving money for First Union. Her own preference was for modern decor—a stark contrast to the other executives' offices, which were decorated in conservative colonial decor. She occupied her new office space comfortably for 1 day.

Upon arriving at work the following morning, she was summoned into her boss' office. Dan Cummings was the senior vice president of human resources. He was well liked and was very accurately tuned into the political rules of the game; his influence in the organization seemed to blossom after he organized the first annual "Dan Cummings Golf Invitational," now in its fourth year of operation. Golfers from the old guard at First Union—those V.P.s and assistant V.P.s close to the senior management group—always felt honored by their invitations. Invitations denoted status in the organization. Meg had taken golf lessons this past summer in hopes of being included in next year's tournament, despite the fact that no female employees had ever received an invitation to the tournament. Even though her boss knew about her golf lessons, she had not been invited that year, and she'd never voiced her disappointment over not being included to anyone.

Upon entering Dan's office, Meg was perfunctorily informed that the president of First Union had expressed concern over the size of Meg's office. A close friend of the building manager, the president had strolled down to the construction site 2 days ago to meet the manager for lunch. The bottom line was this: The president had ruled that the office was too large. Meg was told that the existing office would have to be "modified" to conform with new building regulations set in place just that week. The plan was to tear down her office walls and to rebuild them using the proper 10 feet by 10 feet specifications detailed in the new regulations. Her office, unfortunately, had been built using 12 feet by 12 feet specifications deemed by the building manager to be appropriate.

Her immediate reaction to this troubling news was one of anger. She masked her true feelings behind a demeanor of cooperative resistance. She was very concerned about what this decision would mean to her employees—how they would take the news, and how she could present it to them to mitigate damage to her department's normally healthy morale. She had other concerns, too. She worried that this event would cause her to lose power and esteem among her peers. Meg questioned the building manager later that morning to try to get a handle on how and why such an expensive mistake had been made. He told her that the 12 feet by 12 feet specifications that had been used for her office were set in place by him, personally, to take advantage of the view and to make the best use of the surrounding building structure. Other contacts told her that the former building regulations—more lax than the current, yet similar—had been frequently ignored to suit individual employees' tastes. She couldn't help but feel sorry for the building manager. He had used his skills in office design to try to match form with function; his friendship with the president had apparently not been enough to shield him from personal repercussions. The tone of his voice and his eagerness to end their telephone conversation suggested that he was annoyed about the entire affair. Her empathy for him was joined with confusion. Had he not taken risks in the past by deviating from strict adherence to the regulations? Had he not already considered these risks? And, why was she the first person to fall victim to strict adherence to this regulation?

The Culture and Power Base at First Union

The overall culture of the bank was marked by conservatism. As one might expect when money is involved, cautiousness and conservatism were valued, as was care in retaining tight financial control over depositors' money. Power and influence at First Union were clustered primarily in the line units and at the executive levels of the organization. The mortgage division was particularly powerful. First Union had only recently remodeled the floor on which the mortgage division was located. As the "bread and butter" arm of the organization, the mortgage division enjoyed substantial power because of the revenues it generated and its contribution to the bottom line. Visitors to the newly remodeled offices never failed to remark on the beauty of the mortgage offices and on their distinctiveness from the rest of the bank. Rumor had it that the president of the bank was disturbed about the cost of the renovations, but failed to act on the matter due to the high share of profits that the division generated.

In terms of power distribution across gender, First Union had no ranking female executives above the level of vice president. This fact prompted intervention from the Equal Employment Opportunity Commission, who encouraged First Union to seek out qualified female managers for promotion to executive status. The EEOC's scrutiny was public information, and Meg often felt awkward about being the first female to pave the way. Meg did not have a mentor at a higher rank than she was in the organization. Her philosophy had always been that hard work pays off, and she was not particularly sensitive to social and political cues in the environment. Her male counterparts were very active and visible across the political terrain at First Union, as her boss' golf tournament activities attested. Friendships mattered a lot in the organization, and many of her male counterparts in other divisions were socially connected with their superiors outside of work.

Some of the artwork at First Union seemed to be very telling of values held to be near and dear to the organization. One lithograph was particularly indicative of the gender values in the organization. It featured a series of free-floating female breasts arranged in a decorative manner. The print was located in the president's conference room and was visible to board members, outside clients, and to internal staff members who attended regular meetings in the room. One lower level female manager who visited the room perhaps 15 times had never deciphered the objects in the lithograph. A higher ranking male colleague proudly pointed out the identity of the shapes to her, laughing as he said, "Hey, did you see what this print is made up of?" She was embarrassed by his remark, but joined in his laughter to get past the moment.

What Should She Do?

Meg sat down and made notes about how she would proceed. One thing was sure: If she was going to survive at First Union, she would have to learn how to play ball. As a V.P. in a staff unit, she had to do what she could to elevate her political status in the organization. Her worst fear was that she might lose her job; her very survival might depend on developing more political savvy. She had no one to turn to in the organization for advice and felt that she couldn't afford to make even a single mistake. Meg resolved to supplement her golf lessons with a crash course in organizational politics.

Discussion Questions

1. Make a list of all of the factors that may have contributed to the walls coming down in Meg's office (for example, organizational culture, power dynamics, personal factors, and her use of power tactics).

2. If you were Meg's friend or mentor, how would you help Meg understand her current situation? Do you think she could have done anything differently to prevent this series of events?
3. If you were Meg, how might you view your predicament? What would you do now? How might Meg's coworkers view her predicament?
4. Given her power base, her organization's strategic focus, the Equal Employment Opportunity Commission's attention on First Union, and her track record with the company, what do you think are her long-term prospects? Predict Meg's future with the organization. Justify your answer.

References

Harragan, Betty Lehan. (1977). *Games Mother Never Taught You: Corporate Gamesmanship for Women.* New York: Wade Publishers, Inc.

Korda, Michael. (1975). *Power! How to Get It, How to Use It.* New York: Random House.

Ornstein, Suzyn. (1992). "The Hidden Influences of Office Design." In Peter J. Frost, Vance Mitchell, Walter R. Nord (eds.) *Organizational Reality, Reports from the Firing Line.* New York: HarperCollins Publishers Inc.

Ritti, R. Richard, and G. Ray Funkhouser. (1987). Reading Number 40. "Society of Equals." In *The Ropes to Skip and the Ropes to Know.* New York: Wiley and Sons.

Ritti, R. Richard, and G. Ray Funkhouser. (1987). Reading Number 41. "Spacemen." In *The Ropes to Skip and the Ropes to Know.* New York: Wiley and Sons.

Susan Stites-Doe is an associate professor of management at SUNY College at Brockport, where she teaches organizational behavior, management skills, and strategic management. She earned a Ph.D. in organizational behavior from University at Buffalo School of Management in 1995. Prior to entering academe, she held numerous management positions in retail banking and worked as a marketing analyst at a ferrous foundry.

Melissa Waite is an assistant professor of management at SUNY College at Brockport, where she teaches courses in human resource management, organizational behavior, and general management. She earned her doctorate from the University at Buffalo. Her research interests concern the role that human resource policies play in supporting strategic organizational initiatives. Her work has appeared in *Compensation and Benefits Review*, *Psychological Reports*, and the *Journal of Private Enterprise*.

Rajnandini Pillai is center director, Center for Service Sector Management in the College of Business, California State University-San Marcos. She earned a Ph.D. in organizational behavior from the University at Buffalo School of Management in 1994. Her research and teaching interests are in leadership and cross-culture management. She has managerial experience in the banking industry in India and has consulted with service organizations in the United States.

Briarwood Industries

Carol P. Harvey
Assumption College

Diane Williamson sat at her desk at Briarwood Industries aimlessly staring out of her office window. Today was to be her big day; she expected to be promoted to vice president of marketing. Instead, she just wrote her letter of resignation. Impeccably dressed in her best navy blue suit, Diane looked successful but felt like a total failure.

When Diane came to Briarwood in 1989 as an experienced furniture sales rep, the company was already one of the largest manufacturers of upholstered living room furniture in the United States. However, the furniture industry was stagnant and sales in general were in decline. Assigned to the west coast region, Diane soon became one of the top sales reps in the country. She recognized the potential of warehouse merchandising and capitalized on having one of the major chain's national headquarters in her territory by securing a multimillion dollar contract to supply them with sofas and chairs.

In recognition, Diane was promoted to sales manager of the Seattle office in 1992 and to manager of new product and market development at corporate headquarters in North Carolina in 1995. Most recently, she moved the company into international markets by licensing Briarwood's designs to foreign manufacturers.

But the vice president's job went to Larry Jaccobi, a 12-year veteran of the company, who had the reputation of being efficient but not very creative in his management style. Larry was best known for implementing the company's order-entry system, which equipped the sales reps with portable computers that sent order data directly back to the plant. Having order data rapidly enabled Briarwood to implement a just-in-time inventory system that was projected to save the company millions of dollars over the next 5 years. Diane felt that Larry, although excellent at implementing other's ideas, lacked broad-based experience, and the vision to lead the department.

Diane was startled by a knock at her office door. Sandy McBride, the advertising manager and Diane's closest confidant at the company, heard through the office grapevine that Diane did not get the vice president's job. "What's plan B?" McBride asked. Welcoming the opportunity to talk, Diane expressed her shock and hurt at not getting the promotion. "I just don't understand how this could have happened," Diane lamented. "I came up through the sales ranks. I was the one who had the vision to diversify into office furniture, our most profitable product line. I wrote the marketing plan for our expansion into Canadian and European markets. What else could I have done?"

"Well, Diane, it was well known around here that Larry really wanted to be a vice president. He felt that he had paid his dues and that it was the next logical step. He never missed an opportunity to make his ambition very clear, or his work visible to the top brass. Remember that presentation he gave on just-in-time at the national sales meeting? Then there was the time that he volunteered to represent the company at the labor negotiations with the truck drivers union. Those reports went right to the top. I know that you and Larry never really got along . . ."

Diane abruptly cut Sandy off. "I don't work like that," Diane said. "I wouldn't want to take all the glory for something that was the product of a team effort. Larry looks out for Larry. My style is to do the best job that I can for the company. Good work gets noticed and rewarded. Look at the profit margins for the furniture division. Everyone knows that I am the brains behind that plan.

"And what about the 6 months that I spent in charge of production at the Atlanta plant. I filled in when the company was short-handed. I am not interested in running a manufacturing facility, but when the manager had a heart attack, I did it. I never complained about the assignment or about living away from my family for a year. I have always been there for Briarwood. Fine thanks I get.

"Well, it is too late now. I have resigned. It's Briarwood's loss. I am going to hand deliver this letter this morning."

An hour later, Diane sat in Gary Logan's office. As the retiring vice president of marketing and Diane's current boss read the letter, he expressed his surprise at Diane's action. "I think that you might want to reconsider your resignation. Although you have done a fine job here, quite frankly, your name was not even among the three top contenders for my job.

"We see you as a hard-working, loyal employee but not as corporate-level material. You seem to lack the competitiveness, independence, self-confidence, and level of comfort with risk that this job requires. In fact, this is the first time that you have even expressed an interest in being promoted to my job, and I announced my planned retirement date 3 months ago."

Diane felt her anger building, and said, "You can't be serious? Why wouldn't you realize that I considered myself a viable candidate to move into your position? I hinted at it during my last review. I clearly remember saying that I have done everything that this company has asked of me, and you agreed with me.

"What about the fact that I know that I am making $8,000 to $10,000 a year less than the other managers at my level of experience? I never complained about the salary differences. In fact, I never even brought it up. I thought being a team player counted for something here. I just might call my lawyer." With that statement, Diane left Gary's office but left her letter on his desk.

He left her letter on his desk, unsure how to handle the situation. Gary was glad that he had a lunch appointment with a good friend, Terry Wesley, the vice president of finance at Briarwood. Terry had a lot of female employees. Maybe Terry could help Gary understand Diane's behavior.

Discussion Questions

Note: You may be given special directions by your instructor for the discussion of this case.

1. Is Diane's reaction to Larry's promotion justified? Why or why not?
2. Does Diane have legal grounds to sue the company?

3. Who is mainly at fault for this situation? Why?
4. If Diane leaves Briarwood, what does she stand to lose? What will the company lose?
5. If you were Diane's best friend, Sandy, what advice would you give her about this situation?
6. If you were Gary Logan's best friend, Terry, what advice would you give him about this situation?
7. What can Diane learn from this experience?
8. What can Gary learn from this experience?
9. What are the lessons from this case for men and women working together in organizations?

From Tailhook to Tailspin: A Dishonorable Decade of Sexual Harassment in the U.S. Military

Lori J. Dawson
Worcester State College

Michelle L. Chunis
Boston College

> Tailhook: 1. a hook-like device under Navy aircraft that latches onto cables on the deck of aircraft carriers to assist in their landing. 2. a private association of active duty reserve and retired Navy and Marine aviators and others, primarily known for the debauchery at its conventions (CNN, 2000, August 25).

In 1991, reports of misconduct at the thirty-fifth Annual Tailhook Convention received tremendous media attention, but this was neither the first nor the last of its conventions that drew criticism. In 1974, Senator William Proxmire gave the Navy his "Golden Fleece Award" for using its aircraft to transport conference attendees. Amid growing concerns regarding the 1985 convention, Vice Admiral Edward Martin, Deputy Chief of Naval Operations, sent a memo to the Commander of the Naval Air Force Pacific Fleet, stating:

> The general decorum and conduct last year was far less than that expected of mature naval officers. . . . a rambunctious drunken melee. . . . Heavy drinking and other excesses were not only condoned, they were encouraged. . . . We can ill afford this type of behavior, and indeed must not tolerate it (Department of Defense, Office of the Inspector General, 1992) (DOD, OIG).

After this, letters regarding proper conduct were routinely sent to attendees prior to the beginning of each convention. This was the case for the 1991 convention, where approximately 1,600 people arrived on naval aircraft; 2,000 people registered for the conference; and an additional 3,000 people attended the parties. According to official reports from the Naval Intelligence Service (NIS), these parties were centered around 26 hospitality suites on the third floor of the hotel. In the

"Rhino Suite," a hole cut in a picture of a rhinoceros held a dildo. At other times, the dildo was removed and a partygoer's penis was inserted through the hole. Women entering the suite were forced to perform fellatio on whichever object happened to be protruding from it. The "gauntlet," a large group of men who groped, bit, and fondled women as they passed by, lined the third floor corridor outside the suites (DOD, OIG, 1992).

When the former president of the Tailhook Association failed to respond to her concerns about these behaviors, Lieutenant Paula Coughlin, a Navy helicopter pilot, wrote to the Assistant Chief of Naval Operations, who in turn notified his superior, Admiral Jerome Johnson. Recognizing the severity of the situation, Admiral Johnson immediately had the NIS begin an investigation. Approximately 2,100 witnesses were interviewed as allegations of misconduct grew. The official victim assault summaries included reports of being bitten on the buttocks, grabbed in the crotch, groped on the breasts, pinched, called foul names, and shirts being pulled open. Although these acts clearly violated the Uniform Code of Military Justice (Article 93, cruelty and maltreatment; Article 128, assault; and Article 133, conduct unbecoming an officer), the Naval Inspector General stated that he faced a "What's the big deal?" attitude during the investigation. The fallout from the investigation led to the resignation of Navy Secretary Lawrence Garrett, Admiral Frank Kelso, and several other high-ranking officials, but not a single man stood trial (DOD, OIG, 1992).

The 1991 Tailhook scandal focused attention on sexual harassment in the military and resulted in sweeping policy changes. Based on the recommendations of the Defense Equal Opportunity Council Task Force on Discrimination and Sexual Harassment, the DOD revised its sexual harassment policy, incorporating 48 specific recommendations as department policy in August 1995. During confirmation hearings in 1997, Secretary of Defense William Cohen commented on the importance of upholding the "zero tolerance policy" for sexual harassment, yet sexual harassment and discrimination in the military continue to be pervasive.

TAILSPIN: THE SAGA OF SEXUAL HARASSMENT CONTINUES

In 1996, Maryland's Aberdeen Proving Ground became the focus of attention when a captain and four drill sergeants were brought up on a variety of charges including sexual harassment and rape of female trainees. Army reports alleged that some of the base's drill sergeants made a game of distributing a list of names of women who they believed would have sex with them. In one account, a female private was told to go to the home of Staff Sgt. Wayne Gamble to have sex with him (*New York Times*, 1997, May 14). According to sworn testimony, Gamble reportedly bragged of having sex with over 60 privates. Staff Sgt. Delmar Simpson, sentenced to 25 years in prison for his conviction on 18 counts of rape and 29 other offenses, was described by prosecutor Capt. Dave Thomas as a "sexual predator who was like an animal in the way he victimized the weaker soldiers under his command." After raping one woman for example, Simpson told her that "if you ever tell anyone about this, I'll slit your throat" (Ehrenreich, 1996). In defense of his client, Captain Ed Bradley argued:

> Simpson should be discharged from the Army, but not given a lengthy
> prison term, because he was never a threat to anyone except young sol-

diers. Sending Simpson to jail for the rest of his life will accomplish nothing. The first step toward rehabilitating a broken, humbled, defeated man is compassion (McIntyre, 1997).

No mention was made by Bradley regarding rehabilitation of the broken victims whose lives were shattered by Simpson's abuse.

The controversy at Aberdeen overshadowed other cases of sexual harassment that year, including the retirement of Brig. Gen. Robert T. Newell, after his demotion to colonel for inappropriate conduct with a female subordinate (*New York Times*, 1996, December 27). 1996 also brought a class-action lawsuit by 23 women at Fort Bliss, Texas, alleging that they had been pressured to pose nude and/or perform sexual acts while working at the base (*New York Times*, 1996, August 29).

In the wake of the Aberdeen scandal, the Secretary of the Army set up a Senior Review Panel of high-ranking officers to investigate sexual harassment in the military. One of those appointed was the Army's then highest-ranking noncommissioned officer, Sgt. Maj. Gene McKinney. His tenure on the panel was short-lived, however, when he was accused of sexual harassment by retired Sgt. Maj. Brenda Hoster, who had once worked under him. Following her disclosure, five other women stepped forward, accusing McKinney of sexual harassment. McKinney was court-martialed and faced 19 charges ranging from indecent assault to adultery, including an accusation that he forced one woman to have sex with him while she was nearly 8 months pregnant. If convicted of all charges, McKinney faced up to 55½ years in prison. In the end, he was found guilty of only one charge, obstruction of justice for encouraging a woman to lie to investigators. Why he would encourage someone to lie about an incident that didn't happen is left unexplained. Although demoted to master sergeant, he was allowed to retire and collect the significantly higher pension of a sergeant major (Bennet-Haigney, 1998; CNN, 1998, March 13).

The same week that McKinney was suspended pending the outcome of the investigation against him, three Army instructors in Darmstadt, Germany, were suspended for allegations of sexual misconduct made by 11 female soldiers. Charges included forcible sodomy and indecent assault (*USA Today*, 1997, February 13). Later in 1997, a two-star admiral was relieved of his duties pending investigation of sexual harassment charges; another admiral was dismissed from his post after allegations of inappropriate sexual conduct surfaced (Stout, 1997; *Washington Post*, 1997, August 6).

Deputy Inspector General for the Army, Maj. Gen. David Hale, was allowed to retire quietly while under investigation for sexual misconduct in 1998. Hale became the first retired general in the history of the U.S. Army to be court martialed. He was ultimately convicted on seven counts of "conduct unbecoming an officer" for having inappropriate sexual relations with the wives of four subordinates, who claim Hale used his power over their husbands' careers to pressure them into sex (Plante, 1999a).

Late 1999 found a drill sergeant being demoted to private and sentenced to nearly 4 years in prison for sexual misconduct (Myers, 1999). Earlier that year, the army's top-ranking noncommissioned officer in Europe, Command Sgt. Maj. Riley Miller, was relieved of his duties pending the investigation of charges of sexual assault, sodomy, and kidnapping (Plante, 1999b; Stout, 1999).

This past year, the first woman ever to make three stars in the U.S. Army, Lt. Gen. Claudia Kennedy, had a less celebrated distinction. She became the highest-ranking officer ever to file a sexual harassment complaint against a former colleague. Kennedy made passing reference to having been sexually harassed in an interview in March, 1997:

> "When they investigated it, they found that the person who did a fairly benign thing to me had done very egregious things to two other women. . . ." (McIntyre, 2000).

At the time, Kennedy believed that her informal report of harassment was handled appropriately, and that some record had been added to the personnel file of her harasser, Maj. Gen. Larry Smith. She considered the matter closed and thought little of it, until hearing news that Smith was in line for a prestigious job in the Inspector General's Office, one that would include overseeing investigations of sexual harassment. Kennedy officially reported the incident only after Smith was being considered for the sensitive position in the Inspector General's Office. Kennedy has since retired, and it is expected that a "career-ending reprimand" for Smith is forthcoming (CNN, 2000, May 11). There is some hope that the publicity from a sexual harassment case involving officers at this level will prompt more serious action against sexually harassing behaviors by military personnel. This has yet to be determined.

We end the decade where we began—at the Tailhook convention. The navy severed all ties with the Tailhook Association in October 1991. The conventions continued, but military personnel could attend only if they paid their own expenses and used their own leave time. In 1999, the navy sent a contingency of officials to determine if it should restore ties with the Tailhook Association. After the review was completed, Navy Secretary Richard Danzig decided the association had taken appropriate measures to ensure proper conduct at the conventions and hence renewed ties with the organization. This year marked the first convention where military aviators were officially allowed to attend the convention since 1991. An investigation is now underway to address allegations of what navy spokesperson Rear Adm. Steve Pietropaoli euphemistically referred to as "inappropriate physical contact" by conference attendees (CNN, 2000, August 25).

SEXUAL HARASSMENT: DEFINITION AND PREVALENCE

Reports of the prevalence of sexual harassment in the military are higher than those found in other employment settings. In the largest study conducted to date in the United States, the Merit Systems Protection Board found that 42 percent of the more than 10,000 female federal employees surveyed reported some form of sexual harassment (USMSPB, 1981) and that harassment of women was more common in traditionally male occupations. Several recent studies have found similar results. In contrast, a survey of approximately 10,000 military women conducted by the DOD found that 64 percent of respondents reported some form of sexual harass-

The Equal Employment Opportunity Commission (EEOC) guidelines are the most frequently cited definition of sexual harassment. According to the EEOC:

Harassment on the basis of sex is a violation of Sec. 703 of Title VII of the Civil Rights Act. Unwelcome sexual advances, requests for sexual favors, and other verbal or physical conduct of a sexual nature constitute sexual harassment when:

1. Submission to such conduct is made either explicitly or implicitly a term or condition of an individual's employment,

2. Submission to or rejection of such conduct by an individual is used as the basis for employment decisions affecting such individual, or

3. Such conduct has the purpose or effect of unreasonably interfering with an individual's work performance or creating an intimidating, hostile, or offensive working environment.

The first two sections of this definition are referred to as "quid pro quo" harassment, and the third is referred to as "hostile working environment" harassment. The Department of Defense (DOD) uses this definition, with the replacement of "a person's job, pay, or career" for "employment" in the first section (Dorn, 1997).

ment. The rate of harassment varied by military branch, with the lowest rate, 53 percent, found in the air force, and the highest rate, 72 percent, in the Marine Corps. Men in each branch of the service believed that military leaders were doing a better job of combating sexual harassment than did their female counterparts. Interestingly, there was a direct relationship between gender differences regarding perceptions of how effective military leaders were in trying to combat sexual harassment and the level of sexual harassment in that branch. Those branches with the least gender disparity in those perceptions had the lowest levels of sexual harassment; those branches where men and women showed the most disagreement about how well the leadership was handling harassment reported the highest levels of harassment (Niebuhr, 1997).

WHAT'S THE BIG DEAL?: MILITARY CULTURE AND CORRELATES OF SEXUAL HARASSMENT

Many sexual harassment theories focus on the role of organizational culture as it relates to sexual harassment in the institution. One such theory is the sex-role spillover theory. According to this theory, gender-based stereotypes and expectations dominate the workplace, especially in cases where there is a large gender skew (Gutek and Morasch, 1982). In predominately female occupations, such as teaching and nursing, the expectations of those roles are characterized by the traditionally feminine stereotypes of someone who is supportive, caring, gentle, helpful, and nurturing. In contrast, predominately male occupations, such as police work and military service, are associated with such traditionally masculine traits as assertiveness, strength, decisiveness, and competitiveness (Gutek and Dunwoody, 1987). In these male-dominated occupations, gender roles are more salient than work roles; thus, women are seen as women first and only secondarily as employees (Tangri and Hayes, 1997). When women's characteristics are perceived as incongruous with the needs of the job, they are subject to higher levels of harassment and discrimination (for example, the compassionate female soldier is looked down upon for being too soft). Conversely, women are also harassed and discriminated against when they engage in appropriate work role-related behaviors that are perceived as incongruous with stereotypical gender expectations (for example, the assertive female soldier is looked down upon for being unfeminine.)

Women who find themselves in this "damned if you do, damned if you don't" situation are often subject to sexualized work environments. The pages of one military woman's web site is replete with such stories, like this one from a female ex-Marine: "If I was forceful, I was a 'bitch.' If I was soft, I was not worthy of the uniform, and if I didn't put out, I was a 'bitch' and 'probably a lesbian'" (Anonymous, 1997). A former army recruiter describes a similar situation:

> It seems like every day in this job I run into some type of discrimination or harassment. As a female recruiter, I have been asked to . . . flirt with [male recruits] to get them to enlist. I constantly hear remarks such as: I am a combat arms sergeant and do not know why the Army needs women; I will never enlist a female; why did all of the females who deploy to Saudi have yeast infections; women's bodies look horrible in BDUs (it covers too much); women in the Army are sweaty; most women in the Army are either lesbian or easy, and all women really want is two men to have sex with them at the same time. I personally have been referred to as the bitch, or had statements said to me such as . . . she must be having PMS, and your ribbons must be uncomfortable the way they set upon your chest. When I try to make a complaint with my chain of command (naturally all males), I am coerced to agree that I have a problem or I am just taking these remarks out of context. . . . Bottom line: nothing works! (Anonymous, 1998).

The reaction of many of the 2,100 people interviewed regarding the Tailhook '91 incident provides a good example of the normative nature of sexual harassment in the military. Quoting directly from the official report:

> A common thread running through the overwhelming majority of interviews concerning Tailhook 91 was—"what's the big deal?" Those interviewed had no understanding that the activities in the suites fostered an atmosphere of sexual harassment and that actions which occurred in the corridor constituted at minimum sexual assault and in many cases criminal sexual assault. That atmosphere condoned, if not encouraged, the gang mentality, which eventually led to the sexual assaults (DOD, OIG, 1992).

In any organization, the attitudes of those in charge are directly related to the level of sexual harassment in the organization. When superiors take a proactive stance on education and prevention of sexual harassment, the level of harassment declines (Gruber, 1997). To say that top military personnel expressed dismissive attitudes toward both sexual harassment and women in the military is an understatement. More disturbing than the attitude of those interviewed during the Tailhook investigation was the attitude of top officials in charge of the investigation itself. The DOD report makes repeated references to improprieties by the Under Secretary of the Navy, the Naval Inspector General (IG), and the Commander of the Naval Investigative Service (NIS). These include an unwillingness to properly conduct the investigation, sexist attitudes, and victim-blaming statements.

The dismissive attitude of many top officers is reflected in this comment from the Naval IG, Rear Admiral George W. Davis, VI:

> . . . Once we determined we had a cultural problem then it was our contention in that . . . the corporate "we" had allowed this to take place. And to interview squadron [commanding officers], to ask them why they allowed that to happen didn't make any difference because the whole system allowed it to happen. And frankly, I think a navy captain who had seen that over 4 or 5 years, had seen the Rhino Room with a dildo hanging on the wall, is not going to walk in there in 1991 and change anything (DOD, OIG, 1992).
>
> The DOD report challenges the Admiral's comments by stating: While it is easy to be sympathetic to the attitude—that the Navy has allowed that kind of activity to go on for so many years the attendees that had become enculturated to it could not be expected to change it and therefore should not be held responsible for it—it must ultimately be rejected. For what the Naval IG failed to understand is that the time for attributing misconduct of that nature to a "cultural problem" had long since passed. . . . (DOD, OIG, 1992).

"Long since passed" would be a fitting way to describe the appropriateness of the attitudes expressed by Admiral Williams, the Commander NIS, as well. On several occasions, the commander expressed views that led others to question his suitability to lead the Tailhook investigation. He repeatedly tried to terminate the investigation prematurely, pressuring those individuals directly conducting the interviews to close their investigations. In one meeting, other high-ranking attendees were upset by the admiral's comment that the NIS "did not have a fart's chance in a whirlwind of solving the investigation" (DOD, OIG, 1992).

The admiral's attitudes toward women in the military, or women in general for that matter, were far from admirable. During the course of the investigation, not only did he state that men didn't want women in the military, but that he, himself, did not think women belonged in the military, stating that "a lot of female navy pilots are go-go dancers, topless dancers, or hookers" (DOD, OIG, 1992). A section of the report chronicling the commander's discussion of a sexual assault investigation is perhaps the most telling of all:

> . . . the Commander met with a female NIS agent to review the statement of one of the assault victims. The Commander, NIS, commented on the victim's use of profanity in her statement. (According to the victim's statement, she described that she turned to two of her assailants as they were grabbing her and demanded of each of them "What the fuck do you

think you're doing?" In her statement, the victim also stated that she told her commanding officer that she was "practically gang-banged by a group of fucking F-18 pilots"). The NIS agent related to us the Commander's reaction. . . . Then Adm. Williams—and I'll remember this quote forever. Then Adm. Williams made the quote to me "Any woman that would use the F word on a regular basis would welcome this type of activity . . ." (DOD, OIG, 1992).

Have attitudes of top-ranking military personnel changed over this past decade? Most assuredly some have. Yet sexist attitudes and sexual harassment are still pervasive in every level of the military.

Discussion Questions

1. The Tailhook convention gave attendees informal networking opportunities outside the usual work realm.
   a. What informal networking opportunities exist in more traditional, non-military settings?
   b. How do these opportunities impact employment decisions, promotions, and corporate power?
   c. In what ways are these informal situations different from more formal networking within the confines of the office?
   d. Would some employees be less welcomed, less comfortable, or have less access to these informal networking opportunities?
   e. How would this impact their ability to do their job effectively?
2. How does the sex-role spillover theory apply to more traditional business settings? Cite examples from organizations familiar to you.
3. Discuss the effects of organizational and sociocultural power differentials in traditional work settings.
4. How might men and women perceive the severity of possible sexual harassment situations differently? Are there other group distinctions (race, class, sexual orientation, age) that might influence an individual's perceptions of sexual harassment?

References

Anonymous. (1997, February 7). "Why Women Leave the Military." Available: www.militarywoman.org/whyleave.htm

Anonymous. (1998, November 16). "Harassment Issues—File #3, 1998." Available: www.militarywoman.org/harass3.htm.

Bennet-Haigney, L. (1998). "Military Challenged to Punish Its Own in McKinney Trial." Available: www.now.org/nnt/05–98/mckinney.html

CNN. (2000, August 25). "Navy Investigating Alleged Misconduct at Latest Tailhook Convention." Available: www.cnn.com/2000/US/08/25/tailhook.allegations.02

CNN. (2000, May 11). "Sources: Army Substantiates General's Claim of Sexual Harassment." Available: www.cnn.com/2000/US/05/11/army.sex/index.html

CNN. (1998, March 13). "McKinney Not Guilty of 18 of 19 Counts in Sexual

Misconduct Trial." Available: www.cnn. com/US/9803/13/mckinney.verdict/ index.html

Department of Defense, Office of the Inspector General. (1992, September). "Tailhook 91, Part 1—Review of the Navy Investigations." Available: www. inform.umd.edu/EdRes/Topic/Womens Studies/GovernmentPolitics/M . . . /4/tailhook-9.

DiTomaso, N. (1989). "Sexuality in the Workplace: Discrimination and Harassment." In J. Hearns, D. Sheppard, P. Tancred-Sheriff, and G. Burrell (eds.). *The Sexuality of Organizations.* Newbury Park, Calif.: Sage, pp. 71–90.

Dorn, E. (1997). "DoD Committed to Zero Tolerance of Sexual Harassment." *American Forces Information Service Defense Viewpoint, 12.* Available: www.defenselink.mil/speeches/ 1997/di1209.html.

Ehrenreich, B. (1996, December 2). "Wartime in the Barracks: Here's a Radical Solution to Ending the Harassment of Women in the Military." *Time, 148,* p. 25.

Gruber, J. (1997). "An Epidemiology of Sexual Harassment: Evidence from North America and Europe." In W. O'Donohue (ed.). *Sexual Harassment: Theory, Research, and Treatment.* Needham Heights, Mass.: Allyn and Bacon, pp. 84–98.

Gutek, B., and V. Dunwoody. (1987). "Understanding Sex in the Workplace." In A. Stromberg, L. Larwood, and B. Gutek (eds.). *Women and Work: An Annual Review, Vol. 2,* Newbury Park, Calif.: Sage, pp. 249–269.

Gutek, B., and B. Morasch. (1982). "Sex-Ratios, Sex-Role Spillover, and Sexual Harassment of Women at Work." *Journal of Social Issues, 38,* pp. 55–74.

Hill, M. (1980). "Authority at Work: How Men and Women Differ." In G. Duncan and J. Morgan (eds.). *Five Thousand American Families: Patterns of Economic Progress.* Ann Arbor,

Mich.: Institute for Social Research, pp. 107–146.

Hotelling, K., and B. Zuber. (1997). "Feminist Issues in Sexual Harassment." In W. O'Donohue (ed.). *Sexual Harassment: Theory, Research, and Treatment.* Needham Heights, Mass.: Allyn and Bacon, pp. 99–111.

Kauppinen-Toropainen, K., and J. Gruber. (1993). "Sexual Harassment of Women in Nontraditional Jobs: Results from Five Countries." *Working Papers.* Ann Arbor, Mich.: Center for the Education of Women.

LaFountaine, E., and L. Tredeau. (1986). "The Frequency, Sources, and Correlates of Sexual Harassment Among Women in Traditional Male Occupations." *Sex Roles, 15,* pp. 433–442.

McIntyre, J. (1997, May 6). "Army Sergeant Sentenced to 25 Years for Rape." Available: www.cnn.com/US/ 9705/06/army.sex/index.html

McIntyre, J. (2000, March 31). "Pentagon Investigates Sexual Harassment Charge Filed by Top Female General." Available: www.cnn.com/2000/ US/03/31/army.sex.charge.01

Myers, S. (1999, December, 3). "Prison Term for Drill Sergeant in Sex Case Involving Trainees." Available: www. nytimes.com

New York Times. (1997, May 14). "Allegations of Sexual Misconduct in the Military Persist." Available: www.femi nist.org/911/sexharnews/_military.html

New York Times. (1996, December 27). "Air Force Demotes General." Available: www.nytimes.com

New York Times. (1996, August 29). "Women Complain of Harassment at Ft. Bliss." Available: www.nytimes.com

Niebuhr, R. (1997). "Sexual Harassment in the Military." In W. O'Donohue (ed.), *Sexual Harassment: Theory, Research, and Treatment.* Needham Heights, Mass.: Allyn and Bacon, pp. 250–262.

Plante, C. (1999a, July 14). "Retired General May Now Face Reduced Rank in

Sex Case." Available: www.cnn.com/US/9907/14/army.general.sex/

Plante, C. (1999b, October 23). "Army's Top Enlisted Man in Europe Faces Kidnapping, Sodomy Charges." Available: www.cnn.com/US/9910/23/us.army.assault/index.html

Stewart, L., and W. Gundykunst. (1982). "Differential Factors Influencing the Hierarchical Level and Number of Promotions of Males and Females Within an Organization." *Academy of Management Journal, 25,* pp. 586–597.

Stout, D. (1997, May 31). "New Investigations of Harassment in the Military." Available: www.nytimes.com

Stout, D. (1999, October 23). "The Army's Top NCO in Europe is Charged With Sexual Assault." Available: www.ny times.com

Tangri, S., M. Burt, and L. Johnson. (1982). "Sexual Harassment at Work: Three Explanatory Models." *Journal of Social Issues, 38,* pp. 33–54.

Tangri, S., and S. Hayes. (1997). "Theories of Sexual Harassment." In W. O'Donohue (ed.). *Sexual Harassment: Theory, Research, and Treatment.* Needham Heights, Mass.: Allyn and Bacon, pp. 112–128.

USA Today. (1997, February 13). "U.S. Military Sexual Harassment Charges Surface in Germany." Available: www.feminist.org/911/sexharnews/_military.html

Washington Post. (1997, August 6). "Admiral Relieved of Command After Harassment Complaints." Available: www.feminist.org/911/sexharnews/_military.html

Wolf, W., and N. Fligstein. (1979). "Sex and Authority in the Workplace. A Policy-Capturing Approach." *Academy of Management Journal, 32,* pp. 830–850.

Diversity in Law Enforcement: The Report

Egidio A. Diodati
Assumption College

The executive summary section of the report hit her squarely in the face. The opening paragraph seemed the harshest.

> This department is clearly a male-dominated, paramilitary organization which has demonstrated time and again its inability to integrate minorities, particularly women, into its most central functions. From hiring to training, to promotion, to the design of facilities, this department seems to have dropped the ball, most particularly as far as women are concerned. Researchers for this study noted that on at least several occasions it became accepted procedure to place the lives of women officers in harm's way as a way of testing their readiness. No evidence could be found of a similar systemic pattern toward majority (white male) officers. There is a pervasive subtle (and sometimes not-so-subtle) hostility with reference to gender diversity in this department.

Although researched and written by an independent company, largely comprised of retired federal law enforcement officers, the report had been paid for by the city's Minority Police Officers Organization. Copies of the report had been sent to the department, the television and radio stations, and the newspapers.

The city of Everly police department has a total of 215 officers in all ranks, bureaus, and functions. Of the 215, there are 25 female officers (3 African-American, 3 Asian-American, 3 Hispanic, and 16 white). The 190 male officers are comprised of 20 African-American, 9 Asian-American, 10 Hispanic, and 151 white. The city has an ethnically diverse population of slightly over 125,000 people.

As Linda sat rereading the report in her new office in the Everly city police headquarters overlooking the city hall plaza, she wondered aloud just how long it had taken to get to this point. In her time in the department, she had experienced some minor incidents but nothing that she thought ought to be in the papers. The department was known for cleaning up its own messes. She wondered:

- What was it about the culture of this organization that contributed to this situation?
- What could have been done to prevent this situation?
- What policies, procedures, and training could have been brought to bear?
- In the final analysis, she wondered what could be done to prevent any recurrence of the events that were in the report.

Everyone in the department had known that the report was coming, but it seemed that the report had arrived just as she began her new assignment. Linda Michaelson had recently been promoted to the command staff rank of assistant superintendent of police for administration. Part of that responsibility, as the superintendent had clearly reminded her on her first day, was to "manage the EEO side of the house." "When that damned minority report gets made public, it is going to be a no-win situation as far as the department and the media are concerned. You were in a situation with the department, and we took care of you, right? So, a big part of your job will be to run damage control. Understand?" The directness of his demeanor and the tone of his voice made his meaning abundantly clear.

Prior to Linda's current assignment, she had spent 22 years on the force, rising from patrol officer to assistant superintendent, with what she thought were particularly long stints in what had been described as "high-profile" assignments. She had spent over 5 years as the department's public school safety officer and then been assigned as the DARE (a federally funded drug education program) officer for several years. In her 6 years in the detective bureau, she had been the point of contact for most of the sexual assault cases. Her father had retired from this department as a sergeant and had passed away about 18 months ago from a heart attack. How she wished that he could be here both to see her success and to give her advice. He had always had amazing insight into the invisible workings of the department. She remembered her hiring interview with a board of several lieutenants and captains (all male). One particularly stern-faced captain, near the end of the interview, leaned forward and said, "I only have one question. What does your father have to say about this?" She had told him that her father wanted her to be the best of whatever she chose to do. That's all. The response from her inquisitor was a barely audible, "I'll bet."

So now, Linda found herself putting together a plan to deal with any further incidents of, as the report called it, "hostile work environments." In addition, it seemed like something that the media would really like. The concept seemed alarmingly simple to her but would have some personnel costs associated with it. First, she would set up a bureau within her organization that would be the focal point of all "diversity" complaints. She suggested that it be a part of the Internal Affairs Bureau, the detectives who investigate problems within the department. That way, personnel could be diverted to cases, other than diversity-related ones, as necessary.

But, how would complaints reach the new bureau? The report had shown that most officers knew that the only accepted avenue for personnel complaints generally involved their supervisor and the union representative. For minority officers, the report indicated that this was in effect a dead end. They would not go to either a supervisor or the union for the simple reason that these individuals usually were majority officers and, therefore, could not be trusted. She seized upon something that a number of federal agencies had been using. Give all officers open access to the bureau via a form that could be mailed (or e-mailed) directly to the bureau, bypassing the usual chain of command or the union. The form would be:

- initially mailed to the home of each officer,
- available openly in each precinct or bureau, and
- available to be downloaded over the Internet to be e-mailed back to the bureau.

In her summary to the superintendent, she indicated that departmental action on a particular complaint could range from sensitivity counseling (individual or group) up to and including dismissal from the force. This would, however, have to be consistent with the union contract for personnel represented by the union. The complaining officer would be contacted by the Internal Affairs Division Diversity Bureau with the resolution of any complaint.

The superintendent had liked the idea right away and presented it to the mayor for approval. After a short discussion in the city council, it was approved. Although the superintendent had liked the idea, mid-level field commanders did not react well. One was quoted as saying, "It is just another damn big brother looking over our shoulder. These complaints should go through the usual chain of command, if only so that we can try to resolve them before they get out of hand." The union went on record as not supporting the new procedure, because it was not specifically in the contract for the "bargaining unit." It planned to bring it up in the negotiations for the next contract. In spite of the mixed reactions, the superintendent went forward with implementing the new bureau. He said at the news conference announcing the plan that, "It will go a long way towards preventing problems with minority officers, particularly issues of sexual harassment in the department."

The form IAB-DC (Internal Affairs Bureau–Diversity Complaint) took about 2 weeks to get into the field with full explanation to officers by local supervision. At the end of the first month, the new bureau was up and running, but the results were almost as distressing as the original report. Six complaints had been received from female personnel. A seventh was from three white male officers, who had filed a complaint about the promotion of a minority officer to sergeant. They had found out that the black officer had scored lower on the competitive civil service exam than they had. One complaint had been received from an African-American sergeant who claimed he was being disciplined because of racial harassment.

THE COMPLAINTS

On IAB-DC form no. 1, a young patrol officer named Karen Buckley, who had just completed her probationary period (initial 3 months on the force during which the officer works with other more experienced patrol officers), filed a complaint against an older patrol officer. In the comments section, Officer Buckley stated:

> One day as I passed through a doorway entering the briefing room at the station, Officer Ralph Jones stepped through going the other way, so that he was close to my face. He looked me straight in the eye and whispered, "You don't belong here. This is a man's job." He was so close that I could feel his breath on my face. Several days later, in our locker room (unisex), Officer Jones dropped his pants to his knees, while standing in front of me, in order to "put in his shirt." I said nothing to him. I have mentioned it to my patrol supervisor who told me that Jones is "old school" and that I should just let it roll off my back to avoid alienating other male officers, because then they will all do it. I am not comfortable with any of that. I need your help. It is not right!

The IAB-DC form no. 2 was from a patrol officer named Marcy Smith, who works in the same precinct as the officer in the first complaint. She had been on the force for about 5 years. Specifically, her complaint was:

> I am not sure that this is actually what this form is supposed to be used for, but I believe that I am being punished because of my gender. A couple of months after I had completed probationary period about 4 years ago, I was on patrol alone in a section of the city known for gang activity and burglaries. It was a Sunday at about 1:30 A.M., and I received a call from dispatch about a burglar alarm in an industrial building. I proceeded code 2 (blue warning lights only). While heading there, I heard my patrol supervisor, Sgt. Mack, call the patrol officer in the next sector to back me up—this was standard procedure. Almost right away, I heard the watch commander, Lt. Abrams, recall the other officer to continue to patrol his original sector and not back me up. When I arrived at the location, I found a rear door unlocked, entered with my weapon drawn, and found no one. I had dispatch call the owner and the alarm company, waited for their arrival, and then cleared back to patrol.
>
> At the end of the watch, I asked Sgt. Mack about the backup being recalled, which caused me to enter the building alone. He said he would check with Lt. Abrams. When he came back, he looked angry and told me that if I repeat this, he would deny it. He said that, when questioned, Abrams said that the reason he recalled the backup was because he had heard that I was a "bit tentative in the field" and he wanted to put me to the test.
>
> As a result, in my 5 years as a patrol officer, I have *never* waited for a backup to arrive before entering any situation. I honestly feel that as a woman, I have had to continually be better than the guys just to be considered as good as they are. Last month, Lt. Abrams put me on disciplinary warning because I had received a lost time injury breaking up a fight in a bar where I had gone in without my backup.
>
> I believe that I am being punished just because, as a woman, I have been given different performance standards by my supervision because of my gender. What I specifically want is for the department to drop the disciplinary action against me and remove the letter from my personnel file. I was punished for being a woman!

This second complaint reminded Linda of her own experience when she had been promoted to captain. At the time, she had been upset but at the resolution of the situation, she ultimately felt vindicated. There were no female captains in the department, and she wanted to be the first. She had studied hard for the captain's examination (statewide civil service test) and had taken it with several male lieutenants from her own department, along with about 35 officers from other departments.

About a month later, she had received a call from a friend who worked for the state, who said, "Hey, I heard you did really well on the exam. In fact, I heard you topped the list for your department. Congratulations." At the time, Linda knew that there was an opening for a captain and that the department historically took the top performer from the exam. She had been excited until the superintendent called later that day. He said, "Linda, by now I guess that you have heard that the list is out for captain and you did well. In fact, all three of our lieutenants passed it." Then, he dropped the bomb. "We have decided that all of the candidates for the captain's job have to go through a screening board before we make a choice. The board will have 7 members and will be made up of command staff from this department and captains from other departments. We will have to abide by their recommendation."

Later, as she replayed the call in her head, her emotions were nearly overpowering—ranging from total shock to anger. She really smelled the "old boys" in this one. She called her dad, and his response was worse than hers. He validated her view and told her to "make noise now and make a lot of it, before the cement hardens." When she called the union representative, she was not given much help. Finally, abandoning all loyalty to the department, she called an attorney who, after a brief conversation, agreed to take the case. After the local district court issued a temporary restraining order against the department's intended actions and the local newspaper reporters began to sniff around, the superintendent called to say that he hoped she understood that it was not about her and that she would receive the promotion the following month. She knew that she had earned the promotion for real but resented receiving it this way. She knew what the "old boys" would say about it.

The IAB-DC form no. 3 form was not quite as compelling but still got her thinking. A female investigator named Michelle Repson, with more than 12 years on the force, had submitted a thought-provoking form that showed a series of things. Specifically, the complaint stated,

> It's not serious but it hurts when I put it all together and think about it. Since I have become an investigator and have been teamed up with other officers (mostly men) on a regular basis, a number of petty but bothersome things have begun to occur. Over the course of several years, each time I was assigned a new partner, usually the second or third thing that they ask me is, "Are you straight?" I wonder what would happen if a man were to ask a man that question? Moreover, for the last 12 years I have carried a badge with the word "Patrolman" imprinted on the top. Am I the only one who sees the problem with that? Why is it when I am serious and direct with one of my colleagues, someone asks about "the time of the month"? Has anyone seen the recent studies on male mood swings?
>
> After all of that, the strangest thing I want to point out is just how the wives of my partners treat me when I am introduced to them at social functions. They are usually cold and sometimes downright rude, even when I am with my husband. I can only guess that they are jealous of the time I spend with their husbands or perhaps of the bond that can develop between partners on the job. What do I want? Just smarten these guys up, will you?

The IAB-DC form no. 4 cried out for immediate action. It was from a patrol officer named Marcia Flynn, who had been on the force for about 5 years and who appeared to be having trouble with another officer. Specifically, her report stated,

> For the last year, another officer here in this precinct has been driving me crazy. He just won't take no for an answer. His name is Mick Johnson,

and we started here at about the same time. About a year ago, he asked me out on a date. When I told him that I was really not interested, he smiled and said he was persistent.

A few days later, I found a bottle of perfume in my mail slot in the briefing room. The next day he asked if I had received his gift. I told him that I could not accept it and gave it back to him. When he did it again about a week after that, I told him that he should stop and that it was making me uncomfortable. He called me at home several times to ask me out again. I declined and told him to stop asking. (I have never given him my home phone number.) I continued to get things in my mail slot at the district but he began to deny putting them there when I confronted him. Other officers have told me that he said that I must be a lesbian.

Now, I think that he is stalking me. A couple of weeks ago I was assigned a different cruiser than normal when mine needed repairs. It had been assigned to Mike Blake, an officer who was at training. My supervisor told me to take the cruiser home because I was on nights and had a court appearance the next morning. A couple of days later, the dispatcher stopped me on my way out of the station and said that Johnson had asked how long I had been dating Blake. He said Johnson told him that he had seen Blake's cruiser at my house during the night. Johnson had to have been stalking me. I don't know what to do. I think it is getting dangerous.

The IAB-DC form no. 5 came from a new patrol officer named Karen Wilson. Specifically, she wrote on the complaint,

I have been an officer for 7 months, and in that time I have become very anxious, almost paranoid, about coming into work. It doesn't happen all the time but regularly enough that I never know when something will happen. On a regular basis, at the beginning of my shift as I check my cruiser's glove compartment, I find explicit pornography like magazines opened to gross pages. Other times, when I open my locker I find condoms that have been put in through the slots in the door. Several times there have been sexually graphic cartoons pasted to my locker door. I have talked about this with my supervisor, and he told me to try to ignore it and it will go away when whoever is doing it sees that it doesn't bother me. He explained that police departments for years have been male-dominated organizations, which has resulted in macho behavior. He said it is going to take a while to change the culture and that I should understand. It doesn't seem to be stopping. What should I do?

The IAB-DC form no. 6 was a consolidated complaint coming from three white male patrol officers. The specifics of their complaint were:

We (Michael Davis, Ralph Daly, Tom Nelson) feel that the department has acted in an unfair and biased manner when handing out promotions to sergeant recently. We are three white male patrol officers who recently took the civil service examination for sergeant and did well. We studied hard, and we all have excellent performance records with no complaints in our files. Why did the department promote David Wilson, an African-American patrol officer who scored lower on the examination than we three? We believe that it should have been one of us.

The IAB-DC form no. 7 was the first Linda had seen from an African-American officer, named Frank Peterson. Given the proportionality of African-American officers on the Everly city police department, she found it a bit troublesome that there had been only one complaint. The wording of the complaint soon shed some light on that issue. It was from a sergeant who was being disciplined ostensibly because of his race.

I've been on the job for close to 20 years and have put up with some pretty rough stuff racially, but enough is enough. I am not sure that I should make a complaint at all because, as I see it, the system is white. It really has not changed much from when I first came on the job. Right now, I am in the process of being harassed off the job by a senior officer. He has tried before, but it has not worked. It started when I first became a sergeant (15 years ago). I had just cofounded the Minority Officers Association. He was a lieutenant at the same station as I was at the time and told me one night that I was the "H.N.I.C." and that he did not like "troublemakers." At the time, I invited him to go outside but he declined. Later, I found out that he explained that "H.N.I.C." was an acronym for "Head Nigger in Charge."

The next problem happened about a month later when in the lunchroom one day the phone rang. Lt. Markeson was there when another officer answered it, looked in my direction, and said, "Hey black sambo, you have a call." I literally jumped over the lunch table and grabbed him by the throat. Other officers broke it up, and I ended up in front of the captain with Lt. Markeson charging me with assaulting a fellow officer, and conduct unbecoming an officer. It was a set-up by Markeson, and I should have known it. Luckily, the captain ordered me to apologize to the other officer and Lt. Markeson and said there would be no charges. I begrudgingly apologized to both. One-on-one I told Markeson that it was he who should be apologizing to me. He said he does not apologize to "monkeys or niggers." (This time I figured out he was just trying to bait me to get me to hit him, and I walked away.)

A little later, one night I was covering for the dispatcher when Lt. Markeson left early in his cruiser. About 5 minutes later, he called from his unit and asked that I run a plate. The name looked funny. It was registered to a Joseph Neggers. I called him to tell him I had his plate identification and said I have that plate for you, lieutenant. He replied, "No Dispatch, that is for *you*." I called him a racist asshole over the radio. I was in front of the captain again. This time I received a letter of reprimand.

The incident which I am now up on charges over happened at a retirement party about 3 months ago. I was there with my wife, and we were sitting at our table. Lt. Markeson was sitting at the table near us and shouted to the waiter as he went near our table, "Hey, bring the Petersons some watermelon, will you?" I went over to him and called him a racist son-of-a-bitch. He got in my face and asked, "Do you have the balls to do anything about it *boy*?" I lost it. I punched him and he went down.

I am now on suspension for assaulting a senior officer and conduct unbecoming an officer. My trial board is in about 2 weeks. Can you help me?

Linda wondered what to do with this first group of complaints. A number of decisions had to be made. She had to decide what to do, if indeed the complaints held up after a full investigation.

Discussion Questions

1. What specific action, if any, should Linda recommend for each of the complaints?
2. How should she respond to each of the complaining officers?
3. What organizational changes (procedural, policy, training), if any, should be made to prevent incidents like these from happening again?
4. How would the organizational culture at the Everly police department best be described?

References

Iannone, S. F. *Supervision of Police Personnel.* (5th ed.), Upper Saddle River, N.J.: Prentice Hall Career and Technology, 1998.

Kurkjian, S. "Policing's Nightmare: Minority Officers Face Extra Danger Working Under Cover." *Boston Sunday Globe*, April 2, 2000, pp. 1, 16.

Kramer, M. "Cops Are Too Quick to Use Their Guns." *New York Daily News*, March 19, 2000, p. 47.

Latour, F. "Two Top Officers Face Neglect Charges—But Most Serious Allegations Dropped in Police Case." *Boston Sunday Globe*, May 27, 2000, p. B5.

Shuster, B. "Gender Gap Cited in LAPD Suits." *Boston Globe*, September 18, 2000, p. A4.

Smith, D. *Women at Work, Leadership for the Next Generation.* Upper Saddle River, N.J.: Prentice Hall, 2000.

Field interviews with (majority and minority) state and local law enforcement officers throughout the Commonwealth of Massachusetts

Egidio A. Diodati is an associate professor of management at Assumption College in Worcester, Massachusetts. In addition, professor Diodati provides consulting services to corporations in the areas of network communications, market research, marketing, and management. Prior to teaching, he held management positions with the New England Telephone Company and AT&T. Professor Diodati has lectured and published extensively on the telecommunications industry, economic theory, and diversity topics.

Survival and Change at the San Juan Pueblo Agriculture Cooperative

Terri A. Bitsie
Helen J. Muller
University of New Mexico

> *We have to do prayers . . . to the North, to the West, to the South, to the East and up to the heavens and especially Mother Earth. She's the one that provides these mystical things that are in the Pueblo World . . .*
>
> —PETER GARCIA, TRIBAL ELDER AT SAN JUAN PUEBLO

Several members of the San Juan Pueblo Tribe in northern New Mexico wanted to bring its farmlands back into production to preserve the community's agricultural traditions and to create jobs for tribal members. With an initial loan, they organized a cooperative and cultivated approximately 200 acres of previously idle farmlands for growing a variety of traditional and specialty crops including alfalfa, corn, chile, tomatoes, gourds, and native tobacco. More recently, they packaged and sold native food products under a brand name.

The cooperative struggles to survive and faces two challenges: to endure as a small food-producing business with few resources in a low-margin food products market and to honor the original mission of cultural preservation of agricultural traditions. The board recently embarked upon several organizational strategies to actively involve members and to strengthen management performance. The staff has tried to manage effectively and to generate sales in order to become self-sustaining. Athough members and management remain committed to the original mission, morale suffers from missed targets in production, limited retail distribution, and low volume sales. Board chairman Charlie Marcos ponders about feasible alternatives.

San Juan Pueblo has a rich history of agriculture spanning some 700 years and so sustained itself until World War II. Goods not grown or made on the reservation could be obtained by trading handmade pottery or other arts and crafts. When families needed to purchase store items such as coffee, oil, or fabrics, one family member, working as a domestic or laborer, could make enough money to purchase these supplies. The creation of Los Alamos National Laboratory (LANL) on the nearby "hill" to work on the Manhattan Project brought employment opportunities. Many Pueblo people, particularly women, left their homes to work at LANL. Men also departed from the Pueblo to join the military services. For the first time, San Juan tribal members participated in the mainstream economy.

Over the ensuing decades, traditional farming practices were all but abandoned. Only a few families continued to plant and harvest their lands. As the community became part of the cash economy, tribal members found difficulty returning to traditional farming methods.

Peter Garcia, keeper of the Pueblo's traditional songs and a cooperative officer, recalled some of the changes World War II brought about:

> . . . Los Alamos became a boomtown. There were people that were employed there and they left their lands idle . . . When I left in about 1946 to go to the service, the lands were still plowed, the fields were green in the summertime. And when I came back in 1950, it was kind of a sad situation for me, because, I saw the land idle.

ORGANIZING THE COOPERATIVE

In the late 1970s and in the 1980s, San Juan elders talked about reviving agricultural lands and forming a cooperative to restart production. They lamented how farmlands, once overflowing with bountiful harvests, became idle, and they worried about the water rights that the federal government had secured to them in 1908.

Most important to them was their grandchildren's and great-grandchildren's future. Their hearts ached from knowing that a majority of the pueblo's youth knew little about farming and appeared more interested in mainstream youth culture. Many of San Juan's cultural and religious traditions originated in farming: Stories, songs, dances, and humor tied them to the bounty of the land. If more crops succumbed to lack of production, could the people's culture survive?

In January 1993, the San Juan Agricultural Cooperative officially organized as a nonprofit, nontax-exempt cooperative association that conducted business, initially, as Ohkay T'owa Gardens. Each cooperative member leased his or her respective reservation land assignment to the cooperative in exchange for a $15 per acre annual fee. Most of the 40 members are elderly, and roughly half are widows. Almost all of the elderly members' children and grandchildren did not grow up in the farming tradition, and they lack the skills to plant and harvest; most of the younger tribal members work at wage jobs either on the reservation or in the nearby towns of Espanola and Santa Fe. To address these circumstances, the cooperative organized into (1) a management team—a general manager, a farms manager, and a greenhouse manager to perform day-to-day operations, and (2) a seven-person board of directors—elected from the membership to serve a 2-year term, to provide direction and oversight.

DEVELOPING THE ORGANIZATION

Although the primary purpose for creating the cooperative was to farm the lands, the new board quickly faced a harsh truth. It realized that a return on the harvests had to be made to finance the farm operations and survive. Staff planted hay and alfalfa in the first 2 years. Both crops failed.

Management proposed expanding activities to include food processing. The cooperative embarked upon a new venture in 1995. It created a product line, "Pueblo

Harvest Foods," consisting of processed and packaged farm products to reach a broader market and to create more jobs. At the farm, workers planted vegetable row crops such as green chile, melons, beans and corn, which need a lot of tending. Staff purchased some other ingredients and, these put together, created a line of dehydrated food products that were processed, packaged, and distributed by the cooperative.

Staff expanded the dried-food product line. To sell the dried packaged foods, general manager Lynwood Brown obtained a contract with Wild Oats Market, a natural foods grocery chain headquartered in Colorado. Forty smaller retail specialty shops in the region agreed to carry the product line. A private company, contracted by the cooperative, developed a Web site for online orders (see www.puebloharvest.com). The cooperative, furthermore, exported Pueblo Harvest Foods to a few locations in England and France.

In summer 1996, the business moved into a new, 3,000-square-foot processing facility to handle large production runs. Funds for the $350,000 facility and its equipment came from a combination of federal, tribal, and private sources. Before, a solar greenhouse donated by Sandia National Laboratories had dried harvested vegetables and grown seedlings in the spring.

The focus of the cooperative, by 1999, was the food-processing operation; farming was considerably scaled back. The latter had not generated revenue, even with the addition of vegetable row crops to the traditional crops such as alfalfa, hay, and winter wheat. By now the farm did not supply enough vegetables, so the food-processing operation relied almost exclusively on purchased ingredients. Brown believed that by focusing on food processing in the short run, they would eventually earn enough income to support the farming operation again.

This strategy did not appear to make economic sense. Why build up the food products segments of the business to support the farms? Most people with any kind of business acumen would consider it a money-losing proposition. Brown was aware of the contradiction. He viewed the strategy as the "tail wagging the dog." As he put it, the "balancing act" required the cooperative to "start with the market and work backwards." According to Brown, the board was not concerned with trying to accumulate wealth; it was focused on reviving agriculture. Relying on the food-processing operation to subsidize the farms was a means to this end.

DECISIONS ABOUT PRODUCTION

Brown talked about the compatibility of the cooperative's mission with the realities facing its operations.

> There's a balancing act that goes on . . . holding the two values; one is a
> set of things, you know, around the culture, around preserving the land,
> long-term things, what we are really about . . . one hand. And then . . . the
> requirements of business, on the other hand, has its own demands . . . that
> are very strong. And the market has its particular demands, but it's its
> own task master . . . where you get in real trouble is where you try to
> make the values in your long-term goals completely fit into the require-
> ments of business, because they won't. You'll either . . . end up compro-
> mising the values or going out of business.

Brown felt a responsibility to ensure the cooperative's success, but he was not a member. He had been the tribe's planner for 15 years before he became cooperative general manager. Over the years, he grew to be trusted:

> I'm not a "wanna-be." I never pretended to, never presumed that I could become part of the community. I always viewed myself as a guest in the community, no matter how long I stayed.

The cooperative placed an ad in local newspapers for a manager who would oversee the processing facility's operations. As Marcos told it, although many tribal members needed work, "We had a hard time finding someone with qualified work experience." Jeffrey Atencio, a San Juan tribal member in his mid-30s, applied. Atencio had spent a number of his formative years living as an "urban Indian" in California. After several years in the military where he received extensive computer science training, he returned to his roots in San Juan.

Atencio sees potential for the cooperative to bring pride back to the tribe. He remarked that in most business situations, an individual has to "sacrifice his/her ethnicity in order to get ahead." He said that, at the processing facility, tribal members here had the opportunity to be more than an employee, to buy into the product, the business, the community, and become part of the whole. Atencio has concerns about the operations and its future direction. He hired tribal members on several occasions to work in the processing plant, only to have to let them go:

> Many of the people who come to work tell me, "yes, I want to work, I want to learn," yet they come to work late; they don't stay productive on the job or look for ways to help the company be efficient. Worse yet, some of them have come to work drunk or high. They don't know what it takes to be a good worker.

RENEWAL AND RETRENCHMENT

With the addition of the processing facility, the task began of integrating the new food-processing venture with other activities. Developing the skill level of the board and management to keep pace with the emerging business orientation was an added concern. Few of the board members had management experience. The tribal government also was interested in management training. In the last several years, management of the tribe's various operations shifted from the office of the San Juan Pueblo governor to separate departments and necessitated that each department's staff be ready to administer itself. Although Brown was not referring to Ms. Rio, he recounted observations of how nonnatives present themselves to the Pueblo's Tribal Council when trying to pitch new projects or partnerships:

> I've seen it so many times; somebody comes in with a project, a non-Indian, and they take it to the Council, and they're trying to relate on a conceptual level, and they lay it out and sort of describe it and try to express that they think how this reflects the values of the community, . . . and they're met with blank stares! Or, at least, they don't get a response that they can perceive. . . . They don't understand that their manner, that the

most important thing going on, was all about relationship, not concept . . .
Their manner of forcefully expressing their concept, which is normal behavior in the dominant society, is viewed as rude. It does not engender
trust; it engenders distrust.

The cooperative received a $35,000 grant for management training, and this paid
for two new managers' salaries, tuition, books, and fees to attend the local community
college's associate degree business program. The board believed that the two new managers had the potential to turn around the greenhouse and farms. Members became op-
timistic that the greenhouse and farms would make money. The cooperative even built
a larger greenhouse next to the processing facility. However, in their first year as greenhouse and farms managers, the desired results did not arrive. According to Marcos, the
board believed that their first year as managers was a learning experience that would
carry over to the next year. Alas, the second year resulted in a poor showing as well. Because of the total financial loss for the farms and greenhouse, the board had to lay off
the two recently hired managers. In late 1999, Marcos lamented: "We thought the food
production end of the business would have been stronger by now." Currently, the greenhouse is idle and only a few acres of green chile are growing.

THE FUTURE

Marcos noted that, after 7 years, the cooperative still had not made a profit:

The Coop's marketing activities are not on the volume it needs to be . . .
sales targets haven't been met . . . and the business plan we set for ourselves is not working; I believe it's a matter of implementation. The
Board sets the policy and direction but doesn't manage the business side
or make the decisions.

Marcos offered some alternatives, perhaps some solutions, to "jump start" the
business for the year 2000. He seemed unsure of the new year, saying that it would
"definitely be a rough year." While contemplating about making staff changes, he
suggested that the cooperative members might take on more responsibilities for
running the business. He also considered bringing in an external consultant to make
recommendations.

Brown, on the other hand, did not feel additional training programs or consultants would be necessary. The cooperative had a marketing plan, he noted, but without an infusion of cash, it could not be implemented. Without money, lucrative
grocery contracts to increase product visibility and generate more sales for Pueblo
Harvest Foods could not be obtained. Brown, moreover, dropped to half-time status to pursue his interests with a rural agricultural network. He continued to maintain that he never intended to be a central figure in the cooperative. He had wanted
to help the tribal members organize the cooperative, not manage it indefinitely.

Atencio believed that the cooperative could improve its situation by getting
board members more active in operational affairs, although many board members
lacked business expertise. Atencio was working full-time as the processing manager, and he was working toward certification as a holistic management instructor.

Discussion Questions

1. Distinguish some attributes of the San Juan Pueblo tribal community that are unique to it as a nation and cultural community within the United States.
2. Discuss the purpose of the tribal cooperative and cite the issues that make this intent compatible or incompatible with operating a small business that is able to sustain itself.
3. Analyze the organization's state of affairs—its current state and its future opportunities. What is the role of cultural values in this assessment and how do these influence events and opportunities.
4. Identify some of the critical issues that key decision makers face in sustaining this enterprise and develop alternatives that can be pursued to preserve the cooperative's business.
5. Assume the role of an external organizational consultant who is not a member of the Pueblo. What would be your strategy for interfacing with the tribe and what are some suggestions that you would offer to the cooperative for it to be successful?

References

Ferrell, O. C., and G. Hirt. (2000). *Business: A Changing World.* (3rd ed.). Boston: McGraw-Hill.

Francesco, A. M., and B. A. Gold. (1998). *International Organizational Behavior: Text, Readings, Cases and Skills.* Upper Saddle River, N.J.: Prentice Hall.

Gilbert, R., and H. J. Muller. (2000). "The Business of Culture at Acoma Pueblo." In P. Buller and R. Shuller (eds.). *Management, Organizations, and Human Resources Management.* (7th ed.). Cincinatti, Ohio: Southwestern, pp. 224–234.

Jacobs, S. (1995). "Continuity and Change in Gender Roles at San Juan Pueblo." In Laura F. Klein and Lillian A. Ackerman (eds.). *Women and Power in Native North America.* Norman: University of Oklahoma Press, pp. 177–213.

Muller, H. J. (2000). "A Community Creates a Class on American Indian Business." *Journal of Management Education,* 24(7): pp. 177–206.

Ortiz, A. (1979). "San Juan Pueblo." In A. Ortiz (ed.). *Handbook of North American Indians: The Southwest: Prehistory, History and the Pueblos. 9,* pp. 278–295.

Sando, J. S. (1992). *Pueblo Nations: Eight Centuries of Pueblo Indian History.* Santa Fe, N.M.: Clear Light.

Smith, D. H. (1994). "The Issue of Compatibility Between Cultural Integrity and Economic Development Among Native American Tribes." *American Indian Culture and Research Journal 18* (2).

Tiller, V.E.V. (ed.). (1996). "San Juan Pueblo." In *Tiller's Guide to Indian Country: Economic Profiles of American Indian Reservations.* Albuquerque, N.M.: BowArrow Publishing Company, pp. 457–458.

Terri Bitsie is an MBA candidate at the University of New Mexico's Anderson Schools of Management. She is president of the American Indian Business Association (AIBA) at the Anderson Schools, a student organization that supports native students and native business. She is currently executive director of Teach for

America—New Mexico. She is a member of the Navajo Nation, born for the Red House Clan on her mother's side.

Helen J. Muller is professor of management at the Anderson Schools of Management, University of New Mexico. She is a founding member and faculty advisor for AIBA. With native students, she designed a new course on American Indian business and management. Her research focuses on organizational dynamics in cross-cultural settings.

Jack's Challenge: Sumiko's Dilemma

Nicholas Athanassiou
Northeastern University

Jeanne M. McNett
Assumption College

In his first month as president of a U.S.–Japan joint venture (JV) in the food sector, Jack had restructured the joint venture's management team and terminated the director of finance, Mike Jarone. It hadn't taken him long to realize that Jarone did very little that contributed to the company's success; he had delegated most of his responsibilities to the office secretary, a Japanese woman named Sumiko.

Jack and his wife had had a rough beginning in Tokyo. After 4 weeks, they were ready to pack it in. His wife had expected the local job market to welcome her, as it had in other countries that were tough markets for professional women, such as Saudi Arabia and Algeria. Yet, despite good connections and courtesy interviews with such solid companies in Tokyo as Mitsubishi and Hitachi, she had received no offers. Everything was polite, but every discussion seemed to dissolve into social pleasantries and lead nowhere.

In these first 4 weeks, Jack had found himself unable to get Sumiko to complete a single assignment. She was polite, but she stonewalled every request. Jack was unused to this sort of behavior from a subordinate, and he was puzzled. He knew that harmony was important to many Japanese, and that taking time to plan and work out implementation strategies was important to his colleagues there, but he also wanted to get his office up and running to meet the challenges he had set with corporate headquarters for the joint venture. If he needed to find a new secretary, he wanted to do so quickly. He decided to ask for advice from the most senior Japanese manager in the company. Shin Tomoda, the JV's director of sales, advised Jack to wait it out. He predicted that as soon as Jarone left, Sumiko would devote her energies to Jack's assignments, and they would be completed within the deadlines. Jack also learned from Shin that Sumiko was supervising Jarone's move from Japan to Seattle and tying up his and his wife's business and personal affairs in Tokyo—closing their bank accounts, negotiating the termination of their apartment lease, making arrangements to have the apartment professionally cleaned and even supervising the cleaning, arranging to have their personal and family goods packed, getting his cats transported to the United States, closing his business and social club memberships, and other tasks connected to winding down a foreign assignment, packing out, and reestablishing in Seattle. Jack could barely contain his annoyance. After all, he had fired Jarone, and here Jarone was monopolizing secretarial time. In the states, Jarone would have cleaned out his office the very morning he learned of his termination and would have been escorted out by security. Any other matters would have been handled through the outplacement firm or the legal department. But Jack knew this was Japan, not California.

When he got back to his office, he called Sumiko in and asked her why she continued working for Jarone. Sumiko seemed surprised by the question and began to explain deferentially that after 6 years, she felt an obligation to help Jarone in these last steps. Instinctively, Jack decided not to push this issue. He asked her to delegate where she thought she could and to finish up as soon as possible. He also asked her to give him a copy of her résumé from the files along with her job description and performance evaluations. Jack explained that he wanted to review how they structured their work together. Jack learned that there were no such files and that she had never received a job performance evaluation. Surprised, Jack requested that she outline her job description and submit it to him along with a draft resume so he could gain a sense of her professional background and experience. With so much to do, wasted talent was something Jack wanted to avoid.

This assignment was on his desk the next morning. From the résumé he learned that Sumiko had graduated *cum laude* from Aoyama University, a prestigious women's college in Japan, and then received a master's in accountancy at San Diego State University in California. The job description that Sumiko drafted indicated that she completed many of the responsibilities usually allocated to finance directors. Plus, she sat for and passed the California CPA exam on her first try. Why, with such education and skills, Jack wondered, was she working in a clerical position?

The next time he talked with human resources back in the United States, Jack discussed this situation with the empty position in finance and commented on Sumiko's background. The HR representative who supported Jack, Annette Pang, had not known anything about Sumiko's background or about her actual work because Sumiko was paid through the JV company in Tokyo. Annette reminded Jack of the U.S. partner's commitment to workplace equity and nondescrimination. In addition to following Equal Employment Opportunity (EEOC) legislation, the American company was committed to keeping its best-practices reputation in the areas of support for women and minorities who chose to develop their careers with the company. Jack believed strongly in these values at a personal as well as a professional level. In this same conversation, Jack also learned that U.S. labor standards and requirements would apply to Americans employed by American companies overseas but not to local nationals. The JV company was incorporated in Japan and fell under Japanese labor law and practices.

Jack was a reasonable, logical person. He thought that Sumiko had shown that she could do the job by having done it. What better indication could one have? To him there seemed little risk in doing the right thing. He needed someone to take on the finance director responsibilities, and Sumiko already knew how to get things done and knew the major players.

What had puzzled Jack, though, was that Sumiko, who had essentially run the director's office, had not had a single performance review and was paid, as were the other women in the company, far below the value of her contribution. For example, the average male salary in the Tokyo company was in the range of US $45,600. Drinks and dinners were covered when work required late nights. Jack knew that many of the company men worked late three and four nights a week. Sumiko's salary was $28,300. Jack knew that such a situation would not be acceptable in the United States and certainly not acceptable to the parent company. He wondered how his Japanese partners could tolerate such inequities.

By the end of the day, Jack had talked with his general affairs director, who was responsibility for human resources. He told Mr. Tanaka that he wanted to place Sumiko into the position formerly held by Mike Jarone, at a comparable salary, based on the going rates in the local market. Mr. Tanaka acted dumbfounded. "But we have never promoted a woman to this kind of position. How can a woman be paid so much more than every other woman in the company? What will the Japanese partner company think? How can she be paid more than so many men?" Tanaka's other concern was that promoting Sumiko would isolate her in the organization. She would lose her place in the women's group and not find a place with her new male peers. After a few drinks with Jack at a nearby saki bar that evening, Tanaka mentioned quite out of the blue that if Sumiko took this man's position, she would certainly never marry. Jack thought Tanaka had had one too many drinks and laughed off his comment. Sumiko was young, attractive, and capable of taking care of her own private life.

SUMIKO'S DILEMMA

Sumiko Watanabe thoughtfully sipped her afternoon tea in her Tokyo office and thought about retiring. Retiring? Well, that was the obvious choice, wasn't it? Jack Abelman, who had supported her career development, her growth from an office lady to director of finance for the joint venture company (JV), the American expatriate who had headed the JV for the last 6 years, had just received his next assignment. In 3 weeks, Jack and his family were moving to Brazil, without even a stop in the States. The JV plan, which she learned of that afternoon, was to give leadership to the Japanese side of the JV, to Shin Tomoda, a man for whom Sumiko had little respect. Mark Anderson, another American, would be joining the JV team in Tokyo as director of strategic planning. Sumiko knew that his background was in finance and wondered whether she had the energy to train still another American so that both he and she could be effective in the Japanese environment. Besides, it was not at all clear to Sumiko that she would be reporting to Mark Anderson. Also, Anderson would not know her abilities and would report to a Japanese president. That might be good for the company, but for her she wondered about the impact.

What most concerned Sumiko was that Jack's departure would leave her, the only woman employed at a professional level in the company and the Japanese partner company, without support. Her mentor was leaving. Here she was, almost 38, unmarried, and a career woman. She worked for over 15 years with this major Mitsubishi–U.S. foods company joint venture, starting out as did all women, in a clerical position. Despite her undergraduate degree from Aoyama University in Tokyo, where she studied government and law, and her master's degree from San

Diego State in accounting, where she built her English proficiency and where she became a CPA, she, too, began by making copies, running errands for her male colleagues—to the bank, the dry cleaners, and the drug store—and bringing tea to them and their guests whenever requested.

Those tea lady days didn't bother her too much, now that she was far away from them. In fact, she realized that she had made great friends during those years. She became a part of the women's workforce, a networked collection of clerical assistants who shared their office intelligence to figure out what was really going on in the company. Often far in advance, she knew about budget issues, bonus distributions, and even the extramarital love lives of the top management team members. She had met Marieko, her best friend, while they delivered tea to their male colleagues around the office.

Marieko's life had followed a quite different path. When she was 23, Marieko had accepted the company's offer of marriage introductions to eligible and suitable young company men. She chose and married a man to whom she thought she could grow close, a man with whom she thought she could build a solid partnership. She left the company, had children during her first and third years of marriage, and stayed home with her firstborn son and then her daughter, as do most Japanese women. Her choice was good for her, too, Sumiko realized. Sumiko, though, had politely evaded the company's first offer for such introductions when she was 24 and unmarried and directly declined the second, which came when she was 26. She and Marieko kept up through visits after work, phone calls, and e-mail. They would meet for dinner, and sometimes Sumiko would stop by Marieko's house, which was only 15 minutes from Shinjuku station, the major transfer station on the west side of Tokyo through which Sumiko passed twice a day on her 2-hour commute. Marieko's husband was out most nights until 11 P.M. and Marieko welcomed the company. Their friendship had grown over the years as they compared their points of view and discussed their different situations. Sumiko valued Marieko's perspective, especially on issues related to the office. Often, Marieko would help Sumiko see a whole new way of dealing with a situation in which Sumiko had thought she had no alternatives. Especially after she began her work as director of finance, Sumiko counted on Marieko's intelligence reports on what was really going on in the company. Marieko kept in touch with the office girls, who, once she left the clerical pool, treated Sumiko with respect but no longer included her in their intelligence network.

Sumiko knew that at some time in his career, Jack would "move on," as they say in the American headquarters. It was a strange concept to Sumiko. The JV was working well and had tremendous untapped growth potential. Just when everything was poised for brilliant success, the Americans want to change. The individual's career development seemed to be more important than the success of the company, she reflected.

Sumiko recalled that Jack's first action in Tokyo was to reorganize the office and terminate the previous director of finance, Mike Jarone. She had been angry about this—it was no way to treat an employee. Mike had been her boss; her loyalty was to the position and the company. When Jack had arrived, he began discussions with her about how to reorganize the workflow, what her qualifications were, and what her educational background was. Sumiko was surprised that Jack wanted to talk with her about work allocation. In the process of these discussions, they both came to realize that she had been doing much of Mike's work, with no recognition— Mike had taken full credit himself. That didn't bother her. She enjoyed the challenge and the opportunity to put her skills and training to work to help build the company's success.

Jarone had been an unusual expatriate. He spoke Japanese well for a foreigner, was married to a British woman, and seemed to enjoy his time in Tokyo. He also interacted with her the way he thought a Japanese boss would, which was a little strange (*skoshi hen des*); but his efforts kept the office banter somewhat amusing. His Japanese didn't always get the gender and status markers exactly right, the way a native Japanese male's would, but she knew he tried. At the same time, Sumiko knew that Mike's attempts to be like a Japanese male limited the role she could have in the company, which was the very reason she had chosen an American JV over a totally Japanese company in the first place. Yet she admired Jarone's attempts to try to fit in, even when he was sure to fail.

Sumiko remembered that during the first month Jack was on the job, when Jack had called her in to discuss the office workflow, he was clearly annoyed that she was helping Mike wind up. He told her that it was her choice, that he could get another secretary, but that clearly she had been doing most of Mike's technical analysis work without getting any credit or compensation. Sumiko felt exceedingly uncomfortable at this brazen, frank discussion. It was as if he literally slapped her with facts. She didn't want credit and thought Jack too bold, but she did think about the compensation aspects. Mike's annual salary was in the range of $150,000, while hers was around the U.S. dollar equivalent of $28,300. After she talked this issue over with Marieko, she realized that Jack had accurately described the situation. That week she began to seek out ways to contribute to Jack's goals.

When Jack saw what she could do, he promoted her out of a clerical function and into management (see Figure 4-1). The Japanese side of the JV protested, because women did not assume these roles in traditional Japanese companies, but Jack stuck

FIGURE 4-1 JV Organization

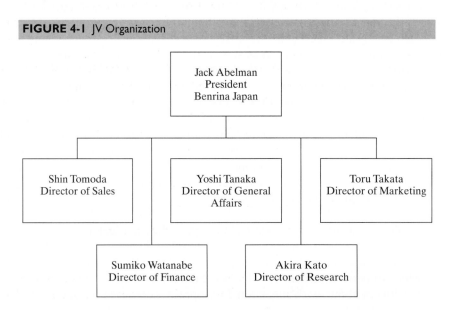

The Cracker Barrel Restaurants

John Howard
University of York, United Kingdom

Discrimination against lesbians and gays is common in the workplace. Sole proprietors, managing partners, and corporate personnel officers can and often do make hiring, promoting, and firing decisions based on an individual's real or perceived sexual orientation. Lesbian and gay job applicants are turned down, and lesbian and gay employees are passed over for promotion or even fired by employers who view homosexuality as somehow detrimental to job performance or harmful to the company's public profile. Such discrimination frequently results from the personal biases of individual decision makers. It is rarely written into company policy and thus is difficult to trace. However, in January 1991, Cracker Barrel Old Country Store, Inc., a chain of family restaurants, became the first and only major American corporation in recent memory to expressly prohibit the employment of lesbians and gays in its operating units. A nationally publicized boycott followed, with demonstrations in dozens of cities and towns.

THE COMPANY: A BRIEF HISTORY OF CRACKER BARREL

Cracker Barrel was founded in 1969 by Dan Evins in his hometown of Lebanon, Tennessee, 40 miles east of Nashville. Evins, a 34-year-old ex-Marine sergeant and oil jobber, decided to take advantage of the traffic on the nearby interstate highway and open a gas station with a restaurant and gift shop. Specializing in down-home cooking at low prices, the restaurant was immediately profitable.

Evins began building Cracker Barrel stores throughout the region, gradually phasing out gasoline sales. By 1974, he owned a dozen restaurants. Within 5 years of going public in 1981, Cracker Barrel doubled its number of stores and quadrupled its revenues: In 1986, there were 47 Cracker Barrel restaurants with net sales of $81 million. Continuing to expand aggressively, the chain again grew to twice its size and nearly quadrupled its revenues during the next 5 years.

By the end of the fiscal year, August 2, 1991, Cracker Barrel operated over 100 stores, almost all located along the interstate highways of the Southeast and, increasingly, the Midwest. Revenues exceeded $300 million. Employing roughly 10,000 nonunionized workers, Cracker Barrel ranked well behind such mammoth family chains as Denny's and Big Boy in total sales, but led all U.S. family chains in sales per operating unit for both 1990 and 1991.

As of 1991, Cracker Barrel was a well-recognized corporate success story, known for its effective, centralized, but authoritarian leadership. From its headquarters,

Cracker Barrel maintained uniformity in its store designs, menu offerings, and operating procedures. Travelers and local customers dining at any Cracker Barrel restaurant knew to expect a spacious, homey atmosphere; an inexpensive, country-style meal; and a friendly, efficient staff. All were guaranteed by Dan Evins, who remained as president, chief executive officer, and chairman of the board.

THE POLICY: NO LESBIAN OR GAY EMPLOYEES

In early January 1991, managers in the roughly 100 Cracker Barrel operating units received a communique from the home office in Lebanon. The personnel policy memorandum from William Bridges, vice president of human resources, declared that Cracker Barrel was "founded upon a concept of traditional American values." As such, it was deemed "inconsistent with our concept and values and . . . with those of our customer base, to continue to employ individuals . . . whose sexual preferences fail to demonstrate normal heterosexual values, which have been the foundation of families in our society."

Throughout the chain, individual store managers, acting on orders of corporate officials, began conducting brief, one-on-one interviews with their employees to see if any were in violation of the new policy. Cheryl Summerville, a cook in the Douglasville, Georgia, store for 3½ years, asked if she were a lesbian, knew she had to answer truthfully. She felt she owed that to her partner of 10 years. Despite a history of consistently high performance evaluations, Summerville was fired on the spot, without warning and without severance pay. Her official separation notice, filled out by the manager and filed with the state department of labor, clearly indicated the reason for her dismissal: "This employee is being terminated due to violation of company policy. The employee is gay." Cracker Barrel fired as many as 16 other employees across several states in the following months. These workers, mostly waiters, were left without any legal recourse. Lesbian and gay antidiscrimination statutes were in effect in Massachusetts and Wisconsin and in roughly 80 U.S. cities and counties, but none of the firings occurred in those jurisdictions. Federal civil rights laws, the employees learned, did not cover discrimination based upon sexual orientation.

Under pressure from a variety of groups, the company issued a statement in late February 1991. In it, Cracker Barrel management said, "We have revisited our thinking on the subject and feel it only makes good business sense to continue to employ those folks who will provide the quality service our customers have come to expect." The recent personnel policy had been a "well-intentioned overreaction." Cracker Barrel pledged to deal with any future disruptions in its units "on a store-by-store basis." Activists charged that the statement did not represent a retraction of the policy, as some company officials claimed. None of the fired employees had been rehired, activists noted, and none had been offered severance pay. Moreover, on February 27, just days after the statement, Dan Evins reiterated the company's antagonism toward nonheterosexual employees in a rare interview with a Nashville newspaper. Lesbians and gays, he said, would not be employed in more rural Cracker Barrel locations if their presence was viewed to cause problems in those communities.

THE BOYCOTT: QUEER NATIONALS VERSUS GOOD OL' BOYS

The next day, when news of Cracker Barrel employment policies appeared in the *The Wall Street Journal, New York Times,* and *Los Angeles Times,* investment analysts expressed surprise. "I look on [Cracker Barrel executives] as pretty prudent businesspeople," said one market watcher. "These guys are not fire-breathing good ol' boys." Unconvinced, lesbian and gay activists called for a nationwide boycott of Cracker Barrel restaurants and began a series of demonstrations that attracted extensive media coverage.

The protest movement was coordinated by the Atlanta chapter of Queer Nation, which Cheryl Summerville joined as cochair with fellow cochair Lynn Cothren, an official with the Martin Luther King, Jr., Center for Non-Violent Social Change in Atlanta. Committed to nonviolent civil disobedience, lesbian and gay activists and supporters staged pickets and sit-ins at various Cracker Barrel locations, often occupying an entire restaurant during peak lunch hours, ordering only coffee.

Protesters were further angered and spurred on by news in June from Mobile, Alabama. A 16-year-old Cracker Barrel employee had been fired for effeminate mannerisms and subsequently was thrown out of his home by his father. Demonstrations continued throughout the summer of 1991, spreading from the Southeast to the Midwest stores. Arrests were made at demonstrations in the Detroit area; Cothren and Summerville were among several people arrested for criminal trespass at both the Lithonia and Union City, Georgia, stores. Reporters and politicians dubbed Summerville the "Rosa Parks of the movement," after the woman whose arrest sparked the Montgomery, Alabama, Bus Boycott of 1955–1956.

Support for the Cracker Barrel boycott grew, as organizers further charged the company with racism and sexism. Restaurant gift shops, they pointed out, sold Confederate flags, black mammy dolls, and other offensive items. The Cracker Barrel board of directors, they said, was indeed a good ol' boy network, made up exclusively of middle-aged and older white men. In addition, there was only one female in the ranks of upper management.

THE RESOLUTION: NEW YORK ATTEMPTS TO FORCE CHANGE

Meanwhile, New York City comptroller, Elizabeth Holtzman, and finance commissioner, Carol O'Cleiracain, at the urging of the National Gay and Lesbian Task Force, wrote a letter to Dan Evins, dated March 12, 1991. As trustees of various city pension funds, which owned about $3 million in Cracker Barrel stock, they were "concerned about the potential negative impact on the company's sales and earnings, which could result from adverse public reaction." They asked for a "clear statement" of the company's policy regarding employment and sexual orientation, as well as a description of "what remedial steps, if any, [had] been taken by the company respecting the employees dismissed."

Evins replied in a letter of March 19 that the policy had been rescinded and that there had been "no negative impact on the company's sales." Unsatisfied, the city of New York officials wrote back, again inquiring as to the status of the fired workers.

They also asked that the company put forth a policy that "would provide unequivocally" that discrimination based on sexual orientation was prohibited. Evins never responded.

Shortly thereafter, Queer Nation launched a "buy one" campaign. Hoping to gain additional leverage in company decision making, activists became stockholders by purchasing single shares of Cracker Barrel common stock. At the least, they reasoned, the company would suffer from the relative expense of mailing and processing numerous one-cent quarterly dividend checks. More importantly, they could attend the annual stockholders meeting in Lebanon, Tennessee.

In November 1991, company officials successfully prevented the new shareholders from participating in the annual meeting, and they used a court injunction to block protests at the corporate complex. Nonetheless, demonstrators lined the street, while inside, a representative of the New York City comptroller's office announced the submission of a resolution "banning employment discrimination against gay and lesbian men and women," to be voted on at the next year's meeting. The resolution was endorsed by the Philadelphia Municipal Retirement System, another major stockholder. Cracker Barrel refused any further public comment on the issue.

THE EFFECT: NO DECLINE IN CORPORATE GROWTH

The impact of the boycott on the corporate bottom line was negligible. Trade magazines reiterated the company's claim that neither sales nor stock price had been negatively affected. Indeed, net sales remained strong, up 33 percent at fiscal year-end 1992 to $400 million, owing in good part to continued expansion: There were now 127 restaurants in the chain. Though the increase in same-store sales was not as great as the previous year, Cracker Barrel at least could boast growth, while other chains blamed flat sales on the recession. Cracker Barrel stock, trading on the NASDAQ exchange, appreciated 18 percent during the first month after news of the scandal broke, and the stock remained strong throughout the next fiscal year, splitting three-for-two in the third quarter.

Dan Evins had good reason to believe that the firings and the boycott had not adversely impacted profitability. One market analyst said that "the feedback they get from their customers might be in favor of not hiring homosexuals." Another even ventured that "it's plausible . . . the majority of Cracker Barrel's local users support an explicit discriminatory policy." Such speculation was bolstered by social science surveys indicating that respondents from the South and from rural areas in particular tended to be less tolerant of homosexuality than were other Americans.

Queer Nationals looked to other measures of success, claiming at least partial victory in the battle. Many customers they met at picket lines and inside restaurants vowed to eat elsewhere. Coalitions were formed with a variety of civil rights, women's, labor, and peace and justice organizations. Most importantly, the media attention greatly heightened national awareness of the lack of protections for lesbians and gays on the job. As the boycott continued, increasing numbers of states, counties, and municipalities passed legislation designed to prevent employment discrimination based on sexual orientation.

THE OUTCOME: STAND-OFF CONTINUES

As the November 1992 annual meeting approached, Cracker Barrel requested that the Securities and Exchange Commission make a ruling on the resolution offered by the New York pension fund administrators. The resolution, according to Cracker Barrel, amounted to shareholder intrusion into the company's ordinary business operations. As such, it should be excluded from consideration at the annual meeting and excluded from proxy ballots sent out before the meeting. The SEC agreed, despite previous rulings in which it had allowed stockholder resolutions regarding race or gender based employment bias.

Acknowledging that frivolous stockholder inquiries had to be curtailed, the dissenting SEC commissioner nonetheless expressed great dismay: "To claim that the shareholders, as owners of the corporation, do not have a legitimate interest in management-sanctioned discrimination against employees defies logic." A noted legal scholar warned of the dangerous precedent that had been set: "Ruling an entire area of corporate activity (here, employee relations) off limits to moral debate effectively disenfranchises shareholders."

Thus, the stand-off continued. Queer Nation and its supporters persisted in the boycott. The Cracker Barrel board of directors and, with one exception, upper management remained all-white, all-male bastions. Lynn Cothren, Cheryl Summerville, and the other protestors arrested in Lithonia, Georgia, were acquitted on charges of criminal trespass. Jurors ruled that the protestors' legitimate reasons for peaceably demonstrating superseded the company's rights to deny access or refuse service. Charges stemming from the Union City, Georgia, demonstrations were subsequently dropped. Meanwhile, within weeks of the original policy against lesbian and gay employees, Cracker Barrel vice president for human resources William Bridges had left the company. Cracker Barrel declined comment on the reasons for his departure.

By 1996, Cracker Barrel annual net sales reached a billion dollars. The company still had not issued a complete retraction of its employment policy, and those employees fired were never offered their old jobs back. In contrast, for a year's work, chairman Dan Evins pulled in over a million dollars in salary, bonus, awards, and stock options; president Ronald Magruder, over four million.

As of Cracker Barrel's fiscal year-end, July 30, 1999, a total of 11 states and the District of Columbia offered protections for lesbians and gays on the job, both in the public and private sectors. With a total of 396 restaurants and 58 Logan's Roadhouse affiliates in 36 states, Cracker Barrel now operated in six of those states with protections: California, Connecticut, Massachusetts, Minnesota, New Jersey, and Wisconsin. (The other states with antidiscrimination statutes are Hawaii, Nevada, New Hampshire, Rhode Island, and Vermont.) Moreover, plans for expansion seemed destined to take the company into areas even less receptive to employment discrimination. As one business editor had correctly predicted, "Cracker Barrel isn't going to be in the South and Midwest forever. Eventually they will have to face the issue—like it or not."

THE PROPOSAL: FEDERAL LEGISLATION

In 39 states it is perfectly legal to fire workers because they are gay—or straight. For example, a Florida bar owner recently decided to target a lesbian and gay clientele and so fired the entire heterosexual staff. Queer activists boycotted, and the bar eventually was forced out of business. Still, for the vast majority of Americans, employment discrimination based on sexual orientation remains a constant threat.

The vast majority of Americans, 80 percent, tell pollsters that lesbians and gays should have equal rights in terms of job opportunities. In every region including the South, among both Democrats and Republicans, solid majorities support federal legislation to remedy the situation. Nonetheless, despite several close votes in Congress, the Employment Non-Discrimination Act, or ENDA, has yet to be passed into law.

Although there are no federal laws to prevent discrimination based on sexual orientation, protections do exist for workers on the basis of religion, gender, national origin, age, disability, and race. Citing these civil rights statutes, the NAACP is supporting a group of employees and former employees in a class-action lawsuit against Cracker Barrel. The suit alleges that the company repeatedly discriminated against African-Americans in hiring, promotions, and firing practices. Further, African-American workers are said to have received less pay, to have been given inferior terms and conditions of employment, and to have been subjected to racial epithets and racist jokes, including one told by Dan Evins. As this book goes to press, the case is yet to be decided.

Discussion Questions

1. How could Cracker Barrel's policy statement have been well-intentioned?
2. What benefits did Cracker Barrel achieve by ridding itself of lesbian and gay employees? What were the disadvantages?
3. How should the perceived values of a customer base affect companies' personnel policies? In a large national corporation, should personnel policies be uniform across all operating units or should they be tailored by region according to local mores?

References

Atlanta Journal-Constitution, 6, 11 July 1993; 2, 3 April 1992; 29 March 1992; 4, 18, 20 January 1992; 9 June 1991; 3, 4, 5 March 1991.

Carlino, Bill. "Cracker Barrel Profits Surge Despite Recession." *Nation's Restaurant News*, 16 December 1991, 14.

———. "Cracker Barrel Stocks, Sales Weather Gay-Rights Dispute." *Nation's Restaurant News*, 1 April 1991, 14.

Cheney, Karen. "Old-Fashioned Ideas Fuel Cracker Barrel's Out-of-Sight Sales Growth and Profit Increases." *Restaurants & Institutions*, 22 July 1992, 108.

Cracker Barrel Old Country Store, Inc. *Annual Report*, 1999.

———. *Annual Report,* 1996.

———. Notice of Annual Meeting of Shareholders to Be Held on Tuesday, November 26, 1996; 25 October 1996.

———. *Third Quarter Report,* 30 April 1993.

———. *Second Quarter Report,* 29 January 1993.

———. *First Quarter Report,* 30 October 1992.

———. *Annual Report,* 1992.

———. Securities and Exchange Commission Form 10-K, 1992.

———. *Annual Report,* 1991.

———. Securities and Exchange Commission Form 10-K, 1991.

———. *Annual Report,* 1990.

"Cracker Barrel Hit by Anti-Bias Protests." *Nation's Restaurant News,* 13 April 1992, 2.

"Cracker Barrel Sued for Rampant Racial Discrimination in Employment." NAACP Press Release, 5 October 1999.

"Cracker Barrel's Emphasis on Quality a Hit with Travelers." *Restaurants and Institutions,* 3 April 1991, 24.

Dahir, Mubarak S. "Coming Out at the Barrel." *The Progressive,* June 1992, 14.

"Documented Cases of Job Discrimination Based on Sexual Orientation." Washington, DC: Human Rights Campaign, 1995.

Farkas, David. "Kings of the Road." *Restaurant Hospitality,* August 1991, 118–22.

Galst, Liz. "Southern Activists Rise Up." *The Advocate,* 19 May 1992, 54–57.

Greenberg, David. *The Construction of Homosexuality.* Chicago: University of Chicago Press, 1988.

Gutner, Toddi. "Nostalgia Sells." *Forbes,* 27 April 1993, 102–3.

Harding, Rick. "Nashville NAACP Head Stung by Backlash from Boycott Support." *The Advocate,* 16 July 1991, 27.

———. "Activists Still Press Tennessee Eatery Firm on Anti-Gay Job Bias." *The Advocate,* 9 April 1991, 17.

Hayes, Jack. "Cracker Barrel Protesters Don't Shake Loyal Patrons." *Nation's Restaurant News,* 26 August 1991, 3, 57.

———. "Cracker Barrel Comes Under Fire for Ousting Gays." *Nation's Restaurant News,* 4 March 1991, 1, 79.

"Investors Protest Cracker Barrel Proxy Plan." *Nation's Restaurant News,* 2 November 1992, 14.

Larry King Live. CNN television, aired 2 December 1991.

Oprah Winfrey Show. Syndicated television, aired January 1992.

Queer Nation. Documents on the Cracker Barrel Boycott. N.p., n.d.

"SEC Upholds Proxy Ruling." *Pensions and Investments,* 8 February 1993, 28.

Star, Marlene Givant. "SEC Policy Reversal Riles Activist Groups." *Pensions and Investments,* 26 October 1992, 33.

The (Nashville) *Tennessean,* 27 February 1991.

20/20. ABC television, aired 29 November 1991.

Walkup, Carolyn. "Family Chains Beat Recession Blues with Value, Service." *Nation's Restaurant News,* 5 August 1991, 100, 104.

The Wall Street Journal, 9 March 1993; 2 February 1993; 26 January 1993; 28 February 1991.

Wildmoon, KC. "QN Members Allowed to Attend Cracker Barrel Stockholder's Meeting." *Southern Voice,* 10 December 1992, 3.

———. "Securities and Exchange Commission Side with Cracker Barrel on Employment Discrimination." *Southern Voice,* 22 October 1992, 1.

———. "DeKalb Drops Most Charges Against Queer Nation." *Southern Voice,* 9 July 1992, 3.

John Howard is lecturer in American history and associate faculty in women's studies at the University of York, United Kingdom. A native of Brandon, Mississippi, he is the author of "Men Like That: A Southern Queer History," 1999, University of Chicago Press and the editor of "Carryin' On in the Lesbian and Gay South," 1997, New York University Press.

The Implementation of Diversity Initiatives: Lessons From the (Battle)Field

Jeffrey A. Mello
Towson University

Diversity initiatives that are developed with good intentions can still result in problems for organizations because there are different kinds of diversity and, more importantly, not all forms of diversity are visible. Deciding which groups to include as part of diversity initiatives can be fraught with political, social, and religious controversy.

This problem is illustrated in a recent case that surfaced in higher education. This case clearly demonstrates some of the unanticipated problems that can result from the implementation of well-intended diversity initiatives. The controversies in this case have important implications for all organizations.

NORTHEASTERN UNIVERSITY

Northeastern University is a privately endowed, nonsectarian university located in Boston. In 1994 the university trustees approved a strategic plan designed to raise the quality of academic programs, heighten student selectivity, and allow recruitment of top faculty.

One component of this strategic plan was a provision that called for the recruitment of openly gay and lesbian faculty members. Because the university already had a university policy that prohibits discrimination based on sexual orientation, in accordance with Massachusetts state law, it was not anticipated that this provision would arouse any controversy. The provision specifically stated that:

> While we have made considerable progress recently in hiring and promoting minority faculty, additional efforts—offering incentives, hiring at appropriate rank, recognizing and rewarding unusually burdensome service demands, and providing ongoing mentoring—are still needed. We must also make similar effort to recruit openly gay and lesbian individuals and persons with disabilities. The success of units in diversifying their faculty and staff will be assessed.[1]

The provision immediately drew the ire of one faculty member who argued, in the university newspaper, that "offering incentives and hiring at the appropriate rank" amounted to giving preferential treatment to gays and lesbians. Further, he argued that such special status for these faculty would alienate others from them, accomplishing the exact opposite of the administration's intent to make the university more inclusive. In lieu of this, he proposed a policy of tolerance "with respect to all beliefs and practices that are irrelevant to a person's position as an employee or student."[2]

This position was supported by three arguments. The first was that gays and lesbians, by virtue of having been raised in heterosexual households, have no distinct culture relative to the cultures that define racial and ethnic minorities. Second, any policy that sanctioned and encouraged the employment of openly gay and lesbian faculty would likely cause individuals from cultures that discourage same-sex relations to feel uncomfortable and unwelcome on campus. Third, and perhaps most controversial, by recruiting openly gay and lesbian faculty, the university was asserting its own moral stance and that by assessing units based on their activity in this area, the administration was forcing its own moral code or standards on others. It was assumed that this position needed to be adhered to if one was to advance in his/her career at the university.

ISSUES RAISED BY THE NORTHEASTERN CONTROVERSY

Although the controversy at Northeastern ignited from a policy that addresses sexual orientation as a component of diversity, the issues raised by the controversy need to be addressed in any discussion of diversity, above and beyond the issue of inclusion of sexual orientation. The first argument presented in opposition to the policy was that no distinctive gay and lesbian culture exists. A critical issue that must be addressed here is what constitutes a culture for any group in our society. Moreover, the argument that there is no distinctive culture based on one's sexual orientation assumes that culture and cultural identity are fixed for individuals in our society. We also need to consider whether cultural identity and the behaviors and values that stem from it might be dynamic and evolve where in the course of one's life, affiliation with groups and cultures changes.

The second argument presented against recruiting openly gay and lesbian faculty is that others will be offended by a university policy that conflicts with their own cultural, religious, and/or personal beliefs. This argument assumes, at best, that racial and ethnic identity and sexual orientation are mutually exclusive. At worst, the argument attempts to set racial and ethnic minorities at odds with sexual minorities. It further assumes that all individuals of a certain racial, ethnic, or religious background share common ideologies. Diversity initiatives need to consider that within our society, individuals may fall into several categories of diversity simultaneously and that within a category of diversity, there may be subcategories, such as lesbian African-Americans or disabled Jews, for example.

The third argument objects to the university administration taking a moral stance and for requiring alleged indoctrination to this position as a condition of favorable continued employment. In this context one needs to consider the question of whether same-sex relationships are universally a moral issue. To some individuals, including the faculty member who composed the letter, they clearly are. Yet to many others, same-sex relationships transcend any morality argument and are a civil rights issue. This raises the question as to what constitutes a moral issue and moreover, what morals set the standards for judgment or assessment of morality or immorality. Diversity initiatives in organizations need to realize that not all employees and stakeholders may frame diversity or morality in the same way. The critical lesson here is that there are no universal standards of right or wrong, appropriate or inappropriate, moral or immoral, or ethical or unethical behavior—just personal opinions that are often based on the teachings of one's culture and the opinions of others.

ARMING ONESELF FOR THE DIVERSITY BATTLEFIELD

Diversity initiatives can provide significant benefits for virtually all organizations. When implemented properly, they can further the mission of most educational institutions and enhance learning environments; they allow public institutions to better understand and serve their constituencies; and they allow all organizations, regardless of ownership, industry, size or age, to attract, retain and develop the best qualified, most motivated, productive employees by moving human resource management decisions away from personal factors that have nothing to do with job performance.

Despite the importance for both individuals and organizations of appreciating and understanding diversity, it is important that those responsible for diversity initiatives realize that diversity can result in a good deal of internal conflict, strife, and harm if not managed strategically. As the Northeastern case clearly illustrates, diversity initiatives designed to facilitate more inclusive and better-performing organizations can simultaneously ignite social, political, and/or religious controversy.

Any diversity initiatives that are undertaken, much like any organizational intervention or change, need public support and commitment from the top echelons of the organization in order to be successful. Diversity requires much more than mere lip service; those who initiate discussions of diversity in organizations need to be aware of the many controversies that such discussions can spark and be prepared to manage the dialogue and disparate opinions that will result. Although diversity initiatives continue to be popular in both the public and private sectors, they can be extremely dangerous if implemented in an uninformed manner, passively or as just another management fad. However, if those responsible for diversity understand the varied contexts and controversies associated with diversity, as discovered in the Northeastern case, the organization then is prepared to design and implement diversity programs that will be critical to the organization's ability to succeed and thrive in the global marketplace of the twenty-first century.

Discussion Questions

1. What are some of the different reasons an organization might consider undertaking diversity initiatives?
2. In what way(s) might diversity initiatives hinder or retard any organizational processes such as teamwork and communication? How can diversity initiatives be designed to minimize their costs while maximizing their benefits?
3. Are any special efforts for recruiting certain groups appropriate or desirable? If so, what should these efforts entail and how will perceived inequity be handled?

Is it appropriate to evaluate units on their ability to diversify their employee population and what might the consequences of such actions be institutionally?

4. How might the Northeastern case be handled differently? Whose input might have been sought prior to announcing either initiative?

Notes

1. "The Connected Community: A Strategic Plan for Northeastern's Second Century." Northeastern University Strategic Planning Committee, February 8, 1994.
2. Furth, P. "University Should Tolerate, Not Promote Homosexuality." In *The Northeastern Voice*, 5(8), p. 2.

Jeffrey A. Mello is professor and chair of the Management Department in the School of Business and Economics at Towson University. He previously was a faculty member at George Washington University, the University of California at Berkeley, and Northeastern University, from where he received his Ph.D. He has been a recipient of the David L. Bradford Outstanding Educator Award, presented by the Organizational Behavior Teaching Society, and has received international, national, and institutional awards for his research. He is the author of *Strategic Human Resource Management* (South-Western) and *AIDS and the Law of Workplace Discrimination* (Westview Press) and has published more than 100 book chapters, journal articles, and conference papers in journals such as the *Journal of Business Ethics, International Journal of Public Administration, Business and Society Review, Journal of Employment Discrimination Law, Seton Hall Legislative Journal*, the *Journal of Individual Employment Rights, Public Personnel Management, Labor Law Journal, Employment Relations Today*, and the *Journal of Management Education*. He serves on the editorial review boards of several journals and is an immediate past associate editor of the *Journal of Management Education*. He is a member of the national and regional divisions of the Organizational Behavior Teaching Society, Academy of Legal Studies in Business, Decision Sciences Institute, Society for Human Resource Management, and the Academy of Management.

The Murder of Barry Winchell: The Ultimate Failure of "Don't Ask, Don't Tell"

Lori J. Dawson
Worcester State College

His roommate takes him to a bar to meet a woman who works there. The roommate doesn't really know her, but he thinks she's pretty. Boy meets girl, falls in love, and makes roommate very jealous. Roommate begins to harass him, makes fun of his new girlfriend, and pretends he was never attracted to her. The roommates come to blows, but seem to make an uneasy peace. The two even double date a bit with another woman who works at the bar. This uneasy peace ultimately falls apart, his roommate continues to spread rumors about him around work, and turns almost all his friends and coworkers against him.

An empty keg brings a Fourth of July office party to a close, and everybody heads off to bed. Everybody, that is, except the roommate and a drunken coworker with a chip on his shoulder. These two stay up and talk trash about the guy. It doesn't take long for the roommate to incite his coworker to exact the ultimate revenge. Fueled by alcohol, prejudice, and his own insecurities, the coworker takes a baseball bat and bludgeons the guy to death as he lay sleeping.

The murder leaves many questions unanswered and raises many more. Was the roommate really jealous because the guy took the girl he liked? Or was it that the roommate really liked *him* and couldn't bring himself to admit it? For that matter, was the roommate attracted to the women who worked at the bar or the men who worked at the bar? Was his girlfriend even a girl? She thinks she is, but the fact is she is a man who looks like a woman. How much did this impact his relationship with his coworkers? How much did his employer know about this? The man with the bat murdered him, but who else is responsible? The roommate? The employer? What can be done when prejudice rears its ugly head in the workplace? This may sound like a bad made-for-TV movie, but unfortunately it is the all too real story of the gruesome murder of Pfc. Barry Winchell at Fort Campbell Army base in Kentucky in July 1999.

Barry Winchell had a pretty normal childhood. Barry got along well with his stepfather, Wally Kutelles. He joined the Boy Scouts, played bass guitar, and went to the prom with the girl he one day hoped to marry. He had a learning disability that led him to become frustrated with school and eventually to drop out. He went into the military to prove himself. He worked hard to be the best soldier he could be. His letters home to his parents were filled with newfound pride in his accomplishments. He received several awards and hoped to someday become an Army helicopter pilot. By all accounts, he was a quiet, well-liked guy who, prior to the last 4 months of his life, had only dated women.

In contrast to Winchell's quiet nature, his roommate, Justin Fisher, was a loud, boisterous guy who lived on the edge. Growing up, Fisher had an alcoholic father and an abusive stepfather. He had trouble fitting in as a teenager, skipped from job to job, and fathered a child. He joined the army, in part, to support this child. He had a volatile personality and was described by one psychiatrist as having alcohol problems and questions about his sexuality. He had a fascination with guns and thugs.

The two roommates clashed from the start. Winchell quietly obeyed orders while Fisher was defiant. Winchell smoked. Fisher hated the smell of it. Winchell once told his brother he thought Fisher was a "psychopath" and told his girlfriend in Florida that he hoped to get a new roommate. Fisher boasted of beating his roommate to relieve stress and referred to Winchell as his "bitch." How much actual physical violence took place and how much was Fisher's macho bragging is unknown, but at least two incidents were reported to authorities. One began as an argument about who should clean the room and ended with Fisher whacking Winchell in the head with a metal dustpan. Fisher refused to let Winchell clean the dried blood from the walls, insisting it be left as a reminder of the altercation. During subsequent arguments, with a nod in the direction of the stain, he would tell Winchell he was going to beat him like he did before.

On another occasion, the two were part of a group of soldiers, including Lewis Ruiz, their squad leader, who went out for a night of bar-hopping in Nashville. As they were leaving, Fisher had several beers with him that he intended to drink in the car on the way home. Ruiz told Fisher he couldn't drink in the car, and Fisher began flinging beer bottles and threatening Ruiz. Fisher hated smoke, and Ruiz got the others to agree not to smoke in the car if Fisher wouldn't drink. That appeased him, and they began to drive back to the base. Winchell decided that because it was his car, he could smoke if he wanted to. When he lit a cigarette, Fisher flew into a rage and began to choke Winchell. The others in the car managed to pull him off and hold him down until he passed out.

On another foray into Nashville, Fisher introduced Winchell to the person who would become his partner, Calpernia Addams. Fisher saw Addams at The Connection, a predominately gay club in Nashville, where Addams worked as a female impersonator. Addams' full, voluptuous lips, impeccable makeup, beautiful green eyes, and long, flowing hair presented a striking figure. Barry and Calpernia hit it off right from the start and began dating shortly thereafter.

At Fort Campbell, Kentucky, the vast majority of soldiers are not conversant in gender politics. The terms *transgendered* and *preoperative transsexual* meant little. Calpernia Addams considers herself a woman, looks like a woman, lives as a woman, and has taken female hormones for several years, but Addams has yet to undergo surgery that would complete her transformation. Barry accepted Calpernia unconditionally. She described their relationship as heterosexual, but he came to see himself as gay for loving her. Addams said Winchell had never been in a relationship with a man, but had questioned his attraction to men in the past.

Fisher, in turn, made what some might consider a confession by proxy. He told Staff Sgts. Michael Kleifgen and Eric Dubielak that he had seen a fellow soldier having sex with another man at a gay bar in Nashville. Through a process of elimination, and in clear violation of the military's "Don't Ask, Don't Tell" policy, Winchell was called in and asked about his orientation. At first, the questioning was veiled, but it turned quite direct with Kleifgen asking Winchell, "Are you gay?" The only way for a gay soldier to stay in the military when those in charge violate the Don't Ask, Don't Tell policy is to violate another: the honor code that prevents a soldier from lying. Winchell answered, "No." For whatever reason or reasons, Fisher did not stop with a report to the sergeants. He spread rumors around base that Winchell was gay. In the 4 months that followed, Winchell was harassed on a daily basis.

Staff Sgt. Kleifgen would later testify, "Pretty much everybody in the company called him derogatory names like 'faggot.'" The situation got so bad that even Kleifgen, who originally thought everyone was "just having fun," tried to get the harassment to stop. He tried to support Winchell, even going so far as to file a complaint against his superior. When nothing was done, he went even higher. Nothing was done about the second complaint, either, despite the fact that this kind of harassment is a clear violation of the army's Code of Conduct that requires soldiers to treat each other with mutual respect.

Those in charge failed to enforce underage drinking prohibitions. Calvin Glover, Winchell's murderer, reportedly had a serious drinking problem. On the night of July 3, 1999, he was drinking beer and telling outrageous stories of drug binges and crime sprees. Among the other soldiers hanging out drinking that night were Justin Fisher and Barry Winchell. Glover pounced on Winchell, who told him he didn't want to fight. Glover persisted, and Winchell knocked him to the ground with a few blows. Winchell, upset from having to come to blows, tried to patch things up with Glover. Winchell tried to offer Glover a drink and shake his hand, saying "It's cool, right?" Glover replied "It's not cool. I could f***ing kill you."

The next day was Independence Day. The soldiers at Fort Campbell were having an all-day party. For the most part, Glover and Winchell kept their distance, but things seemed better later in the evening. As the keg dried up and people headed off to bed, Winchell moved his cot into the hallway to take care of the company mascot, a dog named Nasty. As Winchell lay sleeping in the hall, Glover and Fisher were in his room. Glover went into the hall and repeatedly bashed Winchell's skull with the bat. He returned to the room and handed the bloody bat to Fisher, who washed the blood off it. According to one report, they schemed to dump the body before someone saw it, but Nasty started barking. Fisher went out into the hall and started crying for help as Glover, carrying his bloodied clothes, ran toward the dumpster. As the ambulance carrying Winchell's battered body drove away, Fisher yelled at the driver, "Let him die! Let him die!" (Hackett, 2000; Miller, 2000; Thompson, 1999). Barry never regained consciousness and died later that day.

The chief prosecutor, Captain Greg Engler, hoped for a plea bargain. In exchange for testifying against Glover, Fisher would face charges on three counts of making false statements to investigators, two counts of obstructing an investigation, and one count of supplying alcohol to a minor (Planetout, 2000). Fisher would not be charged with premeditated murder, nor would he be charged as being an accessory after the fact. The maximum sentence for these charges totaled 12½ years. He would be eligible for parole in 4 years.

The Kutelles and most others outside the military believed that there was more than enough evidence to convict both men, but both men didn't serve as driver for the company's commander, affording him the opportunity to hear all sorts of information; only Fisher did. Both men didn't threaten to take others down with him with testimony that would put those higher in command in a disreputable light; only Fisher did. Glover was sentenced to life; Fisher, to 12½ years. Mrs. Kutelles and the Service Members Legal Defense Fund (SLDN), a Don't Ask, Don't Tell watchdog organization, both proclaimed the sentence a "travesty." The SLDN called for the resignation of Major General Robert Clark, commander of Fort Campbell. In the year that followed, an internal investigation found "no homophobia" at Fort Campbell. This is surprising, given the following facts:

- 120 gay service members were discharged from Ft. Campbell that year, compared to 6 the previous year.
- Anti-gay graffiti was found in several bathrooms, including a 2-foot-long drawing of a baseball bat with the words "fag whacker" written on it.
- An anti-gay chant was repeated while running at Ft. Campbell. The chant says, "faggot, faggot, down the street. Shot him, shot him, till he retreats."
- The Pentagon's own study found that 80 percent of those surveyed had heard anti-gay remarks and that 85 percent believed these comments were tolerated in their units. (Miller, 2000).

Twenty-seven members of Congress wrote General Clark asking for some elaboration and explanation. General Clark did not respond. He was transferred to a more prestigious position at the Pentagon.

The military is making progress, however. As Glover's trial was beginning in December 1999, the Pentagon ordered all military personnel to be retrained on the Don't Ask, Don't Tell policy. Commanders of military bases were to tell those in their command of this requirement. This is what one commander, Marine Lt. Col. Edward Melton at Twentynine Palms in California, e-mailed his soldiers, telling them of the training:

> Due to the "hate crime" death of a homo in the Army, we now have to take extra steps to ensure the safety of the queer who has told (not kept his part of the Don't Ask, Don't Tell policy). Commanders now bear responsibility if someone decides to assault the young backside ranger. Be discreet and careful in your dealing with these characters. And remember, little ears are everywhere. (Miller, 2000).

The training alone might not suffice. Winchell's mother offered a different solution in a statement she read at Glover's court martial:

> This has been a horrifying experience for our family. Words cannot begin to describe our pain over losing our son. We knew Barry could be de-

ployed and come into harm's way for our country. We never dreamed
that he would be killed by labeling, prejudice, and hatred at home. "Don't
Ask, Don't Tell, Don't Pursue" did not protect our son . . . It won't protect anyone else's child. This policy must end (Planetout, 1999).

Discussion Questions

1. What responsibilities do employers have in protecting their employees from harassment?
2. In what ways is the military policy toward homosexuals similar to its policies of racial segregation of the past?
3. In what ways does the current policy differ from racial segregation policy?
4. How did the military violate the "Don't Ask, Don't Tell" policy in the case of Pfc. Winchell?
5. Should employers have the right to regulate the behaviors of their employees when they are not at work? Why or why not?

References

Hackett, T. (2000, March). "The Execution of Private Barry Winchell." *Rolling Stone*, 80.

Miller, J. (2000, December 14). "No Fortunate Son." *Pitch Weekly*, 1.

Planetout (2000, January 10). "Second Gay-Bashing Soldier Pleads." Available: wscww.gay military.org/campbell4.htm

Planetout (1999, December 9). "Parole Possible for Military Basher." Available: http://www.gay military.org/camp bell3.htm.

Thompson, M. (1999, December 13). "Why Do People Have to Push Me Like That?" *Time*, 154.

Dilemmas at Valley Tech

Dr. John E. Oliver
Dr. Sarah Ann Bartholomew
Valdosta State University

Dean Harold Warren sat in his office looking at his computer screen, which displayed the Department of Justice Americans with Disabilities Act (ADA) homepage. Dean Warren was wrestling with a real problem. "Does Dr. Johnson's abusive behavior result from a mental disorder that may make him eligible for protection under the ADA, or should I just deal with the abuse and sexual harassment complaints against him without regard to any mental disorder?"

That very morning, Dean Warren had received two complaints. The manager of an electronics store in the local mall had called to tell Dean Warren that Dr. Johnson had actually struck a female employee in the store. The second complaint was from a Valley Tech secretary, who said she had been sexually harassed by Dr. Johnson on a number of occasions.

DEAN HAROLD WARREN

Harold Warren obtained bachelor of science and master of science degrees from Ivy League colleges in New England and worked in industry for several years before attending one of the nation's finest engineering schools to pursue a doctorate. Upon completion of his Ph.D., he taught at a prestigious private university before taking the position of dean of faculties at Valley Tech, where he's been dean for over 10 years.

Dean Warren is known as a confident, incisive decision maker who studied issues thoroughly and solicited the participation of others before making decisions. Once he has heard the opinions of all concerned and makes his decision, he rarely changes his mind. Dean Warren is a goal-oriented leader, and most decisions lead toward the achievement of some objective. He has little patience for side issues that do not lead toward goal accomplishment. In the university culture, in which change comes slowly if ever, Dean Warren is known as an administrator who encourages change. His drive toward improvement sometimes leads those who are slow to adjust to feel stressed and pressured. Those resisting change are usually ignored; those who embraced change are rewarded for their efforts.

DR. RICHARD JOHNSON

Dr. Johnson is a tenured professor who has been at Valley Tech for over 20 years. He was hired during the late 1970s when Ph.D.s in his field were hard to find. Shortly after his arrival, complaints started coming in. It is said that Dr. Johnson is harsh and abusive to students, calling them lazy and stupid and refusing to answer "dumb" questions. Students often avoid his classes. Two foreign students awakened the college president one evening to complain that Dr. Johnson had called them "dumb *ucking" Indians. Faculty members complain of being yelled at and called names by Dr. Johnson. Several clients of the college's Research and Development Institute have called the institute director to complain that Dr. Johnson flirts with the female employees and speaks abusively to others. The wife of one faculty member saw Dr. Johnson ejected from a local health club by a sheriff's deputy for harassing a female member. Students who are employed as waiters and waitresses in the community say he is regularly abusive in his treatment of them.

Academic tenure is awarded to faculty members who are evaluated by their peers and supervisors to be competent in three areas—teaching, service, and professional development. Teaching is often measured by student evaluations and other criteria. Service is measured by positions on college committees, service to the profession, and service to the community. Professional development includes publication in professional journals and books as well as other criteria.

Dr. Johnson's teaching evaluations are the lowest in his department, as a result of his treatment of students. His service on college committees is also the lowest because of his abuse of fellow faculty and his sarcasm. Dr. Johnson's publication record, though, is exceptional and contributes to the national reputation and accreditation of the school. He regularly publishes several articles and books with a number of other faculty in the school. He seems to be nice to his coauthors as long as they provide help in his research. He shows little regard, however, for those who will not work with him. In spite of complaints like these, which began early in his career, Dr. Johnson was awarded tenure before Dean Warren arrived at Valley Tech.

THE RECENT COMPLAINTS

The two recent complaints are the most bothersome. A charge of sexual harassment of a secretary holds a potential high risk for Valley Tech. The secretary has been an excellent employee for 5 years. Her account of the incidents leading up to her reporting them to Dean Warren is particularly troubling. Over a period of time, Dr. Johnson's behavior toward her has become increasingly menacing. She states that Dr. Johnson's actions have made her physically ill and she has begun to have nightmares about him. Something has to be done.

In addition, the complaint from the store manager indicates that Dr. Johnson's behavior has progressed from verbal abuse to physical. The manager has not given Dean Warren specific details about the incident, but has indicated that he feels someone at Valley Tech "should be made aware of the danger." Dean Warren cannot imagine what would prompt a mature professional male to hit a young female clerk in a retail establishment. In fact, Dean Warren cannot imagine why a formal criminal charge has not been filed in the mall incident or in any of the other incidents involving Dr. Johnson over the years.

NARCISSISTIC PERSONALITY DISORDER

While talking with a psychologist at a cocktail party, Dean Warren asked what would cause a person to behave as Dr. Johnson behaved. "That behavior could be indicative of a serious personality disorder that is often associated with violence in the workplace." She continued, "People suffering from narcissistic personality disorder need the respect and admiration of others, but act in ways that tend to alienate those others. Narcissists are preoccupied with themselves and their own desires. They have no ability to see others' points of view or imagine their feelings. They are also alienated from their own feelings because those feelings are unacceptable even to themselves. They are filled with fear, anger, and self-loathing, but unconsciously deny these feelings and project them onto others. In this way, they avoid the intolerable pain that would be caused by owning those feelings. They create a self-image of themselves as good, smart, righteous, superior people.

"Narcissists justify their own unacceptable behavior through rationalization and distortion. They reinterpret events so that others are guilty and they are innocent. Their lack of empathy and respect for others come out as sarcasm and criticism. They overestimate their own abilities and accomplishments and devalue those of other people. They develop self-serving explanations in which positive outcomes are attributed to themselves and negative outcomes are attributed to others. Therefore, they feel free to exploit others to get what they want. Paradoxically, while narcissists need the admiration of others, they alienate them through exploitation, lack of empathy, criticism, and sarcasm. They themselves respond to criticism with either cool indifference or rage."

"What happens to a person to make him that way?" asked Dean Warren. About that time, the psychologist's spouse joined the conversation.

"Could be an abusive childhood," he said. "That's what seems to cause everything else! But don't worry, I think the ADA (Americans with Disabilities Act) makes everybody a victim, so there's probably nothing you can do about it."

"Is that true?" Dean Warren asked, turning to the psychologist.

"It is true that personality disorders are disabilities specifically mentioned in the ADA," said the psychologist, "but I think it's more complicated than that. If you think this guy might have narcissistic personality disorder, you might want to research it before you do anything."

ADA

Dean Warren left the cocktail party and went to his office. He got on the Internet and searched for the Americans with Disabilities Act which was part of the Department of Justice homepage (www.usdoj.gov/crt/ada/pubs/ada.txt). He found Title I of the ADA which was signed into law in 1990. He read and read, but it was difficult to find what he was looking for: clear definitions and information about what to do. He thought that maybe some of the other sites would be of more help.

Dean Warren found other Internet sites explaining the ADA, narcissistic personality disorder, and workplace violence by searching the web (see Figure 4-4). He also consulted Valley Tech's sexual harassment policy (see Figure 4-5) and statement on violent or criminal behavior (see Figure 4-6). After about an hour, Dean Warren began to understand his dilemma a lot better. "This information makes my decision a lot easier," he thought.

a. Narcissistic Personality Disorder

   www.mhsource.com/disorders/nar.html
   www.cmhcsys.com/disorders/3x36t.htm

b. Americans with Disabilities Act (ADA)

   janweb.icdi.wvu.edu/Kinder/overview.htm
   www.ljextra.com/practice/laboremployment/0602psych.html

c. Workplace Violence

   members.aol.com/endwpv

FIGURE 4-4 Internet Sites Found by Dean Warren

It is the policy of Valley Tech to prevent and eliminate sexual harassment in any campus division, department, or work unit by any faculty or staff employee, administrator, supervisor, or student. It is further the college's policy not to tolerate any practice or behavior that constitutes sexual harassment.

1. What is IT?

Sexual harassment occurs when advances are "unwelcome." It is defined as a form of sex discrimination which is illegal under Title VII of the Civil Rights Act of 1964 for employees and under Title IX of the Education Amendments of 1972.

Sexual harassment may be verbal, visual, or physical. It may be indirect or as overt as a suggestion that a person could receive a higher grade or pay raise by admission to sexual advances. The suggestion may not be direct, but implied from the conduct, circumstances, and relationship between the involved individuals. Sexual harrassment may consist of persistent, unwanted attempts to change a professional or educational relationship to a personal one. Sexual harrassment can range from sexual flirtations and put-downs to serious physical abuses such as sexual assault or rape.

Examples of harassment include unwelcome sexual advances; "repeated" sexually oriented kidding, teasing, joking, or flirting; verbal abuse of a sexual nature; graphic commentary about an individual's body, sexual prowess, or sexual deficiencies; derogatory or demeaning comments about women or men in general, whether sexual or not; leering, whistling, touching, pinching, or brushing against another's body; offensive crude language; or displaying objects or pictures which are sexual in nature that would create hostile or offensive work environments. Sexual harrassment creates an atmosphere that is not conducive for effective teaching, learning, and working.

2. WHO is affected?

It could happen to YOU! Sexual harassment is not limited to females only; males as well as females fall victim to sexual harassment daily. Research in higher education indicates that about 1/3 of females enrolled in research universities experience sexual harassment. At moderately sized universities, research indicates that about 1/4 of the female students experience sexual harassment from a professor or supervisor. Incidence research shows 3 to 12 percent of male students harassed (Roscoe, Goodwin, Repp, and Rose, 1987). Fitzgerald (1988) reports that administrative women experience more harassment, and between 20 and 49 percent of women faculty have experienced some level of sexual harassment at work.

3. HOW can I protect myself?

Prevention is the best tool for the elimination of sexual harassment. You should be aware and have knowledge of the sexual harassment policy which has been set forth by Valley Tech, and should not be reluctant to express your strong disapproval of any action taken against you. If you are in a situation in which you feel sexually harassed, overwhelmed, or threatened . . . **do not ignore it, do not resign, and do not stop attending classes.** You should seek assistance at the OFFICE OF EQUAL EMPLOYMENT OPPORTUNITY.

4. WHAT should I do, if confronted?

DO NOT GIVE UP! DO NOT GIVE IN!

You should:

a. Make it clear to the harasser you do not like his/her actions

b. Keep a written record of all harassing activities

c. Notify a few colleagues or fellow students of the problem. They can observe and corroborate your claims

d. Contact your Affirmative Action Officer

e. DON'T blame yourself!

5. If I am a victim, how do I file a report? What can be done?

Any acts, or accusations, of sexual harassment should be reported as soon as possible. The incident will be discussed informally, professionally, and confidentially. If appropriate, an attempt will be made to resolve the problem through informal procedures. (No formal action on the alleged charge will be taken unless initiated by the complainant).

If informal efforts to resolve an incident are unsuccessful, formal procedures exist which allow parties an opportunity to pursue a resolution. A complete investigation will be conducted expeditiously, assuring maximum confidentiality.

If a complaint is found to be valid and charges result, confidentiality is not guaranteed, and appropriate disciplinary action will be instituted.

FIGURE 4-5 Valley Tech Harassment Policy

The Public Safety Department provides police assistance 24 hours. Officers are certified police officers and have been trained to respond to hostile/violent actions. Immediately contact the Public Safety Department if hostile or violent behavior, actual or potential, is witnessed.

1. **Initiate immediate contact with the Public Safety Department to ensure that a timely response has begun before a situation becomes uncontrollable.**
2. **Leave the immediate area whenever possible and direct others to do so.**
3. **Should gunfire or explosives endanger the campus, you should take cover immediately using all available concealment. Close and lock doors when possible to separate yourself and others from the armed suspect.**

FIGURE 4-6 Violent or Criminal Behavior

Discussion Questions

1. Before researching the issues in this case, what was your *initial* reaction to Dean Warren's dilemma?

After researching the issues, answer the following questions:

2. What useful information did you find on the Internet, in the library, or in other sources that will help you make your decision?
3. What did your sources say about personality disorders and the responsibilities of individuals and organizations in managing behavior and accommodations for emotional disabilities under the ADA?
4. If you were Dean Warren, what would you do? Your answers should be based on research findings.
5. What are the potential dangers to the organization of continued employment of Dr. Johnson? Of terminating Dr. Johnson?

SECTION FIVE

Perspectives on Experiencing Diversity: Exercises

Exploring Diversity on Your Campus

Herbert Bromberg
Professor Emeritus, Assumption College

Carol P. Harvey
Assumption College

GOALS
1. To understand how diversity enriches learning/living experiences.
2. To understand how lack of diversity contributes to limited perspectives.

INSTRUCTIONS
1. Describe your college's faculty and administration in terms of its aspects of diversity and/or demographics.

2. Describe your college's student body in terms of its aspects of diversity and/or demographics.

3. What are the similarities and differences between the two groups?

4. How does the degree of diversity in the faculty affect your learning experience?

5. How does the degree of diversity in the student body affect the classroom experience, dorm life, and extracurricular activities? What are its advantages and disadvantages?

6. What could be done in terms of diversity to enrich your college experience?

Herbert Bromberg is a professor emeritus from Assumption College. He has worked for W.R. Grace, Celanese Corporation, and was director of the Chemical and Agricultural Products Division of Abbott Laboratories.

What Is Your Workforce IQ?: American Version

Carol P. Harvey
Assumption College

Read each of the following statements and mark them **T** for true and **F** for false.

_____ 1. The numbers of African-Americans, Asian-Americans, Native Americans, and Hispanics working in the United States represented 7.6 percent of the workforce in 1950 and is projected to exceed 30 percent by 2020.

_____ 2. The Bureau of Labor Statistics predicts that by 2015, the number of women working will represent 61.9 percent of the labor force.

_____ 3. African-Americans make up nearly one-third of the U.S. population earning between $35,000 and $75,000 per year.

_____ 4. More immigrants come to the United States from Mexico than from any other country.

_____ 5. Currently, women represent 12.5 percent of the corporate officers in *Fortune* 500 companies, an increase from 10 percent in 1996. At this rate, women will achieve parity with men at the corporate level in 2064.

_____ 6. There are more Hispanics in the United States than the entire population of Canada.

_____ 7. Although women of color comprise 40 percent of the Division I basketball and track teams, they account for only 2 percent of the Division I coaches.

_____ 8. A 1998 sample of human resource executives revealed that only one in four *Fortune* 500 companies include meeting diversity goals in evaluating managers for their bonuses.

_____ 9. English is the first language for 9 percent of the world's population.

_____ 10. Approximately 64 percent of married women who have children under 6 years of age are currently working.

Total number of true answers _____

Total number of false answers _____

What Is Your Workforce I.Q.?: Canadian Version

Gerald Callan Hunt
Ryerson Polytechnic University
Toronto, Canada

Read each of the following statements and mark them **T** for True or **F** for False.

_____ 1. Over 50 percent of students entering Canadian universities are female.

_____ 2. About 5 percent of the Canadian population is estimated to be gay or lesbian.

_____ 3. Close to 80 percent of Canadian women between the ages of 25 and 44 work outside the home.

_____ 4. Visible minorities will make up almost half of the population of Canada by 2005.

_____ 5. Visible minorities will be responsible for at least a fifth of Canada's gross domestic product by the year 2001, an amount equal to $311 billion.

_____ 6. Disabled people are the most likely group to be unemployed.

_____ 7. 15 percent of the top management positions in _Fortune_ 500 companies are held by women.

_____ 8. Study after study has found that immigrants are less likely than Canadian-born workers to end up on welfare.

_____ 9. At least 10 large organizations in Canada, such as IBM and the Metro Toronto Police Force, now have gay and lesbian employee support groups.

_____ 10. Canada is home to at least 4.3 million first-generation immigrants.

Total number of true answers _____

Total number of false answers _____

Individual Diversity: The Relevance of Personal Values

Self-Assessment

Maali H. Ashamalla
Indiana University of Pennsylvania

GOALS
- To develop student awareness of personal values as a dimension of diversity.
- To understand that no two people have 100 percent agreement on what they value.
- To identify and clarify own values.
- To appreciate other people's values.
- To explore how to deal effectively with individual value differences in work groups and organizations.

INSTRUCTIONS
Option. Part 1 of the exercise can be completed in advance as an outside class assignment.

Part 1: Clarifying My Own Values

Individual Work
Step 1: Form groups of four or five.
Step 2: Read the following list of 15 value items.
Step 3: Rank these items from "1" for the highest value to "15" for the lowest value in terms of how important each item is to you. Start with your number "1" value first and your number "15" value next. Then rank the rest of the items, working from the top and bottom of your list towards the middle. Record the ranking of each value in the space provided to the left of each item.

I VALUE

_____ 1. LEARNING: To develop knowledge, skills, and abilities through inquiry, study, or experience. To search for information and truth. To apply enlightenment, wisdom, or erudition in the conduct of my professional and life situations.

_____ 2. ACHIEVEMENT: To succeed relative to some standards of excellence or in competitive situations. To accomplish a challenging task or goal. To experience self-satisfaction when I rise to the challenge or successfully complete a task or a goal.

_____ 3. POWER: To have influence or control over others; to get others to do what I want them to do. To have the ability to exercise authority, command, and determination.

_____ 4. RECOGNITION: To receive attention, approval, or favorable notice for who I am and what I achieve. To gain acceptance, acknowledgment, or appreciation for my accomplishments.

_____ 5. ETHICAL BEHAVIOR: To believe in and adhere to a set of moral standards. To conform to the accepted principles of right and wrong that govern the conduct of a job or a profession. To be concerned with judgment principles of right and good in relation to human action and character.

_____ 6. REPONSIBILITY: To be capable of making good judgments and sound thinking, of making moral or rational decisions, of being trusted or depended upon. To be answerable and accountable for my behavior.

_____ 7. FAIRNESS: To believe in and act according to what is just, equitable, impartial, unprejudiced, or objective. To show no favoritism, self-interest, or the indulgence of one's likes and dislikes.

_____ 8. INTEGRITY: To value honesty, truthfulness, and incorruption. To respect one's self and to do honorable things even in the face of adversity.

_____ 9. PLEASURE: To have enjoyment, joy, or personal satisfaction; to consciously pursue happiness; to seek gratification and reduce pain.

_____ 10. GROWTH: To develop; to improve my status at work or in the community; to mature personally and professionally. To grow in wisdom or spirituality. To find self-fulfillment in what I do at work and life.

_____ 11. HEALTH: To possess soundness of body and mind; to feel energetic and free from pain or disease; to enjoy a state of well-being and vitality.

_____ 12. HELPFULNESS: To give assistance, support, understanding, or protection to others. To be open, responsive, and willing to contribute to the fulfillment of a need or to the achievement of a purpose.

_____ 13. AFFILIATION: To develop and maintain close mutually satisfying interpersonal relationships with others; to enjoy friendship, camaraderie, companionship, and social relations; to have a sense of belonging to a group, an organization, or a community.

_____ 14. INDEPENDENCE: To be free from the influence, guidance, or control of another or others; to have the discretion to act or judge on my own. To pursue my own goals and interests in a way that best suits me.

_____ 15. CHALLENGE: To use my abilities, energy, or resources; to apply my knowledge and skills effectively and efficiently. To feel good about what I do and the complexity and demands on my creativity.

Part 2: Appreciating Other People's Values

Small-Group Work

Step 1: Choose a member of your group to be the recorder.

Step 2: In order, each group member will share her/his two highest ranked ("1" and "2") values and her/his two lowest ranked ("14" and "15") values and will briefly explain why she/he ranked the values the way she/he did. Other group members will listen and ask only questions of clarification (if needed). No disagreement or criticism should be raised at this point.

Step 3: The recorder will list (on a flipchart or a writing pad) all the values that individual members of your group have ranked "1," "2," "14," and "15". If there is 100 percent agreement among all group members on any of these value rankings, your recorder will move this value from the list and enter it on an Agreement List.

Step 4: Following the same speaking order as before, each group member will report the next two highest ("3" and "4") values and the two lowest ("12" and "13") values.

Step 5: Your recorder will list all the values that individual group members have ranked as "3" and "4" and as "12" and "13." If there is full agreement on a value ranking, the recorder will remove this value from the first list and add it to the Agreement List.

Step 6: Repeat steps 4 and 5, until all items are covered.

Part 3: Small-Group Discussions

1. Discuss the dynamics of your group work. How did you complete Part 2 of the exercise? What went well? What could be changed or improved?
2. What do you think is the major purpose or value of this exercise?
3. Was there 100 percent agreement among your group on any of the 15 value items?
4. What did you learn from this exercise?

Discussion Questions

1. Are all people similar? Are all people different? Are both questions true?
2. What did you notice about how individuals prize, cherish, and affirm their values?
3. Based on your experience in completing this exercise, do you think the potential for value conflicts exists in work settings?
4. What could be some ways of addressing value conflicts in organizations?
5. Diversity is probably one of the universal constants. Agree or disagree with this statement and explain your answer.

Maali Ashamalla is a professor of management at the Eberly College of Business, Indiana University of Pennsylvania. She received her Ph.D. in business administration from CUNY, her masters degree in organizational behavior from Baruch College, NY, and her masters degree in human resources management from Ain Shams University, Egypt. Her research areas include gender and diversity, international human resource management, and management development. Dr. Ashamalla has served as consultant and trainer with business, government, and nonprofit organizations and has conducted management consultant work in over 25 countries.

Common and Uncommon Threads: A Values Clarification Exercise

Jeanne M. Aurelio
Bridgewater State College

Values, beliefs about what is important to people in life, are among the most stable and enduring characteristics of individuals. They are the basis upon which we base our attitudes, personal preferences, and much of our behavior. They are the foundation of crucial decisions and life directions. Much of who we are is the result of the basic values we have developed throughout our lives. We individually formulate our own particular set of values according to our own life experiences, family, thoughts and feelings.

This exercise is intended to (1) enable you to identify values that you hold in common with others and values that you hold that are different from others; (2) give you a chance to reflect upon the possible origins of other people's values, and (3) display the wide range of possible sources of values.

Step 1: Form groups of 8 to 10 people. Be sure to sit facing one another.

Step 2: Each group member: Write three different values that you feel set you apart from others. Use a separate form supplied by your instructor for each value. Do not put your name on the form. Place your form in a pile or container in the middle of your group.

Step 3: Each group member: Randomly draw a form from the container, replacing it if it is your own.

Step 4: Reflect upon how the writer might come to value what is written on the form you selected. Speculate about what life circumstances, experiences, thoughts, and feelings, could lead a person to that value.

Write your speculation here:

Step 5: Read the value you selected to your group and share your speculation about the origin of that value. What would cause a person to hold that value? Are there other possible explanations? What are some of them? No one needs to acknowledge their value when it is being discussed.

Step 6: Discuss within your group other possible explanations for the writer's value.

Step 7: List the values that your group discussed on the board.

Discussion Questions

1. What were some of the very unique or interesting values read in each group?

2. Did anyone read a value that you too had written? Why do you suppose both of you thought you were unique in holding that value?

3. Did anyone read a value that you found hard to understand? Is it reasonable that someone would hold that value? Why or why not?

4. Select a value that surprised you the most. Attempt to develop a justification for that value.

5. What did it feel like hearing others try to justify one of your values?

6. How does this experience apply to understanding diversity in organizations?

Jeanne M. Aurelio, D.B.A., is an associate professor of management at Bridgewater State College in Bridgewater, Massachusetts. She has consulted to numerous public and private organizations on topics including organizational performance, diversity issues, managerial personal effectiveness, and performance counseling. Her areas of specialization include organizational culture and leadership. She has also developed many classroom activities that encourage active learning on the part of students.

Cultural
Assimulator

Understanding Diversity in Our Heritage

Jane Schmidt-Wilk
Maharishi University of Management

GOALS

1. To identify individual differences among participants with respect to cultural and family heritage.
2. To increase awareness of ethnic diversity and its influence on current day practices, values, beliefs, concerns, and preferences.
3. To illustrate diversity with concrete examples drawn from participants' family history.

INSTRUCTIONS

1. Before-Class Preparation—Interview older members of your family (parents, grandparents, great-grandparents, aunts, or uncles) using the questions on the Understanding Diversity in Our Heritage Worksheet. Complete the worksheet and then prepare a short presentation (2 minutes) for the class using the information gained on the sheet. Each presentation may include a visual aid, such as old photographs, costumes or a family tree.

2. Discussion with the Entire Class—Cite something from the presentations that really impressed you and explain to the class why it impressed you.

Jane Schmidt-Wilk, Ph.D., is an assistant professor of management at Maharishi University of Management, Fairfield, Iowa, where she teaches courses in management and organizational behavior. Her research on the development of consciousness and its significance for management education and development has appeared in the *Journal of Business & Psychology*, the *Journal of Management Education*, and the *Journal of Transnational Management Development*. She is also an adjunct faculty of Indian Hills Community College, Ottumwa, Iowa.

Understanding Diversity in Our Heritage Worksheet

Person Interviewed (relationship to you): _____

1. For how many generations have members of your family lived in this area?

2. Where did your ancestors live before they lived here? Did they ever live in another country?

    Which one(s)? When?

3. When did your ancestors leave that country? Why did they leave?

4. How has this cultural heritage influenced your family?

5. What remains today to remind you of this heritage? Give examples. (Examples could include your name, holidays, stories, family traditions, foods, songs, games, expressions, . . . what else?)

I AM . . .

M. June Allard
Worcester State College

GOALS
1. To help you learn about yourself by examining your group members, i.e., dimensions of culture, by which you define yourself.
2. To further examine your self descriptors for indications of your most important group memberships.

INSTRUCTIONS
1. Think about how you would describe yourself to someone you have never met. On each line below, write a single-word description.

I AM a (an) . . .

1. _____	11. _____
2. _____	12. _____
3. _____	13. _____
4. _____	14. _____
5. _____	15. _____
6. _____	16. _____
7. _____	17. _____
8. _____	18. _____
9. _____	19. _____
10. _____	20. _____

2. Put a star by the three most important descriptors.

Increasing Multicultural Understanding: Uncovering Stereotypes

John R. Bowman
University of North Carolina
at Pembroke

GOALS
1. To help individuals become aware of their own values.
2. To show individuals how their culture programs them to react to and judge others in automatic and stereotypic ways.
3. To discover the types and sources of stereotypes about others.
4. To provide an opportunity for participants to see how their stereotypes create barriers to appreciating individual differences.

INSTRUCTIONS
1. Form groups of 4–6 students each. Members of each group should sit in a circle and face each other.
2. Turn to the Uncovering Stereotypes Worksheet.
3. Follow your instructor's directions for completing the blank category boxes to reflect different special populations.
4. Working individually:
   - Complete the First Thought/Judgment column by writing your first thought about or judgment of each category. Refer to the example given on the worksheet.
   - Rate each thought/judgment as positive (+), negative (-), or neutral (0).
   - Complete the Sources column by indicating the source of your judgment for each category.
5. As a group:
   - Turn to the Uncovering Stereotypes Group Summary Sheet.
   - Five categories (family, media, experience, work experience, friends) have already been listed on the summary sheet. Add additional categories (derived from your group discussions) to the sheet.
   - Take a quick count of the number of positive, negative, and neutral thoughts/judgments made by your group for each of the Source Categories and enter totals on the last line.

6. As a class:
    - Discuss which sources lead to positive, which to negative, and which to neutral judgments.
    - Discuss the implications of having negative or positive stereotypes/judgments from different perspectives; for example, among workers, between managers and workers, and at the corporate level.

John R. Bowman is chair and professor of Sociology, Social Work, and Criminal Justice at the University of North Carolina at Pembroke. He received his Ph.D. in Sociology from Ohio State University.

Uncovering Stereotypes Worksheet

Category	First Thought/ Judgment	Rating*	Sources
Working Mother	Neglects children, busy, tired		Own experience, movies
Southerner			
AIDS Carrier			
Smoker			
Hispanic			
African-American Male			
Female President of the United States			

*(+) = positive
(−) = negative
(0) = neutral

Uncovering Stereotypes Group Summary Sheet

Source Categories	Positive (+) Thoughts/ Judgments	Negative (−) Thoughts/ Judgments	Neutral (0) Thoughts/ Judgments
Family			
Media			
Experience			
Work Experience			
Friends			
Total			

A Gender and Communication Exercise

Helen J. Muller
University of New Mexico

GOALS

1. To explore issues of cross-gender communication and behaviors in an environment of peers and to propose constructive solutions.
2. To examine experiences and perceptions about intergender dynamics in the workplace.
3. To practice good listening skills and to increase one's awareness about reactions to the opposite sex's perceptions and problems related to gender-based interaction patterns.

OVERVIEW AND INSTRUCTIONS

This exercise permits single-sex groups of men and women to communicate within their own group about intergender workplace interactions that they experienced and to develop suggestions for improving such interactions. At the same time, the exercise requires one sex group to listen unobtrusively and to observe their own reactions to opposite-sex dialogue.

1. Students are divided into same-sex groups and are then placed in concentric circles, usually with women sitting on the inside circle at the start and men placed around them to form the outside circle. About five to six women is the preferred number of inner circle students that will form a good dialogue group. More than this will inhibit each person from sharing her point of view. About the same number or slightly more men form the outer circle.
2. The second task for the inside circle, usually the women, is to take 15 minutes to discuss the following question with one another: What do I need from the men at my workplace to make my job environment more compatible for me? The women are to focus on actual situations at work (or at the college) that they experienced and to explain actual behaviors, their feelings, and reactions.
3. The task for the men is to sit silently (unobtrusively) and to practice listening and to refrain from making nonverbal grimaces and gestures. They may take a few notes and they are to observe their own reactions and feelings to the discussion. The idea here is to understand the issues raised and to learn about women's perceptions about their own intergender interactions. Notes may also be taken about the group dynamics of the women's group.
4. The second task for the inside circle is to take 10 minutes to discuss the following question: What constructive suggestions do we have for making a productive mixed-sex workplace a reality? Another way of phrasing this question

253

might be: What would I like to say to the opposite sex about how they could improve their workplace interactions with me?

5. Following the two rounds of dialogue for the women's group, the inner and outer circle students switch places for the second phase of the dialogue—usually this happens with the men on the inside circle and the women placed around them on the outside.

6. The second phase of dialogue occurs with the new inside group asking the same questions for the two rounds of dialogue, allowing about 15 and 10 minutes, respectively.

7. Following the first and second phases of dialogue in same-sex groups in fishbowl fashion, the instructor facilitates an interactive discussion among both men and women around the following questions:

   a. What did you learn from listening to the opposite-sex group? Were the situations and suggestions familiar or new—could you empathize with others?

   b. What did you observe about the interaction patterns of group members? Comment on verbal and nonverbal aspects.

   c. Identify listening skills that you drew upon for the observation and identify feelings within yourself that arose during the observation/listening time.

   d. Can you identify behaviors that you practice that were mentioned by others that can enhance constructive cross-gender workplace interactions? What insights did you gain about appropriate behaviors?

8. As a final phase in this exercise, it is helpful to discuss the linkages between classroom readings and insights gained from the dialogues. The instructor can facilitate a discussion about this and draw upon the students for their insights. In particular, Deborah Tannen's work, which may be assigned prior to this exercise, may be appropriate to draw upon for bringing closure to the discussion and the issues raised in this exercise. Assume the role of Dr. Tannen: What comments would she offer about enhancing gender communication and interactions in the workplace that pertain to the discussion that you just had? What are behaviors that undermine people's ability to be effective managers when communicating with the opposite and the same sex?

Is This Sexual Harassment?

Carol P. Harvey
Assumption College

GOALS
1. To help students to understand what is and what is not sexual harassment on the job.
2. To apply the federal government's sexual harassment guidelines to workplace situations. The Equal Employment Opportunity Commission's guidelines define sexual harassment as:

    . . . unwelcome sexual advances, requests for sexual favors, and other physical and verbal contact of a sexual nature when it affects the terms of employment under one or more of the following conditions: such an activity is a condition for employment; such an activity is a condition of employment consequences such as promotion, dismissal, or salary increases; such an activity creates a hostile working environment.

INSTRUCTIONS
Given the guidelines, which of the following incidents are examples of sexual harassment? Explain your reasons for your answers.

1. While teaching Gary how to run the new spreadsheet program on the computer, Lois, his supervisor, puts her hand on his shoulder.

2. Julie, the new secretary to the vice president of manufacturing, frequently has to go out into the plant as part of her job. Several of the machinists have been whistling at her and shouting off-color remarks as she passes through the shop. One of the other women in the company found Julie crying in the ladies' room after such an incident.

3. Paul and Cynthia, two sales reps, are both married. However, it is well known that they are dating each other outside of the office.

4. Jeanne's boss, Tom, frequently asks her out for drinks after work. She goes because both are single and she enjoys his company. On one of these occasions, he asks her out to dinner for the following Saturday evening.

5. Steve's boss, Cathy, frequently makes suggestive comments to him and has even suggested that they meet outside of the office. Although at first he ignored these remarks, recently he made it clear to her that he had a steady girlfriend and was not available. When she gave him his performance appraisal, much to his surprise, she cited him for not being a team player.

6. Jackie received a call at work that her father died suddenly. When she went to tell her boss that she had to leave, she burst into tears. He put his arms around her and let her cry on his shoulder.

7. Marge's coworker, Jerry, frequently tells her that what she is wearing is very attractive.

8. While being hired as a secretary, Amanda is told that she may occasionally be expected to accompany managers on important overnight business trips to handle the clerical duties at these meetings.

9. Joe, an elderly maintenance man, often makes suggestive comments to the young females in the office. His behavior has been reported to his supervisor several times but it is dismissed as, "Don't be so sensitive, old Joe doesn't mean any harm."

10. Jennifer frequently wears revealing blouses to the office. Several times she has caught male employees staring at her.

Invisible Volleyball Game

Barton Kunstler
Lesley University

GOALS

This activity is designed to help explore the following themes:

1. That males and females in our society may experience sports differently from one another.
2. How this sports experience tends to reinforce and exaggerate gender-associated differences in managerial behaviors, attitudes, and values.
3. Whether managerial culture often self-selects for advancement those people familiar with the value and vocabulary of sports culture.
4. Whether understanding and even changing the role of sports in our society, especially in regard to gender-related values and behaviors, can be a source of societal and organizational reform.

INSTRUCTIONS

The following instructions will be reviewed with you by the instructor and will be accompanied by activities and discussion as noted.

1. We are going to play a volleyball game—two games, actually. The women will play one game among themselves, as will the men. We will use an invisible ball and invisible net. As each group plays, the other will observe and take notes. Will either group volunteer to go first? If not, let's flip a coin.
2. Now that we know who is going first, organize a game and start playing. Members of the other group, observe and keep notes on your observation sheets.
3. Now that we have played the game, how did the two groups differ in how they approached, organized, and played the game? Start by making a list of your observations of the other group and then make a separate list of your perceptions of your own group as well. Include such aspects as playing style, teamwork, and organization of the game.
4. Imagine now that each of these two lists represents a profile of someone up for a management job. The person can be male or female. You are the committee deciding this person's future. The instructor will play devil's advocate for either side that you argue. Start with why the person on the women's list would not make a good manager. After giving a few reasons, start defending this person so that a debate will get going on the pros and cons of each of the two profiles.
5. Now do the same with the person on the men's list.
6. How does this argument reflect:
   a. How managers are viewed and evaluated in the workplace?
   b. How these traits and our attitudes toward them reflect current trends and theories in managerial style, behavior, and function?

   c.   The actual experiences you have had in the workplace, in terms of how peo-
        ple are perceived, how they are promoted, attitudes toward men and
        women, and the behaviors considered appropriate for each?
7.   In what ways do childhood experiences with sports contribute to the pattern
     that emerged in our volleyball game? What do you remember growing up, or
     observe in kids today, that is similar to or different from what you observed in
     our game?

Optional Role-Play

The class breaks into groups of at least four people and develops a role-play using the following roles: a male acting according to the male team's profile as described by the class; a female acting according to the female team's profile; a male acting out the female profile; and a female acting out the male profile. After the role-play, each group relates the points it intended to demonstrate and a class discussion ensues.

INVISIBLE VOLLEYBALL GAME OBSERVATION SHEET FOR THE OTHER GROUP

Use this sheet to note your observations of the invisible volleyball game. The following questions are intended to suggest what you might watch for. Feel free, however, to include any ideas that come to you as you observe.

1.   What do you notice about the attitudes of the players towards the game? Be
     specific about the behaviors that lead you to your conclusions.

2.   How would you describe the way the group organized the game?

3. Please note any aspects of teamwork or competition among the players or between the teams.

4. Other observations:

INVISIBLE VOLLEYBALL GAME OBSERVATION SHEET FOR YOUR OWN GROUP

Use this sheet to note your observations of the invisible volleyball game. The questions are intended to suggest what you might watch for. Feel free, however, to include any ideas that come to you as you observe.

1. What do you notice about the attitudes of the players towards the game? Be specific about the behaviors that lead you to your conclusions.

2. How would you describe the way the group organized the game?

3. Please note any aspects of teamwork or competition among the players or between the teams.

4. Other observations:

INVISIBLE VOLLEYBALL GAME SUGGESTED WRITING ASSIGNMENTS

1. Write a one-page discussion of your past sports experiences and how they affected your view of the opposite sex and of your own sex. What kind of gender-related values were promoted in these sports or games programs? Consider some of the details of the experience. For instance, did name-calling or put-downs seem to delineate attitudes about one sex or the other? Did the values that were promoted give you positive or negative ideas about what it was to be a girl or boy, woman or man?

2. Write a one-page response to any or all of the following questions:
    *   Do you think men and woman at work relate differently to teamwork, leadership, and strategizing?
    *   Are managerial skills truly learned to some extent on the playing field?
    *   Are the lessons of the playing field really designed to produce effective managers, or just those who know how to get ahead?

3. Write a response to the following idea from *The Managerial Woman,* by Margaret Hennig and Anne Jardim. Pocket Books, NY, 1977, p. 90: Successful women have always been aware of "the inconsistencies in traditional [sex] role definitions." In what ways in your life did sports reinforce or undermine (or both) such traditional definitions?

Barton Kunstler, Ph.D. is an associate professor at the Leslie University School of Management in Cambridge, Massachusetts, and program director of its general education program. He has developed and delivered programs in creativity, strategic thinking, globalization, diversity, and communications. He is also director of training for the Global Management Consortium's worldwide online trade network conducted through the International Chamber of Commerce.

Transcendus Exercise

Carole G. Parker
Frostburg State University

Donald C. Klein
The Union Institute

GOALS

1. To identify individual differences that may not be apparent among participants with respect to the nature and value of conflict.
2. To increase awareness of participants' assumptions, beliefs, values, biases, concerns, and preferences in relation to conflict that results from their experiences with differences.
3. To enable participants to manage more effectively their experience of diversity and conflict.

INSTRUCTIONS

1. Selection of Transcendents and Earthlings—the class is divided into small groups of 6–8, from which two persons will be identified as Transcendents and the rest as Earthlings. The instructor will provide more information about this process.
2. Planning and Role Preparation—approximately 10–15 minutes. Members of each group of Earthlings and pair of Transcendents meet separately to discuss their assignment and get into their role. Role assignments and information are provided by the instructor.
3. Meetings between groups of Earthlings and Transcendent pairs (approximately 10–15 minutes).
4. Small groups of Earthlings and pairs of Transcendents in their assigned roles come together to explore the nature and purpose of conflict.
5. Entire class is reformed for a discussion.

The original version of the Transcendus Exercise was created by Donald Klein in June 1984 for the use at the Beyond Conflict Training Laboratory in Bethel, Maine, conducted by the NTL Institute for Applied Behavioral Science.

INTRODUCTION TO TRANSCENDUS

In another galaxy, far, far away, there is a planet called "Transcendus." The inhabitants on this planet are physically very similar to the people on Earth and differ from one another, just as Earthlings do. There is one major difference, however, between Transcendents and Earthlings: On Transcendus, there is no conflict.

Word has spread to Transcendus that Earth is a planet on which there is conflict that pervades relationships between individuals, groups, nations, and many other aspects of life. The Transcendent Governing Council has decided to send a team of anthropologists/sociologists to Earth to learn about conflict. Their instructions are to decide whether it would be advantageous to bring conflict, whatever it is, back to their home planet.

The Transcendents work in pairs as they meet with small groups of Earthlings to carry out their study.

INSTRUCTIONS FOR OBSERVERS

The task of the observer is to watch the behavior of group members and note how the group works together. Guidelines on what to look for include, but are not limited to the following:

Observations	Transcendents	Earthlings
1. Who speaks most and least? In what order do people talk?		
2. Does everyone contribute? What happens to the contributions of different members?		
3. What occurs when the Transcendents arrive? To what extent does the group stick to its original plan for interacting with the visitors? Does the plan change? If so, how does the change occur?		
4. What is the level of tension in the group before the Transcendents arrive and after they join the group?		
5. What kinds of emotions are expressed by group members and exhibited in their posture, facial expressions, and actions?		
6. What were your thoughts as an individual sitting on the sidelines observing?		
7. What, if any, emotions were stirred in you as an observer?		

Donald Klein, a community and organizational psychologist, has served as consultant and trainer since 1953 with business, government, and nonprofit organizations. A core faculty member of the Graduate School of The Union Institute and a member of NTL Institute for Applied Behavioral Science, he has published books and articles on organizational diagnosis, transformative change, power, systems simulation, consultation and training, community development, mental health, and the dynamics of humiliation.

Treasure Hunt I: Cross-Cultural Communication

M. June Allard
Worcester State College

INSTRUCTIONS
1. Form groups of three to four members each.
2. Think of ways that countries/cultures such as Italy and Japan regularly exchange ideas and information today and write these below.

   Examples: International student exchange, Olympic events, and so forth.

3. The class will reassemble to compile answers and discuss the exercise.

Treasure Hunt II: Cross-Cultural Inventions and Contributions

M. June Allard
Worcester State College

David P. Harvey
Assumption College

INSTRUCTIONS
1. Guess the culture making the contribution shown in each box and write it on the line in the left column.
2. Research the contribution to determine the actual cultural source and the inventor if applicable, and write it on the line in the right column.

Source: www.historychannel.com

1. _____   _____

2. _____   _____

3. _____   _____

4. _____   _____

5. _____   _____

6. _____   _____

7. _____   _____

8. _____   _____

9. _____   _____

10. _____   _____

11. _____   _____

12. _____   _____

13. _____   _____

14. _____   _____

15. _____   _____

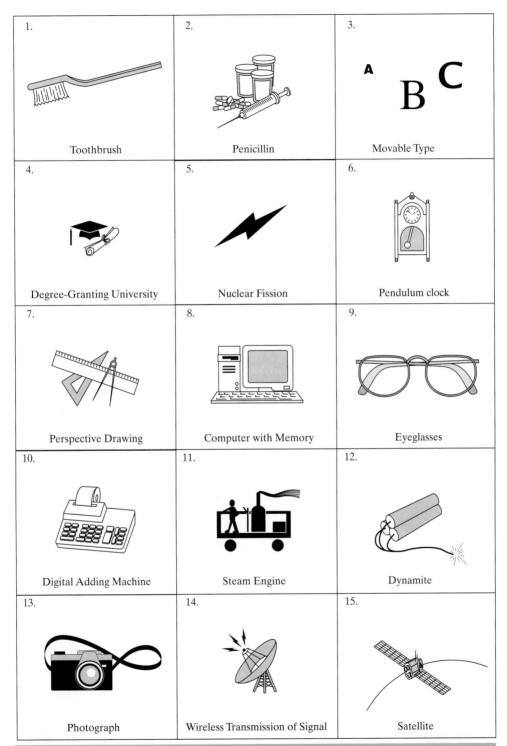

1. Toothbrush	2. Penicillin	3. Movable Type
4. Degree-Granting University	5. Nuclear Fission	6. Pendulum clock
7. Perspective Drawing	8. Computer with Memory	9. Eyeglasses
10. Digital Adding Machine	11. Steam Engine	12. Dynamite
13. Photograph	14. Wireless Transmission of Signal	15. Satellite

FIGURE 5-1   Cross-Cultural Inventions and Contributions Chart

Treasure Hunt III: Nobel Contributors

M. June Allard
Worcester State College

Nobel prizes are probably the most famous international awards. Nobel prizes are awarded in physiology/medicine, chemistry, physics, literature, economics and for peace. Recipients receive a gold medal and diploma on December 10, the anniversary of the death of Albert Nobel. The Peace Prize is awarded in Oslo; the science and literature prizes in Stockholm.

In October 1999, *The Chronicle of Higher Education* carried an article entitled "U.S. Dominates Nobel Prizes in Science, But All Its Winners Are Foreign-Born." That article exemplified modern day exchange among cultures and inspired this closer look at international contributions.

INSTRUCTIONS

Group I: Research the birth countries of Americans winning Nobel prizes. Separately list the winners and their birth countries for each of the prize categories for the past 25 years. Record your findings on the form supplied by your instructor.

Note the different kinds of contributions to the United States by the foreign-born American winners.

Groups II–VII: Research the nationalities (citizenship) of Nobel prize winners. For the prize category assigned to your group, list the winners for the past 50 years. Record your findings on the form supplied by your instructor.

Examine your findings for patterns of cultural concentrations.

All Groups: The class will reassemble to compile findings and discuss trends and implications.

Source: www.almaz.com/nobel/nobel.html
www.almaz.com/nobel

The Aging Population: Exploring Workplace Issues

Pamela D. Sherer, Ph.D.
Providence College

GOALS

1. To familiarize you with age-related facts and workplace issues.
2. To give you practice in identifying age-related resources available through the Internet.
3. To provide an opportunity to explore and understand issues specifically related to the older worker.

INSTRUCTIONS

1. **Preclass Preparation Time:** 10 minutes to complete questionnaire; 2 hours for Internet research and group project planning.
2. **In-Class Activity:** 50 minutes for review of questionnaire and short student presentations on previously assigned age-related topics.

Prior to the day of the class discussion, your instructor will assign you to a group and topic for research. Topics may include:

- Age Discrimination in Employment Act (ADEA)
- Age Discrimination Cases—A Brief Overview
- Company Training Programs for Older Workers
- Government Training Programs for Older Workers
- Phased Retirement Programs
- Recruitment Programs for Older Workers
- Programs Targeted for Older Minorities
- Temporary and Part-Time Work for Older Workers

Your group should be prepared to give a short presentation on your topic and provide the class with (1) a brief summary of your findings and (2) a one-page description identifying key issues and resources. Your instructor may ask you to post the one-page descriptions to your course Web site. Possible Web sites to begin your research:

Administration on Aging	www.aoa.dhhs.gov
National Council on Aging	www.ncoa.gov
Age Discrimination in Employment Act	www.eeoc.gov/laws/adea.html
Committee for Economic Development	www.ced.org
American Society on Aging	www.asaging.org/

Employee Benefits Research Institute	www.ebri.org
American Association of Retired Persons	www.aarp.org
Maturity Works	www.maturityworks.org
Green Thumb, Inc.	www.greenthumb.org
The Older Women's League	members.aol.com/owlil/index.htm
40 Plus	www.socal.com/40plus/
Service Corps of Retired Executives (SCORE)	www.score.org/

THE AGING POPULATION QUESTIONNAIRE

Indicate either **T** for true or **F** for false

_____ 1. Congress enacted the 1967 Age Discrimination in Employment Act (ADEA) to prevent employment discrimination against workers age 55 and over.

_____ 2. By 2030, there will be about 70 million older persons (65+), more than twice their number in 1998.

_____ 3. In the United States, only one-third of workers approaching retirement believe that they could move into less demanding work (at reduced pay) with their current employers. The remaining two-thirds do not expect their employers to accommodate such a transition.

_____ 4. In each of the past four fiscal years, age discrimination comprised about 20 percent of all discrimination charges filed with the Equal Employment Opportunity Commission (EEOC).

_____ 5. In 1998, about half (52 percent) of persons 65+ lived in nine states.

_____ 6. On average, age discrimination settlements and jury awards are substantially lower than those awarded for race discrimination, sex discrimination, or disability cases.

_____ 7. Minority populations are projected to represent 25 percent of the elderly (65+) population in 2030, up from 16 percent in 1998.

_____ 8. The most common situation provoking claims under the Age Discrimination in Employment Act of 1967 are reductions in force, which usually are caused by mergers, acquisitions, or contracting-out operations.

_____ 9. In 1950, there were seven working-age persons for every person age 65 and older in the United States; by 2030, there will be fewer than five.

_____ 10. Workers over the age of 55 are far less likely to receive training to improve their skills than any other age group.

Team Conflict and Generational Diversity

H. B. Karp
Danilo Sirias
Christopher Newport University

INSTRUCTIONS
- The total group is broken into pairs of students.
- Each pair determines who will play Pat and who will play Chris.
- The role-play runs for 10 minutes.
- Each player fills out the rating scales.
- The results are discussed in the total group.

VARIATIONS

1. An observer can be added to each pair.
   - The observer takes notes on what went well and what did not.
   - At the end of the role-play, the role-players fill out the scales.
   - Each player is asked to share their respective ratings.
   - The observer then feeds back the observations that he or she made.
2. At the end of the role-play and before the general discussions, subgroups of same-role players discuss their experience and what might have gone better.
3. Discussions of the scales and general questions can be conducted in small groups, and then the reported out and discussed in the total group.

INTRODUCTION

This role-play takes place in a new and very successful high-tech organization. Pat, the supervisor, had been hired because of good technical skills and an excellent reputation for building teams. Pat is a good manager and is reasonably well liked. Chris is a young software design engineer. Chris has made tremendous contributions to the organization's objectives and appears to be on the "fast track."

Pat thinks that it is essential to build a tighter, more cohesive team out of the group, but seems to be running into resistance to this effort. In Pat's opinion, Chris is the most important player in the group and the least enthusiastic about team building.

In acting out your parts, assume the role as given and then play it the way *you* think you would play it were it an actual situation. When situations arise that are not covered by your role, make up responses that would be consistent with a real-life situation. Remember, it is *you* who is in this situation.

ROLE-PLAYER RATING SCALES

INSTRUCTIONS

Circle the number on each scale that best describes your observations and perceptions of the roleplay.

1. To what extent did your partner listen to you?
        1   2   3   4   5   6   7
Not at all   Completely

2. To what extent did your partner respect your position?
        1   2   3   4   5   6   7
Not at all   Completely

3. Was your partner willing to make concessions to meet your needs?
        1   2   3   4   5   6   7
Not at all   Completely

4. Could you characterize the conflict between you as "productive"?
        1   2   3   4   5   6   7
Not at all   Completely

5. To what extent did the discussion result in a mutually acceptable outcome?
        1   2   3   4   5   6   7
Not at all   Completely

Discussion Questions

1. For those playing "Pat,"
   a. Generate a list of adjectives that describe the behavior of "Chris."
   For those playing "Chris,"
   b. Generate a list of adjectives that describe the behavior of "Pat."

Questions 2–4 are for the entire class:

2. What values appear to be displayed by each of the roles?
3. Describe the relationship between Pat and Chris at the end of the role-play. What do you think the next meeting between them would be like?
4. If you were brought in to facilitate the next meeting, what would you do to enhance the probability of a positive outcome?

Hank Karp, Ph.D., is on the faculty at Christopher Newport University and owner of Personal Growth Systems, a consulting firm that has offered training, conflict management, and executive development since 1979. He has worked with many large organizations such as the Smithsonian Institution, General Dynamics, and Chaparral Steel and has authored over 60 publications including *Personal Power* (Gardner Press, 1995) and *The Change Leader* (Pfeiffer, 1996). He is coauthoring *X Marks the Spot: Building Teams for the 21st Century,* soon to be released by Davies-Black Publishers.

Danilo Sirias, Ph.D., is a faculty member at Christopher Newport University, and he is also a certified academic in the theory of constraints. His latest research relates to teamwork issues and especially the conflicts baby boomers and generation X are experiencing. He is a coauthor of the upcoming book *X Marks the Spot: Building Teams for the 21st Century.* Dr. Sirias has received several grants and awards, including an outstanding paper award for "creative use of scientific inquiry" from the Sigma Xi Scientific Research Society.

* For an abstract or a complete manuscript of the research cited, please contact the authors directly.

A Letter from an American Factory Worker

Dale G. Ross
Michael Whitty
University of Detroit Mercy

A former employee of a large Big Three auto supplier finally began to look at the situation he found himself in and drafted a letter to the president of the company. He wrote:

Dear Mr. President:

It has taken over a year to understand what happened to me on my job. I never wanted to really deliberately come out, but more, I wanted to try to downplay the seriousness of it all. I was hoping that most other people respected me and liked me well enough to accept me for who I am. But I was wrong. These people zeroed in on me when I admitted I was gay. In fact, the bosses' harassment started when I let only one person know my secret. It is now that I am learning how their discrimination has caused me to have low self-esteem, depression, dependencies, shame, guilt, on and on.

I also learned that it's all a pack of lies. I find it hard to write this down, so I have to put it down a little each day. I am usually depressed after I write. I am not doing well financially but I survive. I was soaring for about 2 years when I worked. Now I am barely able to work and pay taxes. I owe federal and local property taxes and I'm not making it. When I think that other peoples' ignorance did this to me, I feel just destroyed.

Let me tell you how it happened that I have the need to come out of the closet. I have always kept my private life to myself, but I do occasionally take on odd jobs for people. One day a person I only knew at work discussed a car problem that he had. I offered to fix it for him. So he had it towed over to my house, and I replaced the head gasket. During the few days his car was at my house, I invited him inside and he met my live-in lover. This was not a deliberate act of coming out, but more just common hospitality. A month or so later, I began being harassed by a production supervisor on the job. I didn't understand his attitude toward me. No matter how hard I tried, he constantly complained to my boss. I complained to the union, I complained to the department management, but I was not defended. So I used my seniority position to bump off to another department. Then weeks later I overhead my old boss talking. He said that I had screwed the department by quitting and they wasted all that training on me. Then the rumors started getting back to me about one bed at my house and two men living there. Where do you think all these strangers heard that? Some friend.

I do feel that you should know what happened to finally cause me to give up and quit. There were several different versions of the same threats against me. The most complete description was from an officer of my own union. He stopped me in the aisle as I was walking by. He asked me why I told everyone that I was gay. I told him that I am no longer willing to hide out and lie and I need to be truthful for myself. It is a hateful thing to have to deny your own identity out of shame, especially when that shame is placed on you by others who are adulterers, drunkards, crackheads, and downright lazy.

According to this union officer, "People who are smiling to your face, some of them you know really well, are talking about doing you bodily harm. Maybe possibly kill you, but I'm not going to tell you who said these things. I just don't want to see you get hurt. So be careful where you go around this plant and watch over your shoulder because some people are not who you think they are." By then, I had been harassed by the bosses and coworkers, I had my truck stolen from a company parking lot, and now a union official (who took an oath to stand by me) believed he was helping me by telling me to be afraid at work, going in and coming out of the shop. I can't even go fishing or hunting with anyone. This guy wants to hurt me, but no names; just hearsay.

I loved my job. I never made any kind of sexual advance in your plant in 4 years, yet so many people were worried that I would. I have never been so insulted in my life. My depression went haywire for awhile and I'm in therapy. It took me over a year to write this. I don't know whether to congratulate you on getting gays out of your shop, or to offer you my deepest sympathy for losing a man.

Bitterly, but with love,
XXXXX XXXXX

Discussion Questions

1.   How do incidents such as this do harm to the business system as well as victimized individuals?
2.   Does diversity training reach down to the front-line supervision in most companies that have some formal policies?
3.   What are the special challenges to diversity training regarding inclusion of sexual orientation? What skillful means would be most effective in a blue-collar setting? What is the union's role?
4.   What might this factory worker's motivation(s) be for writing such a letter?

Dale G. Ross, MSW, ACSW, CSW NCC, has been a private practice therapist/educator in Southfield, Michigan, since 1985. He created and taught two graduate courses on the issues of gay clients for 6 years and has served on four professional speakers' bureaus addressing HIV/AIDS. He also presents programs on dysfunctional group dynamics/issues of the workplace, and on men's issues.

Dr. Michael Whitty, a professor of labor relations and management, College of Business Administration, University of Detroit Mercy for 34 years, has published articles on AIDS in the workplace and on the Americans with Disabilities Act in the *Labor Law Journal*. Among other classes, he teaches sex, race and age discrimination in the workplace and Business Ethics.

Religion and Work

Carol P. Harvey
Assumption College

In today's global society, it is useful to learn more about the religions that may be practiced by coworkers. Without some knowledge, individuals may attribute incorrect meanings to other's behaviors. In addition, organizations may have policies and practices that inadvertently conflict with their employees' religious beliefs. For example, some organizations do not allow vacation time to be accrued, thus preventing pilgrimages, and so forth, that may require a month of leave. Others require all workers to take Christian holidays and do not capitalize on the opportunity to have non-Christians work on days that have no significance to them. For example, Jewish employees may choose to work on Christmas Eve in exchange for having Yom Kippur off with pay. Because many individuals may be reluctant to discuss their religion or to explain its practices in a work setting, misunderstanding of behavior can result.

The following scenarios depict workplace incidents where others are not aware of the religious significance of the individual's behavior. In each case, the employee is put in the limelight because of his/her religion. The supervisor or coworker has no knowledge of the religious practices that are at the root of these employee behaviors.

Form small groups and through the sharing of information (or if given as a research assignment, through library and Web sources) try to determine, in each case, the religious significance of the person's behavior. For each scenario, there is a rational explanation based on the beliefs and practices of the employee's religion.

1. Mary Ellen comes to work with a dark spot on her forehead. Several times during the day, coworkers tease her about forgetting to wash her face and suggest that she visit the ladies' room.

2. David sits with his coworkers at a luncheon provided during a meeting. Chicken with a creamy sauce, salad, and rice are served, but he declines to eat and only sips water. People at the table ask him if he is feeling well. He keeps assuring them that he is fine.

3. Kaleen never attends any company informal or formal social events (drinks after work, trips to a nearby casino, or holiday parties). In addition, in an organization where "open doors" are a strong cultural norm, his door is often closed for short periods of time. During his performance appraisal, his boss tells him that Kaleen needs to become more sociable and accessible if he expects to move into a management position.

4. Rebecca, a high school student in her first part-time job, refuses to allow her photo to be taken for an employee I.D. In addition, she tells the secretary in human resources that she should not have to have Social Security deductions taken out of her pay. When asked about this, she replies that her family has never paid into Social Security.

5. Using the Internet, research a religion that you are unfamiliar with and write an original incident where an employee's work behavior, based upon religious beliefs and practices, is misunderstood by a boss or coworker.

Musical Chairs

M. June Allard
Worcester State College

GOAL
To experience how it feels to be physically challenged; that is, unable to communicate with people in the traditional way.

INSTRUCTIONS
1. Form a group of four to six members and arrange your chairs in a circle.

2. Read the following passage to yourself.
    Fifty students reported for a class that had 35 student desk-chairs: 30 RH (right hand) and five LH (Left Hand). Fifteen RH students then volunteered to transfer to an honors section down the hall, thereby leaving everyone in the original class seated.
    After class, six RH students and one LH student reported their chairs were broken and needed replacing. Later that afternoon the honors instructor called saying eight of the transfer students were not eligible for the honors class and were, therefore, returning to the original class. How many additional RH and LH desk-chairs did the original instructor need for his class?

3. **Working as a group,** use **one** worksheet to come to some consensus on the answer to the question posed in the passage.

4. Your instructor will give you further special instructions on how your group will conduct the exercise.

MUSICAL CHAIRS WORKSHEET

Create an Exercise

M. June Allard
Worcester State College

GOAL

To gain greater information about and understanding of physical and mental disabilities.

INSTRUCTIONS

1. Form groups of five or six members. List the members of your group on the worksheet.

2. Create an exercise to demonstrate/experience a physical or mental disability. Your instructor will provide more information on the specific disability to be addressed by your group.

3. The exercise can take the form of a demonstration, role-play, game, trivia, or whatever. It can be designed for individuals, small groups, or large groups. Be sure that it covers a *broad range of information pertinent to the topic.*

4. Create all appropriate materials such as: introduction, rules, game board and pieces, props, scoring sheets, note-taking sheets, forms, or whatever is needed for the exercise.

5. The criteria to be used to grade the exercise include:
   a. accuracy of information
   b. breadth of coverage
   c. evidence of organization and relevance (e.g., development of meaningful categories or roles)
   d. evidence that additional research has been done and more material has been obtained on the disability
   e. neatness, completeness, and coherence of materials (e.g., readable instructions, meaningful introduction, usable game or observational materials, etc.)

6. Due date: _____ Plan to play/demonstrate your exercise on this date.

CREATE AN EXERCISE WORKSHEET

Group Members: _____   _____

_____   _____

_____   _____

Topic (disability): _____

Title of Exercise: _____

Nature of Exercise
(*check*):   _____ demonstration   _____ role-play

_____ game   _____ other: _____
                                        (please explain)

_____

_____

Brief Description of Exercise:

Materials Needed:

Procedure (steps):

Evaluating Diversity in the Real World: Conducting a Diversity Audit

Carol P. Harvey
Assumption College

GOALS

1. To provide a capstone learning experience so that students are able to see how theory and cases studied during the semester apply in the real world.
2. To improve critical thinking skills by developing and applying criteria to the evaluation of an organization's diversity initiatives.
3. To provide an opportunity to compare and assess the relative levels of commitment that organizations make in terms of implementing and managing diversity programs.
4. To learn about the dynamics of working on a team.
5. To showcase the unique ways that some organizations are working to manage diversity and to illustrate that other organizations are limiting their diversity initiatives to legal compliance.

The purpose of this assignment is to provide a capstone learning experience in diversity management. Student teams will research, visit, evaluate, and make recommendations for systemic changes in terms of diversity initiatives in a real organization.

Dividing the work equitably and preparing the criteria and questions for the interview are part of the assignment. Do not expect your instructor to do these for the group. You will need to follow these steps in order. Students should dress professionally both for the interview and the presentation. Your instructor will assign you to a working team.

INSTRUCTIONS

- As a group, establish some "criteria" for managing diversity in an organization.

- Find an organization that will work with you.

- Conduct *secondary research* by reading their Web page, annual report, and any material that they will give you, such as press releases, articles written about the organization, or employee handbooks.

- Make an appointment to interview at least one company representative or employee. If you can interview people from different functions and levels (human resources, training, managers, and employees), it will provide different perspectives and richer data. All team members do not need to go on the interview.

- Prepare a list of thoughtful questions about diversity in this organization. Your secondary data should help the group to prepare good questions.

- Conduct *primary research* by visiting the organization and conducting an interview(s). Ask for a tour of the organization, so that you may gather additional information through observation. If available, try to obtain copies of company newsletters, value statements, and so forth.

- As a group, evaluate what you have learned about this company in terms of diversity *against your criteria.* Be sure to pay attention to subtle cues (i.e., is there evidence that they really do what they say they do). For example, a manager proudly pointed out that his large retail organization hired physically challenged workers. However, they were all assigned to work in the stockroom, where they were never seen by any customers. The group may add additional criteria that they had not thought of after the interview/visit.

- Each team also will prepare an 8- to 10-page paper, which explains their findings in detail. The paper should be free from spelling and grammatical errors, cite all written Web sources and interviews in a bibliography, and contain exhibits, such as copies of organizational value statements or company newsletters, if appropriate. Your report should detail the strengths and weaknesses of the organization's diversity initiatives. List the criteria (one page), provide some company background/history (one page), evaluate the organization's efforts in terms of diversity, and make recommendations for improvement.

- Each team of students will make a 15- to 20-minute presentation that details the results of their diversity audit. The presentation should include visual material such as transparencies, PowerPoint, handouts, and material supplied by the organization. In addition, groups should rehearse their presentations so that individual speakers do not repeat each other's material and that they do not exceed the time limits. Be prepared to answer questions from the class. At the end of the presentation, the student team should be prepared to answer questions and to assign a letter grade from A–F to their organization.

Index

NOTES

NOTES

NOTES

NOTES

NOTES

NOTES

NOTES

NOTES